THE POLITICS OF RESENTMENT

The POLITICS *of*
RESENTMENT

A   GENEALOGY

Jeremy Engels

The Pennsylvania State University Press
University Park, Pennsylvania

Library of Congress Cataloging-in-Publication Data

Engels, Jeremy, author.
    The politics of resentment : a genealogy /
    Jeremy Engels.
        pages   cm
Summary: "Examines the problem of rhetorical violence in American political
discourse, and maps the history of one form, the politics of resentment. Investigates
key events in American history that have led to a current culture of resentment"—
Provided by publisher.
Includes bibliographical references and index.
ISBN 978-0-271-06710-0 (cloth : alk. paper)
ISBN 978-0-271-06664-6 (pbk. : alk. paper)
1. Rhetoric—Political aspects—United States—History.   2. Resentment—
Political aspects—United States—History.   I. Title.

P301.5.P67E54   2015
306.440973—dc23
2014047331

The Pennsylvania State University Press is a member of the Association of
American University Presses.

It is the policy of The Pennsylvania State University Press to use acid-free paper.
Publications on uncoated stock satisfy the minimum requirements of American
National Standard for Information Sciences—Permanence of Paper for Printed
Library Material, ANSI Z39.48–1992.

Typeset by

COGHILL COMPOSITION COMPANY

Printed and bound by

SHERIDAN BOOKS

Composed in

GARAMOND PREMIER PRO *and* MILLER DISPLAY LIGHT

Printed on

NATURES NATURAL

CONTENTS

ACKNOWLEDGMENTS

I have accumulated some big debts in writing this book—not the bad kind that are crushing, but the best kind that inspire gratitude. Gratitude is one of the most powerful emotions; it is a feeling that can wash away all the darkness of fear and self-doubt (and, in the final analysis, anger and resentment). I feel so much gratitude for all the resplendent people in my life. Without them I would feel homeless and alone. So let me begin this book as I end my yoga practice: with gratitude toward life and friends and fellow rhetorical critics.

In writing this book, I've benefited from my contributions with, and the feedback from, a few dear friends: Kirt Wilson, who always asks the right question, whom I think sometimes understands my work better than I do, and who makes all the cloudy Pennsylvania days seem bright with his friendship; Nate Stormer, who has profoundly influenced how I (and many others) understand rhetoric, but who never takes credit for all the good karma he sets into motion; Christopher Moore, with whom I've spent many a delightful afternoon discussing ancient Greek philosophy, rhetoric, and language; and William Saas, who provided a huge help with the research for the book, and who read the manuscript in its entirety at least twice, providing valuable feedback that has made the book so much better. I take comfort in knowing that Greg Goodale has my back, and I thank him equally for his feedback on my work and for his friendship. I'm blessed with amazing colleagues at Penn State, and to them I give my thanks for great conversational and intellectual inspiration: Matt Jordan, Shannon Sullivan, the late and dearly missed Paul Harvey, Michele Kennerly, Rosa Eberly, Mike Elavsky, Chris Long, Steve Browne, Tom Benson,

Lisa Hogan, Vincent Colapietro, John Christman, Mary Beth Oliver, Sophia McClennan, Joe Rhodes, Cheryl Glenn, Denise Solomon, Josh Wretzel, Aaron Krempa, Jack Selzer, Debra Hawhee, Eric Fuchs, and Mike Hogan. A special thanks goes out to my fearless department head, John Gastil, for his support of this project and of all my work, whatever strange turns it might seem to take. A special thanks, too, to my Latin teacher, Lauren Kaplow, who exhibited tremendous patience with my poor grasp of grammar. Another big thanks to my editor, Kendra Boileau, and the folks at the Penn State Press, for their support and hard work.

This book was made possible by the support of the National Communication Association. NCA awarded me the Karl R. Wallace Award in 2011 to recognize early career achievement and provide support in the study of rhetoric and public discourse. The grant associated with the Wallace Award provided the financial support to jump-start my research for Essay II. Much gratitude also goes out to the Penn State Institute for the Arts and Humanities, which supported the completion of this book with a faculty fellowship in Fall 2013. The IAH is the hub of interdisciplinary humanistic research at Penn State, and I appreciate its intellectual energy.

Rhetorical studies is such a strong and interesting field. Many of you have influenced this book, be it through conference presentations, your published works, or your kind words in passing. There are too many people to mention, but I especially thank Ira Allen, Pat Gehrke, Dave Tell, Nathan Crick, Aric Putnam, and Josh Gunn (in addition to the folks mentioned above). My work has benefited tremendously from all those Saturday afternoon conversations with my rhetoric reading group: Nate Stormer, Megan Foley, and Donovan Conley. I would not be where I am today without the support of my adviser, Stephen John Hartnett (hail to the chief!). Most of all, I have benefited from the opportunity to work with the truly brilliant Penn State grad students. To my advisees Billy Saas, Frank Stec, Jess Kuperavage, John Minbiole, and Cory Geraths—the future rock stars of the field—I've enjoyed every minute working with you. You've taught me so much.

I thank everyone who has made life in State College so enjoyable for the past several years—Mark and Ariel, Josh and Sarah, Josh and Amanda, Chris and Kate, Kirt and Janice and the boys, the folks at Lila Yoga, Erica Kaufman, Webster's, the trainers at One on One, the gentle souls at Callao Café, Eric, Joe. To my teachers, Andrew, Kay, Greg, Erica—thanks. To my family on all sides, thank you for everything. None of this would be possible without your support.

Anna Sunderland Engels gets her own paragraph. After all these years, you continue to inspire me. In the words of the immortal R.E.M., to me, "you are the everything." Thank you for all your support while I was writing this book. It's such a blessing to get to spend our lives together.

Introduction
Democracy and Resentment

On January 7, 2011, Arizona congresswoman Gabrielle Giffords, a Democrat, sent an e-mail to a friend in Kentucky, Secretary of State Trey Grayson, a Republican. Grayson had recently been offered the prestigious position of director of Harvard's Institute of Politics, and, in a rare gesture that crossed partisan lines, Giffords reached out to congratulate him. "After you get settled," she wrote, "I would love to talk about what we can do to promote centrism and moderation. I am one of only 12 Dems left in a GOP district (the only woman) and think that we need to figure out how to tone our rhetoric and partisanship down."[1] Giffords's plea for more civil rhetoric was interrupted the very next day at a "Congress on Your Corner" event in Tucson; in the parking lot of local mall, a vigilante shot her in the head. Nineteen people were wounded. Giffords survived. Six others died.

Tragedy tends to defy precisely what it demands—explanation. Who is the shooter, Jared Lee Loughner, and why did he do it? Many accounts circulated in the days and weeks following the shooting. Some blamed Arizona's lax gun laws. Others the lack of funding devoted to treating the mentally ill. When the local sheriff for Pima County, Arizona, Clarence Dupnik, stepped up to a podium on January 8, 2011, to offer a statement on the shooting, he cited these factors. He then took the conversation in a different, surprising, and for some, an inflammatory direction by blaming political discourse—the very thing Giffords herself had hoped to moderate. This was not, after all, a random shooting; it was a targeted attack on an elected political official. The massacre was, according to Dupnik, a consequence of the resentful, hateful, antigovernment tirades typical of contemporary political rhetoric. For Dupnik, the angry, polarizing, take-no-prisoners, violent talk of the Republican Right—its "vitriolic rhetoric"—was the primary cause of the shooting. Americans searching for an explanation for Loughner's act needed to look no further than talk radio, Fox News, campaign ads decorated with gun sights, and warlike speeches. "To try to inflame the public on a daily basis, twenty-four hours a day, seven days a week, has an impact on people, especially who are unbalanced personalities to begin with," Dupnik opined. "It's time that this country take a little introspective look at the crap that comes out on radio and TV."[2]

When Sheriff Dupnik cited "vitriolic rhetoric" as a factor in the shooting, he sparked a national debate about the metaphors, images (e.g., crosshairs), slogans, and clichés that comprise American political discourse. In the days and weeks following the Tucson shooting, Americans engaged in a number of public discussions that asked: could violent rhetoric have contributed to what happened on that horrific Saturday morning? This question was given a new urgency in the post-Tucson period by a plague of school shootings, by the widespread use of violent metaphors in our public address, and by the anger, hatred, and general nastiness of political discussion in our age of partisan gridlock. We live in resentful times, and it shows in how we talk.

This discussion about the relationship between violence and rhetoric has been complicated by our collective cultural numbness to the violence that fills our various screens. Americans reacted to the Tucson shooting much as they reacted to the mass murder at Virginia Tech in April 2007, to the shooting at Fort Hood in November 2009, to a man opening fire at a midnight showing of *The Dark Knight Rises* in Aurora, Colorado, in August 2012, to the massacre of twenty children and six staff members at Sandy Hook Elementary School in December 2012, to the bombing at the Boston Marathon in April 2013, and to the shooting spree at the University of California, Santa Barbara, in May 2014—we were moved to tears, sure, but we quickly moved on and got back down to it. We have become so used to being moved by the flood of terrible, tragic events that we have adapted by becoming numb to graphic stimuli. This is the "dialectic of postmodern life"—we are moved, and we move on.[3]

Moving on, and on, and on, *ad infinitum*; this is the cultural ethos of our time, designed for a busy and mobile people constantly on the go. Speed is adaptive, but rarely helpful for making wise decisions. There is plenty of evidence that speed kills; speed also makes it difficult to understand killing. Speed encourages us to attune to violence at only a surface-level depth. Citizens moving quickly stop registering the everyday forces that produce and promote violence, and as such we do not get at the marrow of the problem. I believe, therefore, that we should counter the dialectic of postmodern life with a counter-ethos of rhetorical criticism that encourages citizens to look more critically at the operation of the rhetorical forces that shape our world, that manipulate our potentials and vulnerabilities, and that constrain our possibilities for collective action.

In this book I do not answer the question of Loughner's motives. I do not believe that we will ever know why he did it, outside of his own admission (and even then his words would be influenced by the intervening years and all that he has heard). A number of publications, including *Time* magazine—with its January 24, 2011, cover—spoke to the enduring unknowns about the tragedy. Beneath the words "Guns. Speech. Madness," a grainy black-and-white mug shot of the shooter dominated the page, his slight smile infinitely suggestive of dark motives. Superimposed above Loughner's shaved head was a brain-shaped maze terminating in a big red question mark. This cover depicted the ultimate incomprehensibility of the gunman, and I agree that Loughner's mind is unknowable outside of his own words. I do not agree that knowing his mind is the most important thing, or that the question of motive is the most important question for us to ask in the aftermath of Tucson. The optimal question for me is about *force*: what forces are at work in our society that enabled this action and produced such a clearly damaged subject? Here I think that Sheriff Dupnik was on to something: one of the most powerful forces working to produce violence in our culture is political rhetoric.

Rather than moving on so quickly after tragedy, we should continue, expand, and enrich our fruitful cultural conversations about political rhetoric. To confront, challenge, and transcend violent speech must be one of our central political goals today. To do this, however, we must first understand the emotions that give rise to such talk and the feelings that this talk is intended to excite. This includes resentment, long recognized by philosophers, political theorists, and rhetorical scholars to be among the most potent of all emotions associated with democracy. I believe that much of the resentment felt today is the product of widespread feelings of powerlessness in the populace, along with the general sentiment that citizens are victims to forces and changes beyond their control. In turn, much of the violent political discourse we are inundated with today is the direct product of this civic resentment.

To govern the masses, Aristotle taught in his *Rhetoric*, politicians must cultivate in the populace the right feelings, at the right times, in the right proportions—speaking thunder in the face of danger, a lullaby when the people are angry, a psalm in times of trouble. Aristotle had much to say about resentment. He fretted that this emotion was unstable, unpredictable, and ultimately ungovernable; in fact, resentment was the only civic emotion he treated as unqualifiedly negative.[4] The philosophers of the classical period conceptualized resentment as a bitter, eruptive, undignified force that had to be contained. This emotion was especially dangerous, they suggested, because it was characteristic of the democratic poor.[5] In his speech "Antidosis," written in the fourth century BCE, Isocrates observed that the ancient Greek citizenry was *phila-*

pekhthēmōn, "fond of hating"—the people were full of "resentment" toward the wealthy as a political class.[6] Due to Athenians' unearned resentment toward their betters, Isocrates fretted that he and other affluent men had to defend themselves against the charge of being wealthy as though that were a crime.[7]

Isocrates's neologism *philapekhthēmōn* connotes an ongoing practice of resentment toward the rich in Athens. Democratic resentment represented the potential for hostility between the poor and the rich to boil over; it was also the threat of conflict that kept the Athenian elite from using its outsized influence against the citizenry and contrary to the public good. Writing at the moment when philosophy, rhetoric, and democracy were born in the West, Isocrates described resentment as an emotion closely associated with democratic politics. I call our attention to Aristotle and Isocrates from the outset because they encourage us to contemplate the relationship between democracy, rhetoric, and resentment. The explosion of resentment in contemporary politics is not new. What is new is how resentment is framed in public discourse. Opportunistic political leaders have developed rhetorics that allow resentment to be put to troubling uses in democratic politics. It is my goal in this book to describe these rhetorical innovations. My tale is one of reversal and, ultimately, betrayal. I offer this genealogy because resentment is an emotion commonly leveraged today to divide citizens into hostile camps, to turn individual against individual and neighbor against neighbor, to negate the possibility for deliberation between opponents, and to encourage violence. If we want to better understand why contemporary American political rhetoric is so violent, we need look no further than *the politics of resentment*.

Like our Greek forebears, Americans continue to feel resentment; the citizenry remains fond of hatred. But something is different today. Resentment once made the wealthy elite tremble. Now, politicians embrace resentment, making it central to how they govern. These leaders encourage citizens to direct our resentment not at an economic system that benefits the rich and powerful at the expense of the poor and numerous, but instead at our civic equals. The politics of resentment turns citizens against one another, making interpersonal violence seem justifiable and at times righteous. Yet this rhetoric never provides the salvation it promises. It frustrates citizens' desires while upholding the very structures that inflame civic resentment in the first place.

My aim in this book is to explain how resentment went from the bane of political elites to their primary rhetorical instrument for managing democracy and restraining the power of the demos. My goal, in short, is to recount how democratic resentment has been tamed. I will do this by tracking several key transitions in the relationship between democracy and resentment from the classical period to the contemporary moment. Along the way, I will chronicle the primary rhetorical means that political and corporate elites in the United States have developed for directing the emotions of the citizenry. I will describe how and under what circumstances resentment became central to governance during the twentieth century. I will illustrate the master terms in the vocabulary of resentment that Americans have learned to speak. Finally, I will elucidate how the politics of resentment has been put in the service of an economic philosophy (postmodern financial capitalism, or as it is more generally known, "neoliberalism") that is devastating in its consequences for most Americans. At every turn, I take the time to explain why the ambitions of citizens in the United States are constantly frustrated. The politics of resentment encourages us to shout and rage and vent and shoot, but in the end it takes the teeth out of democracy by fracturing the demos. In recent decades, the politics of resentment has been employed to uphold elite, corporate rule over the nation by keeping citizens angry, resentful, frustrated, and acquiescent. The politics of resentment might feel like resistance to power, but its result is the reification of power relations that are harmful to citizens.

Before describing the argument of this book in more detail, let me first say a word or two about how I understand democracy, and then a few more words about how I understand rhetoric. Having done this, I will then describe the conceptual foundations and chronological arc of *The Politics of Resentment*.

Democracy Is Dangerous

What can I say about democracy that hasn't already been said? The word is used to death, to the point that it no longer has much meaning other than the force of a blunt object. Politicians attack one another with the word like it is a stick. Friedrich Nietzsche once argued that "truths are illusions about which one has forgotten that this is what they are; metaphors which are worn out and without sensuous power; coins which have lost their pictures and now matter only as metal, no longer as coins"; for the rest of us, democracy is like one of Nietzsche's coins rubbed smooth—we accept its truth, its value, simply because it has been in circulation so long, because it has been repeated and praised and eulogized and normed and made the foundation of national pride.[8] No matter how bad things are, at least we have democracy.

I think it is clear, however, that contemporary democracy in the United States is on life support, with the body due upon its passage to be handed over to corporate elites in the name of science—the science of neoliberal economics. We live in a time of oligarchic democracy, the rule of the plutocrats, the government of the rich by means of the poor. Americans are encouraged to think of democracy in its thinnest sense, as a national, institutional governing arrangement that calls on citizens to participate on Election Day and be acquiescent at other times—we are taught to conceptualize democracy as a noun, not a verb. Democracy has become little more than another justification for neoliberal, postmodern capitalism.[9] Many heroic teachers fight these trends with ever-dwindling resources, but politicians and our sensationalized media seem intent on training citizens to be frightened, frustrated, apathetic, acquiescent, and, ultimately, resentful.[10]

For those scholars who wish to simply abandon democracy as a guiding social and political ideal, I think the costs of giving up the democratic faith would be too high, given where we are and have been. What needs to be done is to reconsider the rhetorical forces that animate democratic politics and the possibilities inherent to those forces. One such force, I contend, is resentment—though from the outset we must recognize that resentment is an ambivalent emotion that can be harnessed and leveraged for divergent outcomes. Resentment can make democracy dangerous; it can also make it weak, ineffectual, and puerile.

Democracy promises a world where people rise by virtue and fall by sin—and this promise, this assertion, makes democracy dangerous. When speaking of democracy's dangerousness I'm not talking about mobs rioting in the street, an ancient concern that has long accompanied criticism of democracy, and I'm not talking about armed revolution.[11] No, what makes democracy dangerous is the assertion at the very heart of democratic theory that political power should not be given by god or fiat but in fact should be premised on popular input and dependent on the generation of good in common—democracy, in short, makes political power *conditional* and subject to the law of karma.[12]

Democracy is dangerous because while we experience unequal social, cultural, and political power relations as natural, they are anything but. There is nothing objective about how societies are structured, about who is on top and who is on bottom, about who is rich and who is poor, about who is included and who is excluded, about who can speak and who can't. Power as manifested in social organization is always a construction. Democracy becomes dangerous when it cultivates attitudes that empower everyday citizens to act individually and collectively as a check on arbitrary power.

In the classical world, democracy was invested in empowering the group of citizens who, though most numerous, had the least power to control their destinies and the smallest say in politics: the poor. Even today, democracy retains a hint of this ancient meaning: it seeks to empower the most vulnerable groups in society, which includes the materially poor but also those social groups judged by the dominant mainstream to be poor in other ways. The English word *democracy* is derived from the classical Greek *demokratīa*, which means "popular government" or "the power of the citizens": a compound of *dēmos*, the native adult males of the polis, and *krātos*, power, sovereignty, rule. This power, democracy's classical opponents recognized, is the power of the disenfranchised poor united against the wealthy and powerful. The classical Greeks viewed the distinction between rich and poor, the few and the many, as a primary social division. Understanding this, classical proponents of democracy (much to the chagrin of democracy's original haters) imagined it to be a means for common citizens to check the outsized power of the rich, the prominent, and the well connected—those who would be lords of the whole world.[13] At its most dangerous, democracy today seeks to challenge anyone who is invested in upholding social hierarchies that benefit the elite few at the expense of the many.

For the Greeks, democracy was defined not by voting or majority rule. Democracy meant first and foremost fraternity—the transformation of "the many" into a demos because voices assembled in mass are louder and more urgent—and then civic performances orchestrated by the demos designed to keep the rich from tyrannizing citizens.[14] Many Romans understood democracy similarly, as did the Levellers of the English Civil War and the common folks who fought and won the American Revolution—democracy was the power of the many to take control of their destiny by putting the rich and ostentatious in their place. As I understand it, democracy is the assertion on the part of a demos that it has the power to act collectively to create a political world that provides for citizens' needs and sets them up for success. The animating force of democracy can be any number of emotions, including resentment.

The authors of the foundational American text of political philosophy, *The Federalist*, worried that, because the power of the demos is tremendous, democracy represents a potential danger to rights of all minorities in society (of course, they were worried primarily about the rights of the wealthy). Publius was right: democracy can be violent and oppressive if the resentment of the demos is uneducated and unchecked. Democratic outcomes are fundamentally unpredictable—we do not know how a "democratic" politics will turn out, even one born from the best of intentions. Democracy is a wager; it requires a will to believe in the possibilities of collective self-government and the basic goodness of the demos. Either you have this faith or you don't, but if you do, it is likely because you believe in education. One of contemporary American democratic theory's foundational faiths is in the transformative force of education. This was John Dewey's central insight: democracy requires a healthy system of public education that teaches vital skills (such as problem solving and political discussion) and also certain values, such as the dignity of all individuals and the fundamental equality between citizens. Though we tend to think of democracy as a set of activities—voting, polling, public debate, majority rule, congressional deadlock—Dewey taught that in fact democracy represents a personal attitude toward politics.[15] This attitude, of personal dignity, of deliberative fallibility, and of respect toward our fellows, is developed through interaction with others. The care of the self begins in the world of social interaction.

As we will see, democratic education must also teach citizens how to understand, critique, and produce rhetoric, because without an education in rhetoric, democracy will remain nothing more than an unrealized possibility haunting our dreams. Indeed, what is characteristic about the approach of contemporary rhetorical studies (in departments of Communication Arts and Sciences, like my own home department, and also in departments of English) is its focus—be it through training in writing, public speaking, public address, debate, or rhetorical theory—on civic education and democratic ethics.[16] Though rhetoric is all too often tarnished as a sham art, rhetorical scholars recognize that being able to make and understand arguments is essential to democratic politics, for without rhetoric, it is difficult to advocate and agitate and advance one's vision in public or private.

If democracy begins by empowering citizens—individually but ultimately in tandem, through great deeds but ultimately in shared words—then resentment begins in feelings of powerlessness, frustration, and victimhood. Resentment is an emotion foundational to democratic politics—it is not the only democratic emotion, certainly, but a primary political feeling—because power is never distributed equally throughout society and citizens are rarely given access to all they need to thrive. When the karmic force of democracy breaks down—when elites come to live off of politics rather than for politics—when those in power become hubristic and arrogant and unresponsive toward those they govern—when the structures of violence in a society seem immovable—when corporations gain rights that citizens lack—when the avenues to resist are frustrated at all turns—it is natural for citizens to feel they have been wronged, it is natural to feel resentment. Resentment is a very human reaction to the dualistic democratic world, in which citizens are promised a voice and a stake but are confronted by glaring disparities of wealth and shocking inequities of privilege. When dollars are equivalent to speech, and speech is equivalent to political influence, and most citizens have neither enough money nor enough speech, and the wealthiest Americans have almost unlimited amounts of money and speech and influence, then the rest of us are rightfully resentful. While it has never been a compliment to call someone "resentful," resentment is often perfectly appropriate in politics.

Resentment is one of the emotions that makes democracy dangerous. At the same time, resentment is subject to reversal. All too often today, oligarchic elites employ the politics of resentment to enlist the civic urge for a dangerous democracy—the widespread, commonplace desire in the United States to make power responsive to citizens and the economy serve the public good—in their quest for corporate rule. They do this by encouraging citizens to blame one another for economic calamity, dividing society between victims and victimizers ("red states" and "blue states," "real America" and its opponents) and in the process creating a context ripe for symbolic and material violence. And thus we come to the crux of the matter—to the tricky relationship between resentment, ever unpredictable, democracy, ever imperiled, and political speech, ever so angry, in contemporary American politics.

These are days of rage. Americans rage as our life savings evaporate in corporate swindles, as houses and jobs are lost, as healthcare costs soar, as politicians are bought and sold by corporations, as the rich get richer, as government proves unresponsive to pleas for social and economic justice. We rage as citizens are asked to pay taxes that corporations avoid. We rage as students take on crushing debt in pursuit of education, because there is always money for war but not for schools. We rage as long-term promises, the kind of promises we base our whole social system on, prove hollow; we work hard and still don't achieve the good life. The American Dream persists on the screen, on reality TV, and in the NBA draft, but to most people, the system seems rigged. We rage, often mindlessly and unproductively, at mellifluous politicians who speak sweetly and smile contentedly at our anger. The mark of these politicians and their banker buddies is the knowing wink—for they know that today resentment has been made to serve their interest, not ours.

Resentment is a natural, deeply human reaction to injustice and broken promises.[17] The ancient Epicurean mantra of *ataraxia*, equanimity in the face of disturbance, seems inappropriate in contemporary politics; it would be strange if citizens did not feel resentment in the face of such overwhelming structural violence. Though it might seem like our primary trouble today is the overabundance of civic resentment, this is not the case. The problem with our weak democracy is not the *quantity* of resentment but its *directionality*. What I call the politics of resentment involves channeling civic resentment—engendered by economic exploitation, political alienation, and a legitimate sense of victimhood—into a hatred of our neighbors and fellow citizens. Rather than allowing resentment to build up as the unifying emotion through which a demos becomes itself in opposition to an elite, the politics of resentment redirects resentment within the people, thereby taming the force of democracy to act as a path to justice.

Divided against itself, citizen versus citizen, neighbor versus neighbor, Americans find it increasingly difficult to come together and fulfill the promise of democratic fraternity—that of guaranteeing the collective ability to prosper by restricting the outsized power of the few, the rich, the elite, to cause damage to the many, the poor, the middle class. The politics of resentment is one of the most powerful forms of rhetoric ever developed for frustrating the aspirations of American citizens and perpetuating our feelings of victimhood. This rhetoric keeps citizens so weak that we find it difficult to do anything productive about our frustration. The result is a general acquiescence punctuated by explosions of hateful affect. The politics of resentment makes democracy less dangerous to elites, while creating the perfect context for citizens to turn violently on one another.

Ars Rhetorica

Before we can begin to talk productively about the types of violent rhetoric subverting democratic politics, we must first get a handle on the word *rhetoric*, which is one of the most confused and misunderstood terms in our political lexicon. In common parlance, rhetoric means one of two things: *fluff* or *deception*. Both definitions disparage rhetoric as a charade and, as such, capture something honest about Americans' experiences with the chicanery that masquerades as political discourse today. In this book, however, I make a distinction between the duplicitous act of pulling the wool over someone's eyes, the practice of "rhetrickery," and rhetoric more generally.[18]

In political discourse, the word *rhetoric* is rarely used without the diminutive "mere"—"mere rhetoric." Yet for much of Western history rhetoric was not considered "mere" at all. Rhetoric is one of the oldest liberal arts, and for millennia it has been understood to mean the things people say to persuade or advocate change. Generally speaking, rhetoric means symbolic action aimed at changing minds, changing motives, and changing worlds.[19] Rhetoric is therefore more than mere fluff and deception. Who we are as citizens is constituted through rhetoric; directed at an audience, rhetoric orients self toward other. Humans are social creatures, yet our experiences are subjective, limited by our bodies, our culture, and our language.[20] Though Ralph Waldo Emerson once imagined a transcendent, omnipotent eye that could see all, we have no such eyes. Our vision is bounded. Everyone is an other to us: Some others we draw close, some others we ignore, some others we push far away, some others we refuse to recognize as human. In turn, our relationships are contingent on our ability and our willingness to engage the other, to see the other as a fellow.

How we talk shapes how we know and experience the world. Rhetoric matters in our daily lives because how we talk to strangers, to our friends and families, to our enemies, and to the public, will affect the composition of those relationships. In the political realm, how we talk influences our ability to make good decisions and resolve conflicts. If our language allows us to identify with the other, peace is possible (but not guaranteed); if our language demonizes the other, then the road to violence is paved (though we need not walk it).[21] Our rhetorical practices—how we go about trying to persuade others and advocate change—influence the character of our personal relationships and also our politics. Here I agree with Wayne Booth, who suggests in *The Rhetoric of Rhetoric* that "the quality of our lives, moment by moment, depends upon the quality of our rhetoric."[22]

Rhetoric is an artful study in the use of language, and language use is foundational to human being. Indeed, Kenneth Burke defines humans as the symbol-using and symbol-misusing animal.[23] Language causes many of our problems, and is also the answer to those same problems. Humans use and are used by language; language can goad us to think and act in particular ways.[24] This means that we are never completely in control of our destinies. While we use rhetoric to build and do and be, we are also, at the same time, used by rhetoric—and thus one of the great human struggles is to wrestle language into a headlock. If we do not understand how to make our home in language, we will never feel at home in this world.

To study rhetoric is to understand that we as citizens and individuals are subject to many discourses—in fact, these discourses constitute us as subjects, providing us with markers of identity and even supplying many of our wishes and desires. We cannot care for ourselves if we do not first recognize our status as *subjects* in language and rhetoric. The care of the self, in turn, does not mean standing outside of language or finding some sort of authentic experience within it, as the existentialists hoped; it means instead understanding the forces that constitute us as individuals and citizens and then attempting to turn these discourses toward different ends.[25] The possibility for resistance to dominant discourses comes from within the rhetorics, not outside of them, and such resistance will utilize the very same forces and rhetorics, just creatively and irreverently.

Of course, it is notoriously difficult to demonstrate effect, to say definitively that rhetoric caused this person to do that particular thing. Yet there is little question that language can encourage us to see the world in ways that lead to violence (or, alternatively, nonviolence). It is therefore essential that we seize on the exigency created by the Tucson shooting and bring our contemporary rhetorical culture under the microscope. I want to be clear on this point: We cannot say that violent rhetoric was the sole cause of the shooting in Tucson. And we should certainly avoid knee-jerk reactions and recriminations, for such overt moralism following tragedy often does nothing more than shut down critical thought and rhetorical criticism. But two things about the art of rhetoric are clear—and to the extent that we forget them, our conversation about rhetoric and violence will be off point.

First, there is absolutely no question that rhetoric *can* cause violence. In fact, this is the stated point of one of the most celebrated genres of rhetoric in American history, the rhetoric of war. Look back on World War I, or the Vietnam War, or the "war on terror," or any of the other countless wars the United States has fought during its history, and you see clear and indisputable causality between rhetoric and violence.

Second, rhetoric can create an environment in which violence can seem logical, necessary, justifiable, and even righteous. Rhetoric does this by orienting the relationship between self and other, us and them, few and many, in such a way that concord is impossible and conflict is necessary. Rhetoric can inculcate personal attitudes and civic norms, while socializing citizens into an orientation, which actively promotes violence by redefining adversaries as "enemies" and politics as "war."

Here we can learn from the rhetoric of the "culture wars" that have dominated domestic politics in the United States since the 1980s.[26] As is implied in the phrase itself, the "culture wars" imagine the political clash between Democrats and Republicans, liberals and conservatives, as a war—and war carries with it its own rhetorical investments. To say "we are at war" is to express certain political commitments about how we as citizens should conduct ourselves in the world and how we should treat our adversaries. When politics is reconstructed as war, and when politicians use metaphors that are typical of war in their speeches, citizens are encouraged to think of themselves as soldiers locked in battle with their fellow citizens. During wartime, adversaries and competitors become "enemies." And when political adversaries are labeled as enemies—especially if those enemies, to take just a few charges that are typical of culture war rhetoric, are bent on murdering babies, euthanizing old people, appeasing terrorists, instituting fascism, denying God's love, implementing Sharia law, and orchestrating the death of the republic—it is logical, praiseworthy, patriotic, just godly to destroy them. The culture wars naturalize violence, making it the righteous vehicle of a domestic political crusade against filthy miscreants.

Burke observes that "the progress of human enlightenment can go no further than in picturing people not as *vicious*, but as *mistaken*."[27] It makes no sense to talk to monsters, because evil is devious and untrustworthy. Ipso facto, labeling people as devils entails violence. What is innately evil can only be killed. Picturing adversaries as mistaken rather than vicious, however, means that they can be persuaded. Imagining an adversary as mistaken rather than vicious leads toward deliberation, rather than away from it, and it is therefore vital that citizens develop the skills to be able to engage their opponents in good faith.

It is a truism that war is politics by other means. Today those fighting the culture wars have inverted this concept—and in fact, the very premise of contemporary political rhetoric is that politics is war by other means. One of our most pervasive political problems is that citizens are encouraged to imagine their adversaries not as mistaken but as evil: the hosts of wickedness in our democracy. Pundits, politicians, and others blessed with the gift of the gab have cleaved the citizenry into two—the silent majority and its vocal oppressors; red states and blue states; makers and takers; "real" America and its opposite (whatever that may be); the hard workers and the 47 percent. These same people have also radicalized debate into open political warfare between these camps. This is a felicitous rhetorical environment for politics to become violent, especially in a society where weapons are freely available, and a culture that undervalues and underfunds treatment for the mentally ill.

In our age of recession and sequestration, when so many people have lost their houses and their jobs, and when it seems that even the American Dream is faltering, many Americans feel they have been given a raw deal. Such feelings of injustice and victimhood are a very human reaction to powerlessness and frustration. The politics of resentment aims to make these feelings of victimhood politically productive. It does this by *capturing* the resentment Americans feel and *directing* it against civic equals, redescribing them as "enemies" who are said to be the cause of our suffering.

John Rawls argues that the psychological state of resentment involves a calculation of justice. For him, resentment is a moral emotion denoting a just reaction to being wronged.[28] Yet the morality of resentment is scrambled as soon as we take account of what Slajov Žižek labels "objective violence" or what Robert Hariman calls "structural evil"—that is, the normalized violence (including racism and poverty) produced by a social system.[29] When it is a social system, not an individual, that wrongs us, it is much harder to target our resentment. Who should we blame for the ravages of neoliberalism, which places profit above people and treats citizens as commodities? We can blame the wealthy elite who benefit from the system for their open attempts to perpetuate it, and we should, but attacking the "1 percent" or the "robber barons" or the "fat cats" or the "phonies" ultimately means very little if the system itself, and the discourses that sustain it, remain untouched.

In times of suffering, it is human to point fingers and cast stones. Blame gives meaning to suffering, and for this reason civic resentment is intimately related to the problem of scapegoating. It is an economic system that is to blame for much of the pain that Americans feel today—yet it is difficult for us, as rhetorical actors, to condemn a system. It is easier to blame individuals. While Rawls might be correct, and resentment at times might be associated with a desire for justice, Friedrich Nietzsche demonstrates how easily those who are willing to name a scapegoat, and who promise redemption through victimage, can dupe the resentful soul. To be resentful is necessarily to be vulnerable to manipulation.

The politics of resentment represents a shift *away* from the dangerous democratic possibilities inherent in correctly identifying individual culprits with structural violence, and *toward* a misplaced mutual resentment between social groups. In so doing, the politics of resentment tames and normalizes resentment's democratically eruptive force, ensuring a fundamental political ineffectiveness. In the end, the politics of resentment does not actively address the structural and rhetorical causes of suffering, nor does it provide redemption. The politics of resentment does not promote a discussion about what ails society. It does not provide solutions. It is a strategy of distraction that focuses attention on the grievance as an excuse to taunt and offend.

Taming Democratic Resentment

For much of Western history, democratic politics was conceptualized as the means by which citizens came together to protect themselves from the predations of the elite. The animating force of democracy was the resentment of citizens; this resentment inspired them to become a demos fighting for autonomy and self-determination. Unsurprisingly, then, political elites at the top of the social hierarchy have long viewed democratic resentment, not to mention democracy itself, with suspicion. From the very beginning, the art of politics in the West has been concerned with controlling, normalizing, manipulating, and taming civic resentment so that it does not explode into revolutionary acts. This is true in the United States as well. American rituals of nationalism in the eighteenth and nineteenth centuries were designed to domesticate the radically egalitarian, revolutionary message of the Declaration of Independence—which taught that citizens had the right to fight for "life, liberty, and the pursuit of happiness" when they were abused by unresponsive, tyrannical elites. Ensuring that civic resentment does not explode into a populist revolution is one of the central dilemmas of American nationalism.[30]

In Essay I, I describe the central place of civic resentment in democratic politics from the classical period forward to prerevolutionary America. I then outline the two rhetorical innovations the founders of the United States devised for taming democratic resentment. First, the founders offered Americans a new slogan for their politics: *e pluribus unum*, which affirms that Americans are not divided into rich and poor—Americans are one. And how best to teach Americans to see themselves as one? Answering this question was the founders' second innovation—they developed a rhetoric of enemyship that demanded civic unity when confronting national enemies. Encouraging Americans to fear and hate those outsiders who threatened the nation, enemyship redefined the citizenry as comrades in arms, as patriotic citizen–soldiers dedicated to defending the flag. Charged with putting the needs of the nation before their own interest in collective self-determination, enemyship called on Americans to be one but not a demos, to be agents of the state rather than agents of their own destiny. And when Americans did not answer this call, enemyship gave authorities a powerful rhetoric for denouncing civic resentment and tarnishing resistance as un-American. By framing unity as a necessity in times of trouble, enemyship disqualified the conflict between mass and elite as unpatriotic.

In Essay II, I examine how the politics of resentment became central to governance in the United States during the late 1960s through a discussion of the public address of President Richard M. Nixon. During this decade the force of an outward-looking, international enemyship was broken. The dominant metaphor American politicians used to conceptualize politics, that of *e pluribus unum*, collapsed when confronted with social tension and the Vietnam War. Nixon offers a particularly noteworthy example of how conservative politicians seized on the anomie of the 1960s to transform resentment into a force of retrenchment that worked against progressive social change. Though the two master tropes of the politics of resentment—"the silent majority" and "the tyranny of the minority"—had circulated in American public discourse before the 1960s, Nixon pronounced them in a way that fundamentally rewrote ancient democratic practices. Rather than call on the poor to unite to battle the rich, Nixon arrayed the army of the silent majority for an internecine battle against tyrannizing minorities who disturbed the tranquility of traditional political hierarchies. We continue to fight such battles today—the silent majority is the rhetorical precursor to Karl Rove's "red states," Sarah Palin's "real America," and Paul Ryan's "makers." The tyrannizing minority is the racialized fear of "the takers" and "the 47 percent" derided in contemporary discourse.

Beginning in the 1970s and 1980s, the politics of resentment was put in the service of advancing the economic philosophy of neoliberalism, which has become the dominant discourse driving American capitalism today. In Essay III, I tie the politics of resentment to neoliberalism through a close reading of Sarah Palin's address in response to the Tucson shooting, given on Wednesday, January 12, 2011. I focus on Palin because her rhetoric offers a master class in the contemporary neoliberal politics of resentment. By individualizing blame and deflecting civic attention away from the honest consideration of objective violence, her rhetoric also illustrates the profound flaws in how neoliberal economic philosophy teaches Americans to understand violence. Today, the politics of resentment continues to fracture Americans in the interests of defending the vested interests of corporations and wealthy people. The politics of resentment weakens the citizenry even as it encourages Americans to yell and damn our neighbors.

It is when things are taken for granted that they become accepted for truths, and, sadly, the politics of resentment is so familiar today that it is taken for granted. It is my goal in this book to demonstrate that the politics of resentment is not fixed—this violent rhetoric has a history. This book is a diagnosis of rhetorical disorder. My aim is to offer a model rhetorical criticism of the politics of resentment that contributes to the history of the present. When we are born, we are thrown into a world we did not create, alive with conversations we did not begin and built on traditions we did not initiate. This past shapes us, constituting us as subjects. We experience the present *a priori* and interact with it as though it is natural, whole, and seamless. Yet the present is a fragile construction built on a monumental past we are taught to celebrate and revere. Understanding this, Michel Foucault implores scholars to practice a form of genealogical analysis that illuminates how the present came to be.[31] Genealogists study the past in order to map the present, revealing the history of political warfare behind what we accept as "truth" and the forces at work shaping what we accept as "reality." Without question, rhetoric is one of the central forces operating in the construction of the present. To reveal the present as a rhetorical construction is to loosen the hold of the past over our souls and create space for alternative futures.

To narrate the history of the politics of resentment is to denaturalize it, which I understand to be a first step toward challenging and, I hope, defusing this form of rhetoric. The politics of resentment is one force working to shape our present rhetorical realities. It is a chief reason for the nastiness of our vitriolic political discourse. There is no question that rhetoric can cause violence, and the politics of resentment makes violence seem logical, necessary, and even righteous. The politics of resentment colors our political discourse red. There is also no question that we need not accept such skullduggery. In the end, I call on citizens to take action rather than be resigned to the politics of resentment. What this resistance might look like, I cannot pretend to say, for it is impossible to portend the endless creativity of democratic action.

I fear that any book written with the goal of proving the stupidity of those it critiques can only reinforce and intensify the ugliest face of democratic politics. Arrogance has no place in democracy, which calls for humility and circumspection. So I want to be clear from the get-go: in this book I am not interested in bashing conservative Americans. Conservatives are just as much a part of the United States as other citizens. Like most liberals, most conservatives are hardworking people trying to get by as best as they can in a difficult economy. Like most liberals, most conservatives are modern-day Sisyphuses, fighting an uphill battle to provide a better life for themselves, and their kids, in the face of a gloomy economic future in which the middle class is shrinking and inequality is growing at historic rates.

I grew up in one of the most conservative states in the United States—if not the most conservative state—Kansas. "To the stars through difficulty" (*ad astra per aspera*) is the state motto, and this is certainly a moment of difficulty in which the stars are hard to see. On many points I believe my fellow Kansans are mistaken, but I know from experience that they are not bad people. What Kansas illustrates is the folly of bad leadership, and the consequences of poor rhetorical education (though this is not limited to Kansas). In this book I am interested in critiquing a style of leadership that has been employed by conservative politicians since the 1960s to harness, rather than soothe, popular resentment, and to direct this animus at their political opponents. I believe that most Kansans think that when they vote Republican they are resisting dominant regimes of power, that they are being subversive to the welfare state and the errors of big government. The politics of resentment is nefarious because it enlists the honest desire for resistance to power in defense of a neoliberal governance regime that is, ultimately, life-destroying. This is why I say this rhetoric involves a betrayal of democratic desire. I critique the politics of resentment not as an ideological crusader who has a beef with conservatism; I am concerned, as I think all citizens should be, about the violent consequences of this discourse—for it encourages citizens to go to war against their fellow citizens.

I am familiar with the violent consequences of the politics of resentment, for I grew up in Wichita—ground zero for the culture wars—during the 1980s and 1990s. I came of age in a place where angry shouts were considered perfectly appropriate political speech, and bombs political advocacy. I remember the signs and the commercials and the bullhorns and the dread. I remember being completely crestfallen when George Tiller was murdered while serving as an usher at the Sunday morning service of his

Wichita church. I know that we need to defuse the forms of rhetoric that encourage us to see our fellow citizens as evil and to hate them—and this includes the politics of resentment. In the end, this rhetoric deflects attention from the conversations we most need to have, and the struggles we most need to wage. The costs, both human and civic, are much too dear.

Essay I

Reimagining the People:
From *Duas Civitates* to *E Pluribus Unum* to *E Unibus Duo*

According to the *Oxford English Dictionary*, resentment connotes "a sense of grievance," "an indignant sense of injury or insult received or perceived," a feeling of "ill will, bitterness, or anger against a person or thing," and "the manifestation of such feeling." Resentment is a complex emotion involving at least three components: the perception that one has suffered an unwarranted injury (or the forecast that an injury is coming) and thus a judgment of moral wrong; a feeling of hostility at the perpetrator of the injury; and the manifestation of that hostility, in words or deeds. Resentment begins in an immediate and hostile reaction to an insult or an injury; if it is not satisfied or disciplined, and if is repeatedly invoked in memory and through discourse, this resentment can then be intensified into an orientation that shapes outlook, motive, and action—pushing politics ever closer to indiscriminate and stupid violence.

Civic resentment has long made political elites tremble, for they understand that resentment is a political force productive of extraordinary power shifts. Throughout Western history, political authority has been, in one way or another, invested in managing democratic resentment. The politics of resentment represents an innovation in governing, for it does not aim to mitigate citizens' resentment. Rather, it undermines the democratic potential of resentment by redirecting it within the people, thereby using that emotion to uphold political systems that are bad for the citizenry—such as oligarchy, the rule of the super-rich. As it is practiced today, the politics of resentment encourages Americans to direct civic resentment against their fellow citizens and not at social structures that benefit the wealthy and powerful. The politics of resentment cleaves the people into two, into victims and victimizers, and in so doing weakens the collective power of citizens to shape their social world by ensuring that they do not act as a unified body.

The politics of resentment cultivates an internecine war at the heart of democracy. The first step of the politics of resentment is, accordingly, to redefine "the people," encouraging citizens to think of themselves not as a demos but instead as two groups at war. In this essay, I describe how the politics of resentment became a rhetorical possibility available to politicians in the 1960s for reshaping the American democratic landscape. I do so by tracking two pivotal shifts in conceptualizations of "the people" in the United States. These are, of course, not the only important moments in American democratic history—but they are the most vital for a genealogy of the politics of resentment.

The first rhetorical shift occurred during the founding period. When writing and defending the Constitution, the founders rebuked classical Greek and Roman conceptions of democracy as a battle between mass and elite, and institutionalized a different vision of politics organized around the trope *e pluribus unum*, out of many, one. And with this shift came the articulation of a lasting rhetorical strategy for asserting the centrality of oneness to American politics: the *rhetoric of enemyship*, which called on Americans to become a single political body united against an outside enemy. Even if this unity was not realized, and it rarely was, enemyship created a perfect recipe for denouncing resentful citizens taking up the banner of the many versus the few as traitors in league with the enemy. That is precisely the point of enemyship: it weakens democracy by co-opting civic energies and displacing these energies onto desirable targets.

No one rhetoric ever dominates politics. The rhetoric of enemy-ship has never been the exclusive rhetoric of governance in American politics. Over the course of nineteenth and early twentieth century, various American leaders flirted with a politics of resentment. Such a politics only seemed possible at moments of extreme political and social division. When Andrew Jackson vetoed the Bank of the United States on July 10, 1832, he pledged to "take a stand" "against any prostitution of our Government to the advancement of the few at the expense of the many," thereby calling forth democratic resentment by reiterating classical conflict between "rich men" and "the people." The Know-Nothings capitalized on the political division, and general national confusion, of the 1850s to espouse a nativist, anti-immigrant discourse founded on white, Protestant resentment. During the Civil War, resentment became central to political discourse, as *e pluribus unum* fractured into two competing political bodies—this time organized along geographical and moral divisions instead of those of class; and this time literally exploding into war. It was against resentment and in the service of *e pluribus unum* that President Abraham Lincoln spoke those timeless words, "A house divided against itself cannot stand." After the war, "The South Will Rise Again" was a slogan of repressed resentment that frequently broke out into open conflict against a resurgence of postbellum oneness.

Enemyship stands in fundamental opposition to the politics of resentment—in fact, as political leaders talked up the dangerousness of foreign enemies and instructed Americans to get in line because *you're either with us or against us*, enemyship proved, from the late eighteenth to the early twentieth centuries, to be an antidote to any politics that attempted to divide the citizenry against itself. This was often less because enemyship produced actual unity in the populace, and more because enemyship codified unity as a political norm that was then deployed to disqualify dissent as unpatriotic.

The second shift in rhetorics of "the people" I track in this chapter occurred during the 1960s. While the politics of resentment had been practiced before in American politics, it had always been answered—and undermined—by politicians who success-fully leveraged the fear appeals characteristic of enemyship to demand civic unity from citizens. During the 1960s, the force of the imperative *e pluribus unum* faltered in the face of political agitation for equality and widespread outrage against the Vietnam War. Rather than revert to old metaphors of oneness and tried-and-true rhetorics of enemyship, President Richard M. Nixon—here acting as a representation of key trends in conservative political discourse—attempted to capitalize on the widespread social resent-ment of "the silent majority" by embracing division. This is the second shift: from oneness back to division.

Nixon's divisive politics—again, which I take as representative of conservative leadership tactics more generally during the decade—recovered something of the classical sense of democracy as a battle between conflicting social groups. His motto was not *e pluribus unum* but essentially *e unibus duo*, out of one, two. Nixon's rhetoric was not interested in achieving social justice or alleviating civic resentment, however. He avoided triggering the ancient con-flict between rich and poor, he did not empower citizens to stand against sovereign power, and he squashed many communities that stood against the status quo. His rhetoric was invested in promot-ing civic discord, intensifying civic resentment, and then directing this resentment at his political enemies. In this way, Nixon pro-vided politicians with a model for containing the democratic force of resentment and directing it in directions they deemed desirable.

Mass Versus Elite, the Few Versus the Many

How politics is lived depends in large measure on how the body of citizens is imagined. The ways that political actors talk about the people, and the metaphors that are used to conceptualize the rela-tionships of citizens with one another, matter deeply—for our practices and habits of citizenship are developed in accordance with how we talk about and imagine the citizenry and its potential

to become a demos.[1] How we define "the people" largely deter-
mines our *attitudes toward democracy*.[2] Democracy begins with an
imaginative leap beyond the individual to the group, whether
troped as "the people" or "the public" or "the poor" or "the many"
or "the multitude" or "the rabble" or "the takers" or "the lumpen-
proletariat" or simply just "us."

In the West, from antiquity to the Enlightenment, "the people"
had been conceptualized as an entity divided against itself, bifurcated into two social classes battling for power—in ancient Greece
hoī olīgoi and *hoī pollōi*, in Rome plebs and patricians, in colonial
America the rich and the poor, creditors and debtors, the gentry
and the landless. In democratic cultures from classical Greece to
revolutionary-era America, the distinction between the few and
the many, rich and poor, was accepted as fact, and democracy was
the means for the masses to make themselves heard and check the
influence of the rich and powerful.

For the ancient Greeks, democracy referred to the power
(*krātos*) of the people as the capacity to act. Josiah Ober argues
that "*demokratīa*, which emerged as a regime-type with the historical self-assertion of a demos in a moment of revolution, refers
to a demos's collective capacity to do things in the public realm, to
make things happen."[3] The democratic capacity for collective
action in Athens was first asserted after the democratic revolution
of 508–7 BCE and Cleisthenes's reforms of the Athenian constitution. This empowered demos was invested primarily in keeping
social balance in check and ensuring that the rich did not tyrannize the poor. It was when this balance faltered, when the ability
of the mass of citizens to act was frustrated, that the citizenry felt
resentment and, at times, asserted itself as a demos—and thus
the force of democratic resentment was directed into the clash
between few and many, elite and mass, rich and poor.[4] This clash
was so foundational to Greek politics that Socrates could even
subject it to his traditional entelechy in Xenophon's *Memora-
bilia*.[5] It was in the context of this conflict that democracy became
dangerous.

The ethos of democratic Athens was captured in the soaring tones of Demosthenes's speech "Against Timocrates," which proclaimed that democracy represents "a spirit of compassion for the helpless, and of resistance to the intimidation of the strong and powerful." Democracy resists "brutal treatment of the populace, and subservience to the potentates of the day."[6] Greek democracy was designed to protect the poor from the influence of the rich: democracy, in short, was a means to achieving balance and justice, which it did with liturgies, *eisphora*, ostracisms, and punitive fines against the rich leveled by popular courts.

Representing the contrary point of view, Socrates fretted over the noisy terror of an empowered demos in Plato's *Republic*. He claimed that democracy "comes into being when the poor win, killing some of the others and casting out some, and share in the regime and the ruling offices with those who are left on an equal basis."[7] Plato enumerated two key themes in aristocratic Greek thought: first, that democracy was a revolutionary form of government instigated by the poor and founded on force of arms (*di' hoplōn*) and fear (*diā phōbon*).[8] Second, that democracy was invested in achieving equality above all else: *ek īsou metadōsi politeīas*, democracy gives an equal share to citizens. For Plato, this equality ruined good citizens by forcing them down to the level of the dregs, but for common citizens it likely meant the promise of self-determination and a political body not ruled by selfish aristocrats.

Athenian citizens were prone to feeling resentment toward the few because of past attempts to overturn democracy and institute aristocracy or tyranny in Athens. Moreover, they felt resentment because of their pride in democracy and because philosophers and other aristocrats were constantly questioning their capabilities and demeaning democratic government. Resentment was familiar, in short, because it was productive—resentment was the spur to demos-formation, and the might of the demos acted as a defense mechanism for sustaining democracy against those who would happily subvert it and subordinate popular influence to that of an oligarchy, monarchy, or aristocracy, be it of a hereditary elite or philosopher kings. The force of resentment was directed into democratic praxis, and Athenians practiced resentment to protect themselves from the domination of the rich and powerful.

According to Ober, who is one of the foremost experts on classical Greek democracy, popular resentment in Athens after the Thirty Tyrants, during the time of Plato, Isocrates, and Aristotle, originated in the tension between egalitarian rhetoric and the stark reality of economic inequality:

> The existence of economic inequalities created considerable tension in Athens. The demos needed the rich men, since with the loss of the empire the democracy was able to function only by taxing their surplus wealth. The wealthy in turn knew that the state was run out of their pocketbooks; they expected to be, and indeed were, allowed to retain certain social privileges in compensation for their cash outlay. The recognition that the rich were privileged inevitably led to a sense of resentment among the masses, whose dominant ideology stressed political and legal equality. Clearly, if the advantages enjoyed by the rich got out of hand, democracy would end.[9]

Athenian democracy in the fourth century was remarkably stable because it achieved an equilibrium between the masses and the elite: elites agreed to speak in the language of the dominant democratic discourse, and to use their wealth for the benefit of the public, and in exchange they were able to retain many of their special privileges without citizens asserting themselves as a demos and using their greatest power, the power of numbers, against them. Yet there was little question of who was ultimately in charge. The citizenry controlled the fortunes of the wealthy, the interests of the state, and the forums of deliberation and judgment, including the courts where wealthy aristocrats faced public judgment.

In public performances in classical Greece, elites were expected to pay homage to the popular will, to defer to popular decisions, and to use their wealth and power for the common good. Whenever elite Athenians disparaged democratic power and upset the balance between rich and poor, citizens expressed resentment. Aristotle claimed that rich Athenians tended to be haughty (*huperē-phanos*), and, brimming with hubris, they swaggered about the city.[10] The rich were prone to insulting the poor, because "by insulting they think they are superior"; but if insulted, especially by those of "no account," they became angry, "for anger resulting from being belittled is assumed to be against those who have no right to do it, and inferiors have no right to belittle."[11] About public speaking, Isocrates observed, "If you factor in the ignorance that all men have, and the resentment [*tous phthonous*] that arises in us," there were certain characteristics a speaker could not exhibit in front of a democratic audience without triggering civic resentment: *misanthrōpos* (hating people), *huperēphanos* (being haughty and arrogant), and *misōdemos* (hating the demos).[12] If an elite speaker displayed such traits, he would face the justified resentment of citizens.

Resentment might have been an adaptive force central to democratic politics, but that did not make it any more palatable to Greek elites. According to Isocrates, Athenian citizens were "hostile to those who are superior by nature."[13] Such hostility was directed at the rich Athenian aristocrats who called themselves gentlemen, and Isocrates and other Greek writers attributed it to the fact the mass of Athenians were poor. Both Plato and Aristotle described democracy as the rule of the poor, and Aristotle observed that in democracies power was widely distributed but exercised despotically in the interests of the lower class. Isocrates revealed in *Antidosis* that his friends had advised him not to speak truthfully about his life, his career, and his wealth, because "some men" "have been so brutalized by resentment [*phthonou*] and want and are so hostile that they wage war, not on depravity, but on prosperity. They hate [*misousin*] not only the best men but also the noblest pursuits; and in addition to their other vices, they congregate with other criminals and show them sympathy, while destroying those for whom they bear resentment [*phthonēsōsin*] if they can."[14] Due to popular hostility against the rich in Athens, he claimed, he and others had to defend themselves against the charge of being rich.[15]

In *Antidosis*, Isocrates described the psychic state of the demos: they were hateful of the rich, and they were *phthonoūntas*.[16] In translations of Isocrates, *phthonos* is often rendered as "envious," and at times *phthonos* clearly meant straight envy: the masses desired the wealth, status, and privileges of the elite for themselves.[17] There is no doubt that envy is a real emotional force in democratic cultures. Yet labeling democratic resentment as envy has always been a convenient way for elites to dismiss democratic demands as sinful and unworthy of consideration. Whenever a definition of a word clearly serves the interests of a particular political hierarchy we should question it—and that is true of *phthonos*.

In Greek philosophy and literature, *phthonos* meant not just "envy" but also "resentment" and "indignation." In classical Greek, *phthonos* was a synonym for *nemesis*; both had connotations of righteous, and justified, resentment toward someone who overstepped his or her social bounds.[18] Class modulated these words: *phthonos* was generally associated with "upward" resentment of the masses toward the elite, and *nemesis* with downward resentment of the elite toward the masses.[19] The verb *phthoneo* carried connotations of "feel righteous indignation at," and *phthonos* was earned when a person's "arrogance and privilege are not warranted."[20] In the democratic culture of Athens, *phthonos* was tied to the maintenance of equal power between mass and elite. Someone who tried to rise above the mass without demonstrating the proper qualities and respect was subject to *phthonos*.[21]

The translation of *phthonos* solely as "envy" is therefore problematic—an error fueled by Aristotle, who in his *Rhetoric* broke with colloquial usage and distinguished *phthonos* from *nemesis*. It is important, given the centrality of resentment to democratic politics, to recover how Aristotle characterized this emotion in his *Rhetoric*, which was unquestionably the most important treatment of the emotions in classical Greece.[22] Aristotle defined *to nemesan*, which was an emotion typically associated with the upper class, as "indignation" and marked it as a valid social emotion; yet he defined *phthonos*, an emotion typically associated with the lower class, as "envy" and marked it as socially abhorrent.[23] *Phthonos* was, in fact, the only emotion he dismissed as necessarily reprehensible.[24] By stigmatizing *phthonos* as envy, and disqualifying the emotion from civilized rhetorical discussion, Aristotle worked to subtly disarm and disqualify the possibilities for radical democratic action based in resentment of the rich and powerful on the part of the poor and numerous.

From the Greek democracies forward, the conflict between few and many was central to the democratic imaginary, inspiring both revolutionary action to achieve dignity and an equally intense fear in those at the top of the social hierarchy. This was also true in Rome. The basic social distinction between citizens and the Senate or elders, between the people and the Roman elite, was built into the institution of Roman politics with the office of the Tribune of the Plebs. Moreover, the Senate and the people, via the *tribunus plebis*, were said to manifest different and often antithetical forms of power—the Senate *auctoritas patrum*, the people *potestas* and *imperium*.[25] The battle between rich and poor was allegorized in a number of prominent Roman myths, including the fratricidal tragedy of Romulus and Remus, and displayed in the very logo (*SPQR, Senatus Populusque Romanus*) and language the Romans used to represent politics to themselves and the world.[26]

The "struggle of the orders" between the people and the aristocratic elite drew to a close during the fourth century BCE, with the plebs winning a share of power. Livy described Roman politics as "duas civitates ex una factas," two cities having been made out of one, "each side with their own magistrates and laws."[27] The *duas civitates* Livy spoke of were the rich and the poor, the few and the many. The philosophers of ancient Greece and Roman accepted this class distinction as the basic fact of political life. For classical proponents of democracy, resentment was not some arbitrary emotion, but a political force guaranteed by the clash between mass and elite. Resentment was an inevitable feature of the emotional landscape of democratic politics.

The Roman rhetorical theorists recognized, as had the Greeks before them, that resentment was a dangerous emotion. Some, including the politician and historian Sallust, attempted to transform popular anger at the Roman aristocracy into shared indignation.[28] Quintilian described Sallust as a first-rate historian, equal to Thucydides and superior to Livy.[29] Two speakers in Sallust's histories, Macer and Memmius, directed popular resentment against the nobles. Macer described the power of the people, as sanctified in the office of the tribune of the plebs, as "telum a maioribus libertati paratum," a weapon from the ancestors having been provided for the purpose of defending liberty. Macer concluded, "I have decided that to enter into battle for liberty and be defeated is better for the strong man than not to have struggled at all."[30] Sentiments like this revealed democracy at its most dangerous, for Macer called on the many to band together to protect their liberties and resist the elites attempting to dominate them. Both Macer and Memmius rallied the plebs not in order to promote bloodshed and mass violence, they claimed, but instead to affirm the ultimate power of the people—the power of the sovereign, democratic, resentful refusal to tolerate the slights of their social "betters." This indignant, resentful "no," directed by the many against the few, was a powerful rhetorical weapon in the democratic fight for dignity, equality, and the common good.

Other elites saw democratic resentment very differently, including Cicero. Indeed, the rhetoric of Sallust and Cicero represent antithetical responses to the resentment at the heart of the ancient democratic conflict between rich and poor.[31] For Cicero, though it was imperative that the orator be skilled in riling up an audience, one of his primary jobs was also to calm the audience and bring them to peace (*otium*). *Populares* speakers like Sallust fought against civic acquiescence, while *optimates* orators like Cicero tried to promote it. In his *Oratio Lepidi*, Sallust denounced the "otium cum servitio" of the masses, their passivity and quiet in the face of oppression, because he equated quiet with slavery: "quieto servitio." Taking the polar stance, in *Pro Sestio* Cicero described his social ideal as "cum dignatate otium," tranquility (*otium*) joined with worthy standing—that is, social peace led by the best men.[32]

In *On Rhetoric*, Aristotle claimed that the opposite of anger, *praotēs*, often translated as "calmness" or "satisfaction," was a useful emotion for the elite rhetor to be able to create in a popular (perhaps disobedient) audience. Cicero, too, talked up rhetoric's power to quiet a murmuring multitude. "Nothing is so easy as to divert a crowd from pain and often from ill will by means of a timely and terse and wise and lively phrase," he concluded.[33] He maintained in *De Oratore* that the speaker should be able to *revocare*, to call back an audience from the paroxysm of passion.[34] It is worth noting here that Cicero explicitly (and repeatedly) mentioned *invidia*, which is how he tended to translate the Greek word *phthonos*, as well as *iracundia*, anger (a translation of the Greek *orgē* and an emotion often associated with resentment), and *iniuria*, the belief that one had been injured, as three of the emotions that an orator should be skilled in calming.

The philosophers of the classical period tended to conceptualize resentment as a bitter, eruptive force that had to be contained or calmed. Cicero certainly understood resentment in this way. Yet an essential aspect of any genealogy of resentment is also narrating the story of how popular resentment is domesticated to productively serve the interests of a particular political regime. The rhetorical tradition is vital to such a story, for rhetorical scholars—with their acute understanding of language and persuasion—have often been on the leading edge of such theorizing. Understanding this, we can look with fresh eyes on Cicero, for he attempted to conceptualize resentment as a stable intensity and thus as a force that could be made predictable and governable.

In *De Oratore*, Cicero described how the orator could best con-
jure key political emotions—including love (*amor*), hatred (*odium*),
anger (*iracundia*), resentment (*invidia*), pity (*misericordia*), hope
(*spes*), joy (*laetitia*), fear (*timor*), and anxiety (*molestia*)—in an
audience, and also how to assuage those emotions when they were
not advantageous to the speaker.[35] These emotions acted as political
forces that could be enlisted in the battle for hierarchy and the
rule of the best men (or, alternatively, in the battle for democracy).
Cicero was particularly concerned to describe the rhetorical force
of *invidia*. Cicero judged *invidia* the most democratic of all the
emotions, the most dangerous, and the most difficult to tame: it "is
by far the most violent of all emotions, nor does it require less
power for its repression than for its stimulation."[36]

Drawing the same distinction between *nemesis* and *phthonos*
that Aristotle worked so hard to establish in his *Rhetoric*, and again
proving the philosopher's lasting impact on rhetorical conceptions
of the emotions, Cicero distinguished *indignatio* from *invidia*,
explaining that "indignation is not the same as resentment."[37] The
meaning of *indignatio* was close to the Greek *nemesis*, and like
Aristotle, Cicero worked diligently to take indignation out of the
hands of the masses. *Indignatio* became for Cicero an emotion that
an elite speaker conjured up in an address to move an audience,
rather than a popular emotion that could be used to rally the plebs
against the Roman nobles. In fact, Cicero transformed *indignatio*
into a technical term for a rhetorical maneuver that a good man
speaking well performs in the peroration of a speech. In conclud-
ing an address, a speaker must do three things: he must sum up the
oration, he must engage in *indignatio*, arousing ill will against an
opponent, and he must arouse sympathy (*conquestio*). In *De Inventione*, Cicero observed, "The *indignatio* is a passage which results
in arousing great hatred against some person, or violent offense at
some action," and he lists fifteen topics appropriate for the *indignatio* part of the peroration.[38] Having made indignation the
domain of the elite speaker, what was left to the masses was *invidia*,

and *invidia* was an inherently illegitimate emotion, a sign of bad character and, in many cases, Cicero implied, madness.

Invidia originated in a social balance gone haywire—especially when someone had unjustly or arrogantly risen up the social ladder, ascending above those who were once equals, or when an elite man conducted himself with hubris, as such men often did: "Now people are especially resentful of their equals, or of those once beneath them, when they feel themselves left behind and fret at the others' upward flight; but resentment of their betters also is often furious, and all the more so if these conduct themselves insufferably, and overstep their rightful claims on the strength of pre-eminent rank or prosperity."[39] Cicero continued to describe how resentment, *invidia*, could be fueled if it was in the speaker's interests to do so: "If these advantages are to be made fuel for resentment [*invidia*], it should before all be pointed out that they were not the fruit of merit; next that they even came by vice and wrongdoing; finally that the man's deserts, though creditable and impressive enough, are still exceeded by his arrogance and disdain."[40] Most importantly for the elite speaker, it was necessary to be able to soften this emotion:

> To quench resentment [*invidia*], on the other hand, it is proper to emphasize the points that those advantages were the fruit of great exertion and great risks, and were not turned to his own profit but to that of other people; and that, as for any renown he himself may seem to have won, though no unfair recompense for his risk, he nevertheless finds no pleasure therein, but casts it aside and disclaims it altogether: and we must by all means make sure (since most people are resentful, and this failing is remarkably general and widespread, while resentment is attracted by surpassingly brilliant prosperity) that the belief in such prosperity shall be weakened, and that what was supposed to be outstanding prosperity shall be seen to be thoroughly blended with labor and sorrow.[41]

Cicero understood resentment as a dangerous democratic emotion, but it was also a political force that could be domesticated with the proper rhetorics. Cicero was remarkably clear and straightforward in his treatment of the rhetoric of *invidia*: resentment could be cultivated by stressing that success was unearned and directed against the common good; resentment could be mollified by contending the contrary, that success was won through hard work and at great personal expense, and that great wealth was directed toward the good of all. *Invidia* was powerful because it was endemic to democratic politics—and because, with the right words, the force of resentment could be turned against a speaker's opponents. Humans were naturally resentful of "brilliant prosperity" (*florenti fortunae*), and in any society where there was such prosperity and hence economic stratification, resentment was an emotion present for rhetorical action. Cicero would continue his discussion of *invidia*—especially the rhetorical methods for calming it (derived in large measure from Stoicism)—in *Tusculan Disputations*, where he described several forms of emotional distress that could be consoled through rhetoric, including "the bite of poverty."[42]

These themes—the definition of democracy as the competition between the rich and the poor, and the centrality of resentment (*phthonos/invidia*) as an emotional force animating democratic politics—resounded far beyond the classical era. These ideas were at the heart of Machiavelli's writings on popular government. Like Sallust, who was one of his chief inspirations, Machiavelli believed that this conflict was productive because it nurtured an active concern in the populace for protecting liberty.[43] The competition between rich and poor formed a constituent theme in the writings of the Levellers and Diggers who, during the English Civil War, demanded economic justice for laborers and a formal recognition that the powers of government came from the people.[44] Americans echoed this discourse when they imagined politics in the early republic—they understood their society to be, like ancient Rome, bifurcated; they, too, lived in a world of *duas civitates*. As Gordon

Wood notes, "By the 1780s the most common conception used to describe the society was the dichotomy between aristocracy and democracy, the few and the many. The essential struggle of politics was not between the magistracy and the people, as the Whigs had thought, but between the two social groups of the people themselves."[45] One of the foundational political goals in on-the-ground politics during the Revolution was to ensure that elite, rich men did not dominate the masses and that citizens were not steamrolled by their rulers. Rightly understanding the potential of democracy as a powerful force of civic organization, and hoping to contain the mighty potential of the citizenry to become a demos fighting for equality and self-determination, the framers took aim at this definition of politics with the Constitution.

The Poor-as-Faction Trope

Contrary to the misperception cultivated by politicians and pundits today, the United States was not born a "democracy." Democracy was portrayed as an enemy to political virtue and national stability in the years following the American Revolution.[46] "The evils we experience flow from the excess of democracy. The people do not want virtue; but are the dupes of pretended patriots," Massachusetts's Elbridge Gerry commented at the Constitutional Convention.[47] In *Federalist* No. 10, James Madison claimed that democracies "have, in general, been as short in their lives, as they have been violent in their deaths."[48] In 1788, at the height of the controversy over ratification, Fisher Ames announced that "a democracy is a volcano, which conceals the fiery materials of its own destruction. These will produce an eruption, and carry desolation in their way."[49] "If wisdom then has improved on the democracy of the ancients; faction has also refined on the means of defeating the end of those improvements," the *New-York Herald* announced in 1795.[50] "This form of government," promulgated an essayist in 1803, "is extolled by those men, whose weakness and ignorance have constantly impeded their progress to the attainment of excellence and fame. This is their last resort."[51] John Adams concluded in 1814 that "democracy never lasts long. It soon wastes, exhausts, and murders itself. There never was a democracy yet that did not commit suicide."[52] Notice the violent, catastrophic imagery in these quotations: democracy was a volcano, a plague, a cancer, a storm, a wildfire—in short, democracy was a violent imposition of the popular will and thus a powerful, nigh uncontrollable force tantamount to a natural disaster.[53] For these early American critics, who echoed ancient aristocratic critiques of democracy like Plato's *Republic*, democracy was a politics of last resort in which the filthy rabble was elevated to prominence while the good and noble and true suffered.

During the founding period, democracy was feared because it existed in a state of exception beyond law.[54] Democracy was not yet the national, institutionalized, bureaucratized system of government that we know today. Instead, democracy emerged when people asserted their right to nullify laws and decisions they considered contrary to the community's interests. In the thirteen colonies, mobs, riots, and other popular forms of protest were widely accepted democratic methods for the community to enforce its sovereign will and to right a perceived wrong. Democratic action was dangerous; it was a way for poor citizens to make real the popular slogan "government by the people, for the people."

As it had for the Greeks, democracy in the early American republic meant the enactment of the people's power to limit the influence of the rich and powerful, a power that was often expressed in acts of collective political will known at the time as "regulation." Crushed by a deep economic recession, seeking debt and tax relief, and weary of becoming the "foot-stool" of the wealthy, in the mid-1780s citizens all along the seaboard rose up in a series of rebellions—with the popular uprising that became known as Shays's Rebellion in Massachusetts in 1786–87 being the most prominent example.[55] According to the first historian of this event, George Richards Minot, the insurrection was the product of "hostilities between creditors and debtors, between the rich and the poor, between the few and the many"—hostilities first exposed during the Revolutionary War that exploded into open conflict between the rich and the poor in 1786–87.[56]

The men who gathered to write the U.S. Constitution in the summer of 1787 also interpreted Shays's Rebellion as a conflict between rich and poor.[57] With the uprising in Massachusetts very much on their minds, those gathered at the Constitutional Convention repeatedly expressed their determination to prevent the poor from dominating the rich. In Philadelphia on June 6, 1787, Madison observed that "all civilized Societies would be divided into different Sects, Factions, & interests, as they happened to consist of rich & poor, debtors & creditors, the landed & the manufacturing, the commercial interests, the inhabitants of his district, or that district, the followers of this political leader or that political leader, the disciplines of this religious sect or that religious sect." He then expressed his persistent, all-encompassing concern that "in all cases where a majority are united by a common interest or passion, the rights of the minority are in danger." This worry was supported by the study of world history and "verified by the Histories of every Country antient & modern. In Greece & Rome the rich & poor, the creditors & debtors, as well as the patricians & plebeians alternatively oppressed each other with equal unmercifulness."[58]

At the Constitutional Convention on June 18, Alexander Hamilton observed similarly that "all communities divide themselves into the few and the many. The first are the rich and well born, the other the mass of the people. The voice of the people has been said to be the voice of God; and however generally this maxim has been quoted and believed, it is not true in fact. The people are turbulent and changing; they seldom judge or determine right."[59] The lesson for Hamilton was to balance out the pernicious influence of the masses, who happened to be poor, by increasing the power of the rich, specifically by giving rich Americans a "permanent" interest in government (via an aristocratic senate with long terms in office).

While *vox populi vox Dei*, the voice of the people is the voice of God, was a common proverb in Renaissance and Enlightenment political discourse, Hamilton denied that that the *vox populi* shared any characteristics with the *vox Dei*. Instead, he expressed his hope that the new Constitution would place its faith in a rich elite rather than the poor masses.

Both Madison and Hamilton affirmed the classical worldview of *duas civitates* at the Constitutional Convention.[60] Yet when it came to justifying the Constitution, they adopted other political vocabularies. Madison, especially, rejected the classical politics of the few and the many in his public discourse. Madison's *Federalist No. 10*, an essay recognized by historians and political thinkers to be one of the most important works of political philosophy in the history of the United States, was significant in 1787, and remains so today, because it rearticulated the classical politics of the few and many into the modern language of "factions." Indeed, one of Madison's central rhetorical moves was *reductio ad factum*, the downgrading of the many from the very center of politics to a mere faction competing with other factions for influence. According to Madison, the poor was a "faction" whose interests stood contrary to the permanent and aggregate interests of the body politic.[61]

Enlightenment philosophers tended to agree with the ancients that societies were always divided between rich and poor, or, in more modern language, between property owners and the landless (hence, creditors and debtors). How they addressed this social fact differed widely. Take Jean-Jacques Rousseau, who opened *The Social Contract* (1762) with the classic lament, "Man was born free, but he is everywhere in chains."[62] In his discussion of inequality in society, Rousseau proclaimed that the modern state did not repress but instead produced violence. For Rousseau, society was formed to protect private property, which, he claimed in his *Discourse on the Origin of Inequality* (1755), was the origin of social oppression: "The first person who, having enclosed a plot of land, took it into his head to say *this is mine* and found people simple enough to believe him, was the true founder of civil society." He continued,

"What crimes, wars, murders, what miseries and horrors would the human race have been spared, had someone pulled up the stakes or filled in the ditch and cried out to his fellow men: 'Do not listen to this imposter. You are lost if you forget that the fruits of the earth belong to all and the earth to no one!'"[63] Because society was premised on artificial distinctions enforced by violence, and because modernity entailed inequality, social life produced democratic resentment; backlash from the downtrodden was a constant threat, making society unstable.[64] Rousseau argued that society's laws did not contain violence but instead produced it in the interests of protecting artificial property distinctions. Rousseau's solution was to minimize government and promote civic education in its place.

Madison could not have disagreed more strongly with Rousseau's conclusions.[65] He rejected Rousseau's argument that private property was an artificial system contrary to nature and supported by the violent repression of dissent. Instead, he followed Enlightenment liberalism generally, and John Locke specifically, by naturalizing economic stratification as an inevitable feature of modern life. While Rousseau argued that there is nothing natural or inevitable about who is rich and who is poor, Madison audaciously claimed that property distinctions were not contingent but were, on the contrary, produced by "the diversity in the faculties of men," by which he presumably meant intelligence and initiative.[66] Society's elite, he reasoned, were likely such because of their superior faculties. Viewing hierarchy as natural, Madison claimed that it was the job of government to protect private property. He thus ceded Locke's point that "the great and chief end therefore, of Men uniting into Commonwealths, and putting themselves under Government, *is the Preservation of their Property.*"[67]

Madison acknowledged that the oppression of the masses by the moneyed few was a problem; yet, the essays of *The Federalist* were much more concerned with the mischief caused by the poor-as-faction. Madison thus repeated the old fear, first articulated by philosophers and aristocratic elites in ancient Greece, that the people were avaricious and that democracy was just another name for stealing. The poor, somehow, stood contrary to the permanent, aggregate interests of society as a whole. It is interesting that Madison labeled those without property a faction in the first place—how, after all, could a majority of the community have an interest contrary to the interests of the community? Yet this was precisely what Madison feared—a fear that would be given a catchy name in the next century by Alexis de Tocqueville: "the tyranny of the majority." To the extent that societies were organized around protecting private property, the poor could be defined as a faction—even though they were the majority—precisely because it was their collective interest to infringe on property rights by stressing equality, or even worse, redistribution.

Of course, by Madison's logic, rich Americans were also a faction—a fact that he acknowledged in *Federalist* No. 10. Yet here we see the perverse casuistry of American liberalism at its moment of institutionalization in the federal Constitution. Labeling wealthy Americans a "faction" undermined the legacy of classical democracy by elevating the interests of the rich to the same level as those of the poor. Moreover, labeling the rich a faction was an empty symbolic gesture—for the interests of the rich, factional or not, were protected by the Lockean law of the land inscribed in the Constitution.

Madison flatly rejected the suggestions of activists like the Levellers and philosophers like Rousseau, for he disagreed that economic inequality could be managed by promoting material equality. About democracy Madison wrote, "Theoretic politicians, who have patronised this species of government, have erroneously supposed, that, by reducing mankind to a perfect equality in their political rights, they would, at the same time, be perfectly equalized and assimilated in their possessions, their opinions, and their passions."[68] On this point he was emphatic: "reducing" humans to "a perfect equality" was not the answer.[69] Government had no interest in balancing out the economic power of the rich. On the contrary, in one of the most twisted facts of the founding period, the framers argued that government had the opposite interest: to augment the power of the rich and their control over politics.[70] At a time when the classical republican vocabulary was being overtaken by the discourse of liberalism, the United States was born a *government for the poor, by the rich*.[71]

Moreover, Madison, Hamilton, and the other founders rejected the concept of a mixed constitution that would have affirmed the poor as a class whose interests should be represented in government. The idea of mixed constitutions, of *duas civitates ex una factas*, was ancient, articulated in Book IV of Aristotle's *Politics* and Book VI of Polybius's *Histories*. The idea was also central to Enlightenment political philosophy. Surveying world history, Algernon Sydney concluded that "the best Governments of the World have been composed of Monarchy, Aristocracy, and Democracy."[72] Rather than divide government based on the interests of the few and the many, the Constitution chose a division based on separation of powers. By denying any governmental interest in promoting equality, Madison also affirmed that the Constitution did not create a "mixed government," and that it was not invested in protecting the poor at the expense of any other social class. He derided the democratic demand for equality as manifested through economic reforms ("an equal division of property") as the lunacy of the Levellers, as an "improper or wicked project."[73]

Writing under the handle Publius in *The Federalist*, Madison and Hamilton maintained that the United States was no longer *duas civitates ex una factas*, as Rome and classical Greece were. Instead, the founders forwarded a different metaphor for the new nation: *e pluribus unum*, out of many, one.

E Pluribus Unum

When writing and defending the Constitution, the founders acknowledged and then rebuked classical conceptions of democracy as a battle for power between rich and poor. Casting aside the metaphor of *duas civitates*, the founders of the United States institutionalized and attempted to actualize a very different vision of politics organized around the trope *e pluribus unum*, out of many, one. No longer would politics consist of the rich and the poor battling for supremacy; in the United States, Americans would speak with one voice—whispering, singing, shouting, "We the People."

For something as significant as our national motto, memorialized in our federal letterhead and on the national currency we carry around in our pockets and purses, the phrase *e pluribus unum* carries with it a less-than-inspirational origin. Though we do not know for sure, America's greatest slogan-maker, Benjamin Franklin, was probably its inventor. It is likely that Franklin yanked the words from the title page of *Gentleman's Magazine*, a London publication first published in 1731 that combined articles from various publications into a single periodical. The earliest known usage of the complete and exact phrase *e pluribus unum* occurred on the title page of this periodical.[74]

Franklin was friends with Edward Cave, the editor of *Gentleman's Magazine*. He published several essays in the rag and attempted to bring the publication to the colonies. Furthermore, Franklin's nephew, Benjamin Mecom, started a short-lived publication in 1758 called the *New England Magazine of Knowledge and Pleasure* that borrowed the bouquet image and its attendant Latin phrases from Cave's publication. Mecom's magazine featured the following couplet in its issue of October 1758: "Alluring *Profit* with *Delight* we blend; / One, *out of many*, to the Public send." Variations on the "oneness" theme can be found in antiquity, but none is more likely a source for the national motto than the quotation as found on the title page of *Gentleman's Magazine*.[75]

Surprisingly, before the 1770s and 1780s *e pluribus unum* was never a battle song or rallying cry, easy as it might be to imagine it as a call to arms. In fact, the figure of the bouquet from *Gentleman's Magazine* bears much in common with a similar phrase in line 103 of the poem called "Moretum" ("Garden Herbs"), often attributed to the great Latin poet Virgil, and commonly misidentified as the inspiration for the U.S. national metaphor. Yet Virgil's phrasing was different; his poem contained the phrase *color est E pluribus unus*, which referred not to a political motto but instead to a poor person preparing his dinner by combining several ingredients together into a salad.[76]

The concept of constituting oneness from plurality was articulated in Franklin's design, in 1776, of the Continental currency (the "Continental Dollar," or "Fugio cent"). On the reverse of the Continental Dollar (both paper and coin versions) is the phrase "WE ARE ONE," surrounded by a chain comprising thirteen interlocked rings, each representing one colony bound together in a common fate. Franklin recognized the Continental currency as a crucial response to the rhetorical situation of a contentious and quarrelsome Congress. The adoption of the "WE ARE ONE" motto on the Continental Dollar likely informed, if it was not itself informed by, the suggestion of *e pluribus unum* for the Great Seal of the nation.

In 1776, a congressional committee consisting of Thomas Jefferson, John Adams, and Franklin convened to work on the national seal. After enlisting the help of the French artist Pierre Eugene du Simitiere, this committee tossed around a number of ideas for the design, including a multicultural coat of arms representing the diverse nations "from whence America has been peopled": Moses parting the Red Sea; the children of Israel wandering in the wilderness; the mythic Saxon chiefs Hengist and Horsa; and Hercules taking instruction from Virtue while denying the seduction of Sloth.[77] Franklin originally proposed the national slogan to be "Rebellion to Tyrants Is Obedience to God"; Jefferson was so impressed by this motto that he included it on his personal seal. Yet Congress was unimpressed by the committee's final design submitted on August 20, 1776—which suddenly and without explanation included the phrase *e pluribus unum*. Two subsequent committees retained the phrase, as well as the idea of the all-seeing eye (the "Eye of Providence") and the date 1776 in Roman numerals (MDCCLXXVI) in their designs of the seal. A second committee on the seal met in May 1780. A third and final committee met in May 1782. Finally, in June 1782, Congress handed Secretary of Congress Charles Thomson all the materials compiled by earlier committees. Congress accepted Thomson's final design for the Great Seal on June 20, 1782, including *e pluribus unum* as a national motto.

In the 1780s, the founders of the United States pivoted from talk of faction to talk of oneness. The rhetoric associated with oneness was devised to temper the ancient conflict between mass and elite—which Madison reinscribed in the language of "faction"—by asserting that all Americans, no matter how rich or poor, were equally involved in the national, patriotic project and were equally subject to its rules. The founders feared the rabble and were interested in protecting themselves, and the fortunes of other wealthy Americans, from the mob's grasping hands. The motto *e pluribus unum*, which collapses distinction and promotes the unity of an exceptional people, was their answer to the ancient problem of democratic resentment. Before the Revolutionary War, the oneness theme referred to the combination of several distinct elements into a stronger union—strength through confederacy.[78] As the U.S. motto, however, *e pluribus unum* quickly came to refer more to the flattening of distinction into a singular, national identity.

The rhetoric of *e pluribus unum* was a savvy if cynical move to protect the interests of the rich by arguing that they were indistinguishable from the interests of the poor. The founders claimed that the nation's interests transcended those of individual and class, yet of course the rich men who wrote the Constitution were the ones who defined the nation's interests.[79] Born as an empty slogan, as much an aspiration as a reality, *e pluribus unum* had to be given rhetorical force so that it could be enacted. Jefferson might have believed, as he wrote in 1774, that Americans were "Insuperabiles si inseparabiles," invincible if not divided—but how to make Americans of one mind?[80] With its call for oneness, *e pluribus unum* demonstrated a lasting rhetorical strategy for accomplishing it: the rhetoric of enemyship.[81]

Unlike friendship, whose bonds are forged by mutual affection, enemyship fabricates bonds of mutual antagonism for the enemy. At its most forceful, enemyship asserts a bifurcated, Manichean world of us against them: *you're either with us or against us.* Even when this rhetoric is not successful in making the world over in its image—as it rarely is—it is nevertheless still powerful, for it creates a rhetorical schema for discrediting democratic dissent. Repeated time and time again, enemyship produces civic norms—such as patriotism, deference to sovereign authority, and the martial debt owed to those who died to defend our freedom—that undermine the ancient democratic conflict between few and many. In declaring the United States to be a nation of oneness through their rhetoric of enemyship, the founders fundamentally altered the practices of citizenship associated with American politics. Over the long run, enemyship has proven an enduring rhetorical technique for disciplining democratic resentment.

Hobbes's Gamble

The idea of enemyship is ancient, with precursors dating back to the foundations of Western civilization. To take just one example, in his speech *Panegyricus*, Isocrates proposed mitigating the internecine squabbles between the Greek city-states, and between the few and the many, by waging war on a common enemy—the Persians. "The plan" for unity, he observed, "is simple and easy; it is impossible to have a secure peace unless we join together to make war [*polemēsōmen*] against the barbarians, and it is impossible for us to be unified [*homonoēsai*] until we gain our advantage from the same sources and run our risks against the same enemies."[82] About the *Panegyricus*, Isocrates observed, "What speech could be about finer and greater deeds than one which exhorts the Greeks to a campaign against the barbarians and counsels us to have a united purpose [*homonoias*]?"[83] For Isocrates, *polemeō*, making war, was the path to achieving *homonoeō*—being at peace, or, more literally, being of one mind.

Many Roman elites shared this thought. In Book III of Livy's *Ab Urbe Condita*, the tribunes of the plebs (who were tasked with fighting for the people) repeatedly complained that the nobles used foreign conflict to ally social tension and negate the demands of citizens asserting themselves as a demos. Roman nobles waged war, the tribunes fretted, not to advance the republic's interests but to distract the Roman people from rising up to defend their liberties from elite abuse.[84] About war and danger, Livy wrote, "Dum haec in foro sedandae discordiae causa aguntur"—such were the means undertaken to calm discord in the Forum.[85]

Although the idea of enemyship was ancient, it was the seventeenth-century philosopher Thomas Hobbes's genius to describe a political philosophy in which enemyship could become the central technique for managing democratic resentment. Hobbes was the Enlightenment author of the philosophy of oneness, and his dream of an England united under kingly rule was captured in the famous frontispiece to the first edition of *Leviathan* (fig. 1). Hobbes's sovereign promoted oneness by naming a public enemy who represented an existential danger to the entire commonwealth, and by making this danger seem more immediate and serious than any demos's demands for economic justice or collective self-determination. Hobbes's guideline for producing union and taming democratic resentment was simple: constitute unity through fear, a fear shared equally by rich and poor, by the aristocratic and the democratic "factions."

Hobbes's writings in the 1640s and 1650s were driven by the desire to justify a state in which acquisitive individuals—modern subjects as liberalism conceived them—could be disciplined to peacefully coexist. Hobbes pondered how best to convince self-interested individuals, desirous of power and property above all else, to band together into nations. He was also concerned about the terrible power of a resentful demos. Hobbes understood that

FIG. 1   Frontispiece to the first edition of Thomas Hobbes's *Leviathan*, 1651.

the force of democracy was at its most potent in a politics that had been bifurcated into rich and poor, the few and the many. Unlike Machiavelli and the Levellers, Hobbes saw no value in this conflict, and he foreshadowed Madison's *Federalist* No. 10 by describing the rich and the poor as "factions." The factions of "Patricians, and Plebeians of old time in Rome, and of Aristocraticalls and Democraticalls of old time in Greece, are unjust, as being contrary to the peace and safety of the people, and a taking of the Sword out of the hand of the Sovereign."[86] Dividing power between "the Aristocraticall, and Democraticall, factions" was, he mused, a death sentence for the modern state and the king's sovereign power.[87]

For Hobbes, the evils of democracy were on display during the English Civil War that raged from 1642 to 1651, a conflict that claimed over 180,000, including the head of King Charles I. Hobbes blamed the chaos on those "democratical writers" who, in "the Reading of the books of Policy, and Histories of the antient Greeks, and Romans," had spread the idea that monarchy was incompatible with liberty.[88] "From the reading, I saw, of such books, men have undertaken to kill their Kings, because the Greek and Latine writers, in their books, and discourses of policy, make it lawfull, and laudable, for any man so to do; provided before he do it, he call him Tyrant," Hobbes concluded.[89] In the strongest possible terms, he condemned those political actors who, heads chock-full of classical ideas about politics, spouted off nonsense about monarchy and democracy that justified killing their king.

Hobbes's philosophy was designed to eliminate the ancient democratic conflict between rich and poor. In the process of ordering multitudes, his Leviathan mitigated the age-old conflict between few and many by providing these "factions" with common enemies to fear. Oneness was peace because, to the extent that the people believed they were one and acted accordingly, there was no conflict inside the commonwealth. No longer would citizens have any reason to fear their neighbors; no longer would the poor fight the rich. All were equal under the benevolent protection of the iron-fisted potentate.

Hobbes believed that the people, rejoicing in the safety that the king provided, would abandon their hopes for economic justice or populist revolution in exchange for that protection. The frontispiece to the first edition of *Leviathan* models Hobbes's ideal political oneness.[90] Rejoicing in the safety that the king provided them, Hobbes believed that the people would abandon their hopes for economic justice or populist revolution in exchange for that protection.

If you look closely at the famous image you see that the king literally organizes the body politic—his body is composed of the commonwealth's people. And if you look even more closely, you see that all of the commoners are looking in the same direction, their eyes fixed on the glory of the sword-and-scepter-wielding sovereign. The oneness of the Leviathan demands that every citizen turns his or her gaze in the same direction, toward the king, who is the sovereign (represented by the mitre), and the wielder of violence (represented by the sword). Hobbes's king represents a specific vision of political force and the monopolization of violence. In seventeenth-century political thought, the king's violence served two primary functions: meting out punishment for the guilty, and defending the populace from its enemies.[91] Thus, the monarchs of this period governed by staging spectacular punishments, including macabre and expensive festivals of sovereign violence. They also called on their subjects to unite to confront their enemies: to face the enemy was to be one. In Hobbes's *Leviathan*, we see two forms of governance; *sovereign violence*, which, according to Michel Foucault, was simply too expensive to endure much past the eighteenth century, and, accordingly, was supplanted by disciplinary mechanisms and biopolitical strategies for controlling populations; and *enemyship*, which has persisted to the present.[92]

Hobbes summed up the essence of modern governance as "protego ergo obligo," from protection follows obligation.[93] This is Hobbes's gamble: that citizens would trade many of their natural rights, including the right of revolution (which early liberal thinkers repeatedly affirmed), for protection from danger, so long as the danger was of sufficient enormity. He bet, in short, that citizens would give up the democratic power gained by cleaving the polis into *duas civitates* in order to achieve the stability and peace of oneness.

Hobbes's gamble has proven throughout the centuries to be one of the most effective techniques for taming democratic resentment. The founders of the United States adapted Hobbes's philosophy to their own needs, taking his gamble and developing a rhetoric of enemyship that has been deployed to discipline democracy through the assertion of patriotic norms of oneness since the founding period.

My description of the founders' debt to Hobbes's rhetoric of governance might be surprising given that the Revolutionary War was clearly a war fought against Hobbes's vision of the state. Sovereignty was one of the most significant issues that divided Americans from the British during the 1760s and 1770s. Hobbes articulated a theory of indivisible and unlimited sovereignty residing in the king, yet the American theory of sovereignty was born out of a set of material conditions that allowed for precisely the opposite: in the colonies, power was divided, local, and popular.[94] The founders still faced many of the problems that Hobbes addressed, however. While the Constitution divided sovereignty between the judicial, legislative, and executive branches, between the federal, state, and local governments, and, presumably, between government and the people, it had to compel assent to the laws, persuade citizens to work together for the common good, and temper the democratic impulses that exploded in revolution in the 1770s. It had, in short, to make Americans obedient to government rather than the other way around. In addressing these problems, the framers created a federal government capable of harnessing the power of enemyship to manage the conflict between the few and many at least as well as the kingship Hobbes imagined. The United States is therefore the mirror image of the Leviathan: republican, not monarchal, but cut from the same rhetorical cloth.

Hobbes the monarchist taught the founders of the United States two vital lessons about governance. First, that government can manage populations by providing protection from enemies because security is one of the most basic, if not the most basic, of human needs. And second, that political authority can be won by cultivating fear. Government would prove its authority by providing Americans with safety from danger. Hamilton commented in *Federalist* No. 8, "Safety from external danger, is the most powerful director of natural conduct. Even the ardent love of liberty will, after a time, give way to its dictates."[95]

In the early American republic, enemyship involved three maneuvers. First, politicians named a public enemy shared by all Americans, replacing resentment with fear as the dominant political emotion. Americans in the seventeenth and eighteenth centuries had become accustomed to experiencing the fear of god; in a time of revolution, political fear became the means to oneness, for as Thomas Paine observed, "mutual fear is the principle link in the chain of mutual love."[96] By making Americans fear, politicians displaced the ancient divisions of democratic politics. Second, politicians construed the relationship between us and them in such a way that communication with the enemy was no longer possible, making it that much harder for enemies to reconcile and transforming the relationship between us and them from one of dialectic to one of absolute hostility. Finally, politicians escalated the crisis "from argument to arms" by cultivating widespread civic fear with a disquieting rhetoric of imminent danger and attack.[97] With enemyship, the founders of the United States adapted the basic insight of Hobbes's philosophy into American politics: *protego ergo obligo*, from protection follows obligation. The path to disciplining civic resentment was fear.

A Union of Resentful Citizens

Philosophers have long disagreed about the moral status of resentment and this emotion's capacity to contribute to social stability and hierarchy. Several Enlightenment philosophers, including the Anglican bishop Joseph Butler, Adam Smith, and Thomas Reid, broke with Hobbes on this question. They claimed that resentment was an emotion fundamental to morality and essential to governing liberal individuals, those modern souls living in disenchanted times. These philosophers hoped to normalize resentment, making it predictable and hence governable.

According to Butler, whose astute account of resentment in *Fifteen Sermons Preached at the Rolls Chapel* (1726) has proven one of the most influential in political philosophy, there are two types of resentment: a "sudden," defensive, bodily reaction to an insult or an injury (in other words, "anger"), and a "settled" or "deliberate" resentment that is felt in any rational being in response to moral evil and "to injury and wickedness in general."[98] In its "deliberate" state, Butler believed resentment to be foundational to the moral sentiments and the emotion that activates our sense of right and wrong. Both forms of resentment were reactive, and both manifested themselves most forcefully in actions of retribution: with the first targeting the injurer, the second targeting not the person but the moral vice itself, and with the first being individual, the second communal. Butler believed that resentment was foundational to modern governance because it would draw people together into communities determined to mite out justice, and also because it would deter criminals from acting immorally, lest they face the justified resentment of the community. For Butler, deliberate resentment and the communal acts of reprisal it entailed distinguished civilization from Hobbes's state of nature, where individuals were free to pursue retribution as they saw fit outside the oversight of the community. Butler's distinction between the two types of resentment became central to Enlightenment writings on the subject—Lord Kames adopted it and renamed sudden resentment "instinctive"; Thomas Reid called sudden resentment "animal" and deliberate resentment "rational."

Adam Smith was one of the many Enlightenment philosophers Butler influenced. He developed Butler's thinking further in *The Theory of Moral Sentiments* (1759). Here he dubbed Butler's deliberate resentment "proper resentment," and he contended that this type of resentment addressed a key deficit of moral motivation in many people that could drive citizens to fight for social justice.[99] Smith's *Theory of Moral Sentiments* described a microphysics of power based on the internalization of cultural norms in the absence of a watchful god. For Smith, by internalizing social norms and then judging their own actions in relation to those norms, individuals became self-regulating; by encouraging citizens to monitor one another, society became self-regulating. Resentment was vital to this process of self-regulation. For Smith, it was a deeply human emotion: "nature has implanted in the human breast" a "consciousness of ill-desert."[100] Sudden resentment was natural and deeply human; through instruction and self-discipline, Smith believed that humans could develop a sense of deliberate resentment that would draw them into the community and commit them to upholding the community's norms.[101] Proper resentment involved adopting the attitude of the "impartial spectator," or what Smith called "the man within the breast," when evaluating one's emotions and conduct: a criminal deserved punishment if he was "the natural object of a resentment which the breast of every reasonable man is ready to adopt and sympathize with."[102] Rather than merely a mindless rage for revenge, proper resentment represented the desire for a specific form of retaliation: "to bring him back to a more just sense of what is due to other people, to make him sensible of what he owes us, and of the wrong he has done to us."[103] Proper resentment was a demand for accountability and acknowledgment of wrongdoing in the context of a community committed to justice. In its proper form, resentment addressed a key deficit of moral motivation in many people and became a spur to acting toward justice.

An astute student of language who gave lectures on rhetoric and belles lettres in the late 1740s at Edinburgh and the early 1750s in Glasgow, Smith believed resentment to be a powerful emotion for moving people to appropriate behavior. The philosophers of the Scottish Enlightenment, including Smith, imagined that people were naturally sympathetic, with minds like "mirrors" reflecting the emotions of others.[104] For Smith, then, it was possible to coordinate human cooperation through resentment directed against criminals and other wrongdoers.[105] Resentment was the means to social order and hierarchy: he prophesized an *e pluribus unum* of resentful citizens forged in opposition to criminals and other wrongdoers. Smith claimed that communities of resentment could be built by triggering a sympathetic response to another citizen's resentment: "When we see one man oppressed or injured by another, the sympathy which we feel with the distress of the sufferer seems to serve only to animate our fellow-feeling with his resentment against the offender."[106] When confronted with the "most deadly of crimes" such as murder, humans feel "an immediate an instinctive approbation of the sacred and necessary law of retaliation."[107] While Hobbes (of whom Smith and the other participants in the Scottish Enlightenment were deeply critical) called on the sovereign to create order by naming public enemies that the people would fear, Smith attempted to turn resentment toward civic justice by encouraging the collective denunciation of wrongdoers who were subject to the shared feelings of proper resentment.[108]

It is a self-perpetuated (and self-perpetuating) myth about liberalism that its goal is to place the individual outside the workings of power—hands off, says the liberal philosopher in the name of negative liberty. Here, Hobbes: "A FREE-MAN, is he, that in those things, which by his strength and wit he is able to do, is not hindred to doe what he has a will to do."[109] Yet liberalism advances a rhetorical economy of power just like any other philosophy of government; it is a strikingly affective economy that orders by working on the emotions of citizens. In Hobbes, there is norming through fear.[110] Smith's laissez-faire individual would be ruled by resentment.

The Scottish Enlightenment exercised a profound influence on the outlook of the founders of the United States, especially their conceptions of the art of rhetoric.[111] However, the framers did not

adopt Smith's insights about resentment as a moral force foundational to government. At least on the question of resentment,
Smith's meditations proved untimely. In *The Federalist*, "resentment" was something to be avoided, and Publius imagined a politics that could manage and perhaps even purge public resentment
from the public sphere.[112] Rather than Smith's blame culture, the
founders pledged their allegiance to a politics of public reason,
valorizing a rational, un-affected public discourse—urging Americans to speak, when they had to, with "the mild voice of reason."[113]

Yet the founders were not above appealing to the emotions of
the citizenry. In fact, they believed such affective appeals to be
foundational to the art of government. In *Federalist* No. 49, James
Madison countered those anti-federalists who called for a second
Constitutional Convention by noting that the charged partisan
atmosphere of the moment would not allow for reasoned discourse. At this time, "the passions, therefore, not the reason, of the
public, would sit in judgment." This was a problem because "it is
the reason of the public alone, that ought to control and regulate
the government. *The passions ought to be controlled and regulated
by the government.*"[114] The public could speak when it was rational,
and only then (hence the power of "reason" as a disciplining force).
In a remarkable statement that shows the intended reach of the
new government—which would be far from hands-off—Madison
announced that it was the job of government to control and regulate the passions of the public. And thus early politicians spoke in
an affective register, targeting the emotions of citizens to win their
allegiance to the Constitution and the new political order. "The
government," Hamilton wrote, "must be able to address itself imme-
diately to the hopes and fears of individuals; and to attract to its
support, those passions, which have the strongest influence upon
the human heart."[115] Consequently, the founders employed all of
the available means of persuasion to target the hearts of citizens,
including the basest forms of rhetoric (or better, of *rhetrickery*):
slander, doublespeak, innuendo, and fearmongering. Understanding reason in its Hobbesian sense—as the desire for peace at any

and all costs—the founders set American politics on the path to becoming a politics of fear.

Shirking collective rituals of resentment like those imagined by Smith—for the history of this emotion was too dangerous—American politicians adopted enemyship as their primary rhetoric of governance for managing democratic aspirations during the eighteenth and nineteenth centuries. It is likely, given resentment's volatile history within the field of a democratic politics of the few and the many, that this emotion did not seem to be a realistic force suited for governance. Had they tried to harness civic resentment, the framers would have discovered that without a powerful discourse for generating civic norms that stabilized and normalized resentful responses—without, in short, a *rhetoric of resentment*—there was no way to stabilize and normalize civic resentment. As we will see in Essay II, it was the development of just such a rhetoric that allowed the politics of resentment to become a technique of governing in the mid-twentieth century.

The U.S. Constitution, like Hobbes's *Leviathan*, demands obedience from citizens in exchange for safety. Repeatedly, during the eighteenth, nineteenth, and twentieth centuries, enemyship has distracted Americans from their political and economic grievances. Enemyship has long been the dominant rhetorical strategy in the United States for countering the old democratic discourse of *duas civitates*, which was animated by civic resentment, with a new metaphor of *e pluribus unum*. For much of American history, enemyship was the rhetorical means for promoting obedience, disqualifying class conflict, and encouraging allegiance to the Constitution.

The founders of the United States found that enemyship had three predictable effects on the populace. First, enemyship created a national identity where there was none, defining what it meant to be an "American" by positing an enemy that was fundamentally "un-American." Enemyship rhetorically constituted "the people" as one. Second, enemyship persuaded Americans, who were deeply divided on issues including religion, language, ethnicity, slavery, taxation, industrialization, urbanization, and the franchise, to come together into a more unified national community. Enemyship did not preclude dissent, but it did produce working coalitions by finessing citizens' psychological attachments to and investments in war. Enemyship was the rhetorical means of enacting the trope of *e pluribus unum* and using this trope to challenge the democratic politics of the few and the many. Third, enemyship distracted Americans, redirecting their anger away from a distant government intent on augmenting the influence of the rich at the expense of the poor, and toward a national enemy. In the founding period, enemyship acted as a safety valve for citizen resentment. It continued to be a tried and true rhetorical strategy for achieving desirable political effects well into the twentieth century.

American Enemyship

Americans living in the 1960s were no strangers to enemyship, for this rhetoric has a long (though largely unwritten) history in the United States.[116] Enemyship helped assert norms of national unity after a terrible Civil War. Enemyship fueled American support for the two world wars. Even after World War II, Americans continued to portray the world in terms of an enemyship of us versus them—one national enemy, the Nazis, was simply replaced by another, the Soviets.

The transition from WWII to Cold War was seamless and, according to many historians, instantaneous. In fact, it has been argued that the United States dropped "Little Boy" on Hiroshima on August 6, 1945 (killing between 130,000 and 150,000 civilians), and "Fat Man" on Nagasaki on August 9, 1945 (killing between 60,000 and 80,000 civilians), not to compel Japan to surrender— for all intents and purposes, President Truman and his advisers knew that Japan was defeated, and Japan knew this, too—but instead to impress and intimidate the Soviet Union with the superior technological knowhow of the U.S. military.[117] There was then, and remains today, substantial debate over whether the bombs were necessary to force Japan to surrender. The sticking point for the Japanese leadership in the summer of 1945 was whether the United States would allow the office of the emperor to continue after the nation's inevitable defeat. General Dwight D. Eisenhower and Truman's chief of staff, Admiral William D. Leahy, both opposed the use of the atomic bombs as unnecessary and, ultimately, immoral. Yet President Truman approved the bombs "without hesitation, without even contemplating an alternative."[118] Why? In his influential 1965 book *Atomic Diplomacy*, Gar Alperovitz claimed that the bombs were a spectacle designed to cow the Soviets from their activity in Eastern Europe and establish American dominance as the leader of the free world.[119] The atomic bombs at once ended World War II and began the Cold War.

Looking back on the decade, in his 1969 *An Essay on Liberation*, Herbert Marcuse observed that the rhetoric of the state "not only defines and condemns the Enemy, it also creates him; and this creation is not the Enemy as he really is but rather as he must be in order to perform his function for the Establishment."[120] The Cold War was characterized by the escalation of conflict with fearful rhetoric about missile gaps, Karl Marx, and atheist evil. Politicians during this period defined the American people as a militarized brotherhood of patriotic citizen–soldiers bonded in their shared antagonism for the red menace.[121] And thus the lessons of the founding period cut straight through centuries. Fear remained at the heart of politics, and Hobbes's gamble continued to be a dominant means by which politicians demanded popular obedience and subdued the democratic resentment of the few.

For Kenneth Burke, a crucial feature of language is that it can act as a motive for behavior. Humans use and are used by language; language can goad us to think and act in certain ways. I accept Burke's argument that when we use language, our behavior becomes subject to it—often more so than the other way around. To understand human behavior, then, it is necessary to study the nature of language. Thus is clear during the Cold War, when talk of the Iron

Curtain, falling dominoes, and containment justified American intervention in Asia in the 1950s and 1960s, including Vietnam. The Vietnam War was the product of Cold War enemyship. The language of the Cold War goaded American politicians into viewing the world in such a way that intervention in the postcolonial Vietnamese Civil War seemed logical and necessary. American intervention in Vietnam was born from the strident anticommunism of postwar American liberalism. After the assassination of President John F. Kennedy, who had first sent American "advisers" and then troops to Vietnam as a show of American strength in the fight against communism, which suffered a major setback with the Bay of Pigs fiasco, President Lyndon B. Johnson escalated American involvement in Vietnam steadily and dramatically, especially after the Gulf of Tonkin Resolution in August 1964 (though its charges were later proven to be false).[122]

The enemyship of the Vietnam War was stoked by a rhetoric of national innocence: as demonstrated by the nation's sacrifices during and after World War II, Americans were a guiltless people innocently and tirelessly working to create and maintain peace and the rule of law in the world. President Johnson framed American intervention in Vietnam by contrasting Vietnamese force with American political freedom, Vietnamese irrationality with American rationality, and Vietnamese aggression with American defensive action.[123] With these three topoi, Johnson reframed war in Vietnam as necessary for defending freedom and reason against an irrational, violent, aggressive enemy who could not be brought to reason. Just-war theorists have long argued that if any war is justifiable, it is a war for self-defense, and Johnson framed American war as defensive action against an aggressive enemy. His enemyship claimed American innocence and asserted imperialism as just war.

Enemyship orchestrates political action by reducing the complexities of modern life to simple binaries and easy platitudes. Historically, enemyship has proven alluring because it provided citizens with moral certainty in a topsy-turvy world while fostering the illusion of heroic agency in the fight against evil.[124] Citizens must be invested in the rhetoric of enemyship or else it will fail. Inheriting and escalating an unnecessary and unjust war in Vietnam that was also unwinnable, President Johnson found himself unable to unify Americans by touting Cold War platitudes. This was due, in large measure, to technological changes associated with the medium of televised communication. With embedded reporters and new technology, this was an era of unprecedented media access to the battlefield. Every night, the horrors of war greeted Americans in their living rooms. As death counts rose and news of disaster and atrocity reached the American public, and as anxiety produced by the draft shook up a generation of young men and those who loved them, the spell of enemyship broke. The civic and human costs were simply much too high. This crisis in enemyship set the stage for the ascendance of the politics of resentment to become a dominant rhetoric of governance in the United States.

E Unibus Duo

In order to temper the resentment of the masses and disarm the conflict between mass and elite giving democratic politics force, the founders of the United States adopted a new metaphor for American politics: *e pluribus unum*, out of many, one. For much of American history, enemyship was the means for making *e pluribus unum* a reality. Yet it was not the only strategy for disarming democratic resentment. During the nineteenth and early twentieth century, the other significant prop for an idealized, republican oneness was "the American Dream," one of the central cultural fictions of American politics.[125] The Dream promises that any American, no matter how poor, can be successful if they only work hard and show individual initiative. This is the first commandment of American citizenship: *Pull yourself up by your bootstraps*.

The American Dream is a crystallization of beliefs implicit in the Protestant work ethic.[126] Benjamin Franklin was the Protestant ethic's most prominent spokesperson in the eighteenth century, and he made it clear in his *Autobiography* that success requires hardening oneself to sin, temptation, and the outside world. Worldly accomplishment is built on self-discipline, diligence, and honest, unwavering self-vigilance. Salvation in this world and the next depends solely on one's initiative and state of mind. Here we see the great appeal of the Protestant ethic, for it makes the individual the agent of his or her own glory.

From a young age Americans internalize a number of clichés: shoulder to the wheel; from rags to riches; pull yourselves up by your bootstraps. We are taught that anyone—even the most humble—can become president. The brilliance of such clichés is immeasurable. The Protestant ethic squeezes hard work from poverty while keeping idle, potentially disobedient hands busy. There is no need to riot if the path to success is clear. The Protestant ethic has often functioned to neutralize revolution and to naturalize social hierarchy. If industriousness and ingenuity lead to success, then it is easy enough for the rich and powerful to claim that their spoils were earned by industry and ingenuity. Ironically, then, the Protestant ethic can make even the most ostentatious displays of wealth seem legitimate. The eighteenth-century philosopher David Hume suggested that it was a basic fallacy of moral thought to mistake what *is* for what *ought to be*; here, we see the opposite problem, as what *ought to be* is mistaken for, and ultimately justifies, what *is*. But no matter. A fallacy is only a fallacy if it is recognized as such and called out.

Alongside enemyship, the American Dream has proven to be an effective technique for managing democratic resentment and promoting a sense that *we're all in this together*. If everyone can be successful, then there is no need to begrudge the success of the rich and mighty. In this way, the American Dream undermines the democratic conflict between the few and the many and invests American liberalism with a sense of *e pluribus unum*. The trouble with the American Dream, of course, is that it has never been open to all—it has always been the exclusive privilege of certain races and classes. In 1776, Abigail Adams urged her husband John to "remember the ladies," but the framers did not, nor did they remember those whose labor allowed many of them to participate in politics, institutionalizing slavery and racism right into the legal fabric of the Constitution with the Three-Fifths Compromise. During the early nineteenth century, the American Dream rested on slavery and gendered oppression. Many of the most important speeches of the nineteenth century were given to sound out this foundational hypocrisy of American life. And thus Frederick Douglass declaimed white Americans for their hypocrisy in his fiery address "What to the Slave Is the Fourth of July?" as did Sojourner Truth in her speech "Ain't I a Woman?"

After the Civil War, the American Dream continued to apply almost exclusively to white men, as Reconstruction upheld white privilege over black Americans.[127] In 1925, Langston Hughes demonstrated that even the most powerful, transcendent poetry associated with American democracy—such as Walt Whitman's poem "I Hear America Singing," part of his epic *Leaves of Grass* (1867)—forgot about people of color. Hughes's poem "I, Too, Sing America" illuminated the shadows of the Progressive era. Forced to hide in the kitchen and eat dinner alone when white company came over, Hughes's narrator laughs and grows stronger contemplating tomorrow, the next day, when he would be so strong and beautiful that no one would banish him from the scene. "I, too, am America," he reminds us.

From the beginning, the American Dream was a privilege for some maintained at the expense of others. Unsurprisingly, then, one of struggles animating American democracy during the nineteenth and twentieth centuries was a battle for access to the benefits of the American Dream. During the 1960s, many Americans who had been excluded from the promises but not the responsibilities of *e pluribus unum* spoke out against their plight—as when Martin Luther King, Jr., told Americans of his "Dream" on August 28, 1963. During the 1960s, courageous African Americans, women, students, and gay men and women rallied to make real the claim that *we are all in this together*—not in the sense that everyone was equal in their debt to the nation (this is the rhetoric of the "contract of blood" long associated with American enemyship), but that everyone was due the promise of the American Dream.[128] These activists demanded a genuine civic fraternity that frightened those who were never sent to the kitchen to eat. Moreover, these activists demanded that white Americans acknowledge, and honor, the often-unnoticed and frequently mocked sacrifices they made in the interests of the common good. This put further pressure on the national slogan, *e pluribus unum*, by tapping into ancient traditions of dangerous democracy. Unlike enemyship, which makes oneness real as a shared patriotic obligation, social activists during the 1960s attempted to make the oneness materially real by elevating the interests of the poor and oppressed to national attention. They aimed, in short, to promote genuine democratic equality for all.

Oneness had long been the dominant metaphor for conceptualizing the American people, and enemyship the dominant means of enacting *e pluribus unum*. In the late 1960s, the oneness metaphor began to buckle under its own weight, unable to handle the conflicting demands placed on it by contending forces. The fiction of national oneness was fractured by civil rights protestors who exposed the hypocrisy of the American Dream, by feminists who demanded social justice, and by protestors who actively fought against the Vietnam War. Some activists on the Right worked to reassert their exclusive access to the American Dream and to rebuff those who made contrasting claims on their "birthright"—a counterrevolutionary battle for privilege that has persisted to the present day.

In the past, and for much of American history, enemyship had proved an effective means of solidifying the status quo and upholding order in the face of demands for equality. As war became the grounds for agitation and division, rather than the means of unification and hierarchy, Americans questioned the war, and in so doing they also questioned enemyship. Of course, this was precisely the type of questioning that peace activists had been demanding for centuries. Yet the breakup of a militarized oneness during the 1960s did not bring social justice or peace. Instead, a fractured people set the stage for the politics of resentment.

Essay II

The Rise of the Politics of Resentment

Since the age of classical Athenian democracy, political observers have noted that popular government is premised on deliberative rhetoric. Without good deliberation, democracy suffers. The ancient truism that democracy needs deliberation, ratified today by professional and lay philosophers and political theorists alike, is also an argument for the importance of rhetoric in democratic governance. For Aristotle, deliberation was one of the three genres of rhetoric—the study of rhetoric, in other words, encompasses and encapsulates democratic deliberation.

The obvious importance of deliberation to democratic politics should not distract us from exploring the other rhetorical forms that are equally foundational to democracy—including, to fill out Aristotle's schema, epideictic rhetoric, which assigns praise and blame, and forensic rhetoric, which assigns guilt and innocence. Each form of civic discourse—deliberative, epideictic, and forensic—is equally essential to democracy. Democracy suffers just as much when epideictic and forensic rhetoric break down or are abused.

It is vital that citizens be able to determine guilt and victimhood, for while politics in the United States at least theoretically makes government responsive to citizens and guarantees political equality, there are nevertheless many opportunities for citizens to be victimized. This is the dark side of American politics—majority government necessarily includes sacrifice and loss.[1] The American Dream is only open to some, and not all sacrifices done in the spirit of *e pluribus unum* are recognized. Over the years, Americans have therefore developed a vocabulary of slogans and catchphrases to capture the ways that victimhood is experienced in our democracy: "Don't Tread on Me"; no taxation without representation; corrupt bargain; the Monster Bank; tyranny of the majority; "The South Will Rise Again"; the Man; black power; "Hell, No, We Won't Go"; the great silent majority; three-word chant; unfunded mandate; "No Blood for Oil"; Nobama; "I Want My Country Back!"; "We Are the 99 Percent"; makers and takers; "You Are Not a Loan."

The rhetoric of victimhood, in its various guises, is necessary to a healthy democratic politics. Such rhetoric can raise awareness about abuses both seen and unseen, setting the agenda for social activism, productive deliberation, and civic fraternity. But it does have a dark side. Rather than promoting deliberation, the rhetoric of victimhood can fracture the citizenry and manufacture consent by manipulating vitriolic emotions such as resentment. Here we shift from one rhetorical phenomenon to another: from a rhetoric of victimhood to what Kenneth Burke calls the rhetoric of *victimage*.

As Burke explains, "the victimage ritual" is a practice of scapegoating traditionally associated with rhetorical praxis in the West. For Burke, humans have a natural propensity for social order because we are, first and foremost, language users, and language tends toward hierarchy. Language creates certain expectations for order, and the language of the American Dream, in particular, creates the expectation that when we work hard we will succeed (and, conversely, that if we fail to succeed it is because we did not work hard enough). When this order breaks down—when, say, we lose our house to foreclosure or our job to recession—it is only natural to feel guilt for such a violation. We ask ourselves, *What if I had only worked harder? Should I have done more?* Sometimes we just throw our hands up in frustration and plead, like Job before us, *Why, God?* The rhetoric of the American Dream encourages us to take the blame for our failures, but such mortification is difficult to sustain if we are to get out of bed. As Nietzsche suggests in his *Genealogy*, it is not easy to live with debts that can never be repaid (be they material or symbolic). And thus for Burke people ease their guilt, and find redemption for their sins, by blaming someone else for the evils that befall them—this is victimage.

Burke argues in *Permanence and Change*, "If order, then guilt; if guilt, then the need for redemption; but any such 'payment' is victimage."[2] Or, as he explains in *The Rhetoric of Religion*:

> Here are the steps
> In the Iron Law of History
> That welds Order and Sacrifice:
> Order leads to Guilt
> (for who can keep commandments!)
> Guilt needs Redemption
> (for who would not be cleansed!)
> Redemption needs Redeemer
> (which is to say, a Victim!).
> Order
> Through Guilt
> To Victimage
> (hence: Cult of the Kill) . . .[3]

Victimage does more than praise or blame, more than assign guilt or innocence. This rhetorical strategy fundamentally transforms the conversation, making public discourse less about finding consensus and more about achieving expiation, less about giving reasons and more about plotting revenge.

Burke believes that the victimage ritual is "curative"—in other words, it works.[4] While victimage may be an "error in interpretation," an example of "faulty means-selecting," nevertheless, "we must remember that the technique of purification magnificently met the pragmatic test of success. It was, for instance, quite effective in unburdening a people of their sins."[5] Of course, to say that victimage is "curative" is not the same as saying it is healthy. In fact, this type of rhetoric clearly falls under the category of the manipulative engineering of consent, and thus Burke searches for rhetorical alternatives to the victimage ritual.

I understand the politics of resentment as a rhetoric of victimage born out of an engagement with structural violence. Although Burke described victimage as a successful rhetorical strategy for unloading guilt, I think we have plenty of reason to doubt the "curative" nature of the politics of resentment. The politics of resentment is not curative; it does not grant the redemption it promises. This rhetoric fails to be curative for two reasons: first, because it does not address the actual forces causing civic suffering, which are structural and institutional in nature; and second, because it misdirects civic resentment away from structures of oppression and the elites who benefit from such structures, and calls instead on Americans to blame their civic equals for their pain. This rhetoric promises redemption, but because it is unwilling to talk about the structural causes of violence, and because it undermines the force of democratic fraternity, it is unable to deliver on that promise. The politics of resentment works to capture popular resentment and direct it away from structures of oppression and toward our neighbors and fellow citizens. In so doing, the politics of resentment leaves untouched the legitimate target of civic resentment, an economic system that benefits oligarchic elites at the expense of the masses. The politics of resentment transforms democratic resentment into hate among and between socioeconomic equals, thereby making democracy much less dangerous to elites while making it more violent for the rest of us.

Historically, the dominant metaphor that Americans have used to imagine their politics was *e pluribus unum*—out of many, one— but the politics of resentment has a different slogan, and aims to create a very different state of affairs: *e unibus duo*, out of one, two. Rather than calling on all citizens, rich and poor, to unite to confront their national enemies, the politics of resentment embraces division—though it rearticulates the division between *duas civitates* along cultural and moral, rather than political, lines. The politics of resentment rewrites the conflict at the heart of democracy: it is no longer mass versus elite or rich versus poor; it is now liberal social reformers and those vocal "minorities" they represent versus good, hardworking, moral conservatives who do not shout but who do believe fervently in defending the status quo. This politics fundamentally alters the possibilities for democratic resentment by cleaving the people in two and calling forth a culture war at the heart of political and social life.

I focus in this essay on President Richard M. Nixon's rhetoric. I do so because he modeled a prominent politics of resentment on the national stage that sought to both capture the resentments that many Americans in the "silent majority" felt during the 1960s and channel those resentments in a politically expedient direction. During the 1960s, Nixon represented a rhetorical movement. Indeed, he modeled a rhetoric also voiced by Barry Goldwater, George Wallace, and Ronald Reagan; and it was his vice president, Spiro Agnew, who practiced the politics of resentment at its most offensive during the late 1960s. Nixon's politics of resentment was not a *reversion* to old political norms but instead an *inversion* of ancient democratic dogma. Nixon radically altered American definitions and practices of democracy by redefining the conflict at the heart of democracy. It was no longer the rich versus the poor or the few versus the many. Instead, he divided "the people" into "the great silent majority" versus the tyrannizing minorities seeking to oppress it. Nixon's politics of resentment was a *perversion* of the classical legacy of democracy as the political empowerment of the masses. In this brave new world of legitimated political warfare, democracy was not about political discussion or finding the common good, but instead became an arena for open battle between civic enemies. It was in this context that the politics of resentment became central to American political life.

The Silent Majority

Democratic politics, especially in its more modern, majoritarian varieties, inevitably means trusting one's fate to one's adversaries. Danielle Allen argues that for democracy to be successful it must take questions of sacrifice and loss seriously. In majority politics, there are winners and losers. The dark side of democracy is that some people lose more often than others do. "The hard truth of democracy is that some citizens are always giving things up for others," she writes, and "only vigorous forms of citizenship can give a polity the resources to deal with the inevitable problem of sacrifice."[6] This vigorous form of democratic citizenship is interested in keeping score. Democracy is a government of numbers: it counts everything. Sacrifice in the private realm is easily forgotten because few people see it. Sacrifice gains validity when it is public, where it is visible—for there it can be recognized, remembered, and honored.[7] Identifying the victims of structural imbalance is vital to democracy, for if the same people lose repeatedly, they will eventually stop playing. And if they choose the bullet over the ballot, violence over talk, the democratic culture is compromised as debating partners take up arms.

Allen is critical of the oneness metaphor for "the people"—derived from Thomas Hobbes's philosophy—because the democratic people are never one. Even during the rarest, most fervent moments of oneness, such as in the aftermath of great national tragedies, there are always differences of opinion and conflicts of interest. This means that a hallmark of good democracy is its successful management of differences and conflict. The trouble is that the metaphors like *e pluribus unum* erase the differences and struggles that underlie democratic culture. Allen therefore argues that democratic theorists should work to replace the Hobbesian rhetoric of oneness with a more realistic and productive metaphor of wholeness.[8]

In a democracy, we have to be able to think in terms of the whole—of what will benefit everyone *in toto*. But we also have to think about what kinds of sacrifices are legitimate and illegitimate, and we have to remember that the whole is fractured and that sacrifice is an enduring reality of democratic life. Wholeness is a metaphor of a heterogeneous polity that cannot be reduced to one. It recognizes that while "we" might be part of a democratic community, there will always be differences, conflicts, and incompatible desires. Rather than whitewashing the prominent, persistent, and ultimately irresolvable problems facing democracies, Allen believes that wholeness will force us to tackle them head-on.

In formulating her democratic politics of wholeness and balanced sacrifice, and in theorizing the rhetorical strategies best suited to promote trust in a democracy, Allen is most interested in the lessons of the civil rights era. She begins her discussion by reading one of the most famous images from that period: Elizabeth Eckford attempting to enter the whites-only Little Rock Central High School on September 4, 1957, in the aftermath of the *Brown v. Board of Education* verdict (fig. 2). While Eckford and the other girls were denied entry to the school, this picture is significant to Allen because it "rendered visible democracy's 'public sphere,' as it existed in 1957," forcing Americans to consider issues of race and civil rights that they had up to that point avoided.[9] Images of Eckford "provoked, and do so even today, specific epiphanies about the nature of democratic citizenship."[10] These images forced Americans think seriously about the individual habits and the constitutive metaphors used to imagine and practice democracy. These images, in all their horror, were educative.

I do not dispute Allen's elegant reading of this photograph. However, I want to focus on something different. For Allen, this image "leads us finally to the discovery that wholeness, not oneness, is the appropriate metaphor with which to discuss the aspirations of a democratic populace to integrity and solidarity."[11] To extract this lesson about wholeness, Allen focuses on the unintentional heroism of Elizabeth Eckford and the steely look of determination on her face. I want to focus instead on the spiteful expression on the face of one of Eckford's tormentors, Hazel Bryan. We must focus

FIG. 2   Elizabeth Eckford and Hazel Bryan. Little Rock,
Arkansas, 1957. Will Counts Collection, Indiana University
Archives (P0026600).

on this look of unadulterated hatred, manifested in a grimace or
yell and stoked by the forced integration of white schools, because
it leads us finally to the discovery that the politics of resentment is
central to political culture in the United States. Indeed, this picture,
taken in 1957, forecasted one of the central political divides of the
1960s: between, on the one side, those (like Eckford) who were
courageous enough to stand up against discrimination, joined by
the politicians they inspired to fight for a more equitable and just
United States; and, on the other, those (like Bryan) counterrevolutionary soldiers who resented civil rights legislation and the attempt
by civil rights activists to open up the American Dream to the racial
minorities who had long been excluded. Many politicians found
great success during the 1960s by tapping into this resentment, winning votes for their cause and in the process completely remaking
the American political landscape.

In 1964, President Lyndon B. Johnson signed the Civil Rights
Act into law. "What the ceremony marked was not merely a law

but a liberal apotheosis—an apparent liberal national consensus," Rick Perlstein writes.[12] President Johnson was planning an ambitious democratic agenda for his Great Society, which was intended to eradicate racism, segregation, and poverty while enriching the lives of all citizens through environmental justice, Medicare, and public broadcasting. Johnson successfully leveraged rhetorical appeals to civic oneness in the aftermath of Kennedy's assassination and won handily the 1964 election over Barry Goldwater, who practiced an inchoate politics of resentment. The Republican Party was in terrible shape—it nearly closed its national office because it couldn't raise funds to remain open.[13] The day after the election, November 5, the *New York Times* printed an article titled "White Backlash Doesn't Develop," dismissing the Republican hope that anti–civil rights violence like that in Birmingham, Alabama, the year before would spread throughout the country, paving the way to victory. "Rich and poor, Protestant and Roman Catholic and Jew, farmer and city-dweller and suburbanite—all showed marked shifts toward President Johnson in yesterday's election," the paper observed. "The white backlash, on which Mr. Goldwater had counted so strongly, failed to materialize."

Of course, the white backlash did develop. Fears among white suburban citizens that the American Dream was somehow slipping away from them, and that they were subject to political, economic, and cultural changes outside their control, were widespread. The stage for victimage was set by such changes. The long history of racial distrust, as well as traditions of white privilege going back to the founding period of the United States, functioned as an explosive opening act to the national drama.[14] The backlash Goldwater had counted on began as images of looting, fire, and murder filled the TV screens of Americans across the nation with the Watts riots in the summer of 1965. Suburbanites who had fled the big cities for the safe comfort of cul-de-sacs began to fear for their lawns and their lives—and the suburbs were the future, concluded Kevin Phillips. It was to them that Nixon would appeal.

Phillips was a Harvard-trained lawyer who worked as an "ethnic specialist" for Richard Nixon's presidential campaign in 1968, analyzing voting patterns and tailoring messages for different ethnic audiences. Though political commentators at the time mocked Phillips—in his popular *The Selling of the President*, Joe McGinnis chastised Phillips's demographic analyses and chuckled about how he explained all of Nixon's negative polling in terms of "excluded Catholics"—Phillips was nevertheless an astute observer of the changing political culture.[15] He believed that it would be possible, if he developed the right rhetoric, for Nixon to break up the New Deal coalition that supported FDR's big government projects, picking off the blue-collar workers and the Southerners who were up to that point vital elements of the Democratic Party. Though Democrats were strongest in the big cities of the Northeast, in what Phillips dubbed the monstrous "Megalopolis" of Boston, New York, Philadelphia, and Washington, D.C., the suburbs were quickly strangling this area of "Black Influence." Deploying a metaphor that captured with terrifying, violent clarity the Nixon campaign's racial politics, Phillips claimed that the suburbs were a "white noose" surrounding "the increasingly Negro cities."[16] The "emerging Republican majority," he concluded, would be tied to the two faces of "Negrophobia": white fear of blacks and white resentment of liberal social engineering that would open up the promise of the American Dream to other races.[17]

Johnson's plans for social engineering did not work, Phillips claimed, and Phillips reminded Americans that the more liberals tried to improve the lives of minorities, the more violent those minorities became. As the smoke billowed into the air, newspapers began to call for law and order in place of civil rights. A popular book by George Hunter titled *How to Defend Yourself, Your Family, and Your Home* was published in 1967, instructing white suburbanites how to kick and shoot and kill when the riots, like wildfire, spread to their neighborhoods. This book advised Americans to read the NRA's monthly magazine, *American Rifleman*, for its new column, "The Armed Citizen," which praised American vigilantes.[18] Everywhere, white America was gripped by fears of a black revolution—kind of a Denmark Vesey scare for the twentieth century stoked by television and radio.

Simultaneously, students became increasingly agitated on campuses across the nation, demonstrating against the war. These students challenged the post-WWII rhetoric of *e pluribus unum*. The challenge faced by these protestors was that the rhetoric of patriotic oneness had become central to American politics. To challenge it was to challenge tradition—and this tradition had become a privilege for certain groups who benefited from enemyship (and also for those who, in the world wars, had fought to honor the "contract of blood" demanded by the American rhetoric of enemyship). Opinion polls showed that the majority of Americans were deeply resentful of student protestors, who spit on authority, mocked the wisdom of their elders, and called for revolution.[19] The more violent these students became, the less legitimate they seemed to the broader American public. Senator William J. Fulbright, chairman of the Foreign Relations Committee, concluded that racial violence and the Vietnam War were eating at America's soul. He observed, "The Great Society has become a sick society."[20]

Amid this sickness Nixon was resurrected. Left for dead after his narrow defeat to John F. Kennedy in the 1960 presidential election, Nixon spent the decade rehabilitating his image, and his second try was winning. He succeeded by putting into play Phillips's observations about the "white noose" and developing a rhetorical strategy that activated and directed the resentment of those who had fled the cities for quieter neighborhoods. Understanding that his rhetoric could not be overtly racist—he could not win a national campaign by going all George Wallace on the American public (though Wallace himself did pretty well in 1968)—Nixon employed a number of coded racial appeals that activated racial resentment without concretely calling on Americans to be "Negrophobic," to adopt his adviser Phillips's terminology for the driving force of 1960s politics.[21]

Nixon's campaign slogan "law and order"—first used by Goldwater in 1964, and then used to great effect by Ronald Reagan as governor of California in the late 1960s—and the TV commercials that brought this mantra into the dens of suburban homes, is a perfect example. Nixon's rhetoric acted as something of a "textual wink" to his constituency, who understood the import of his appeals even if this was not explicitly stated.[22] Nixon's politics of resentment worked by mimetically linking two groups—the angry minorities rioting (and taking welfare) in the inner cities, and the disobedient young men and women challenging endemic American traditions of *e pluribus unum* with their campus activism. Of course, this linkage was already common cultural currency in the late 1960s. Indeed, on October 6, 1969, *Newsweek* ran a cover story titled "The Troubled American: A Special Report on the White Majority," which began, "All through the skittish 1960s, America has been almost obsessed with its alienated minorities—the incendiary black militant and the welfare mother, the hedonistic hippie and the campus revolutionary."[23] This linkage was possible not only because the aims of these two groups often overlapped, and not only because they often cooperated in demonstrations and protests, but also because, Nixon said, both groups victimized everyday Americans with their disobedience, with their drugs, and with their violence. To speak of one was to capture popular resentment directed at the other.

Rhetorical scholars have long noted the divisiveness of Nixon's campaign rhetoric against Hubert Humphrey in 1968; according to Andrew W. King and Floyd Douglas Anderson, he practiced a "rhetoric of polarization."[24] Once elected, and having broken up the New Deal coalition with his Southern strategy, Nixon did not leave behind the either–or, us-versus-them, no-compromise, win-at-all-costs rhetoric. His governing rhetorics continued to be divisive and polarizing, for he was working to cement new rhetorical norms for American politics organized around a divided polis. "A campaign rhetoric will be one of either–or choices, a war-like rhetoric seeking defeat of the enemy and victory for the candidate.

A governing rhetoric will be one of decorum in which confrontation usually leaves some opening for accommodation," observes Theodore Otto Windt, Jr. "It is the former that Nixon mastered, not the latter. What Nixon did is merge a campaign rhetoric into a governing rhetoric."[25]

Nixon was a master at dividing in order to consolidate his political base. He was also a master at choreographing resentments in order to win votes and secure support, turning division into victimage and justifying the rage of one side at the other. For the political scientist Joseph Lowndes, "the key" to Nixon's rise "was a rhetorical constituency variously called the 'silent majority,' the 'emerging Republican majority,' 'the Forgotten Americans,' and 'Middle America.' This invented political demographic was meant to appeal to voters primarily on the basis of white racial resentment."[26] This rhetorical term, *the silent majority*, was one of the two master tropes of the politics of resentment as Nixon practiced it.

Of course, the concept of the silent majority was not Nixon's invention. In 1883, William Graham Sumner, one of the founders of American sociology and the first professor of that discipline at Yale University, published *What Social Classes Owe to Each Other*—with his answer being very little. Sumner was fed up with the populist reform spirit of the 1880s. Reformers, he claimed, touted the highest ideals, but in reality they were little more than common thieves picking the pockets of "the forgotten man." For Sumner, the schemes of social reformers "may always be reduced to this type—that A and B decide what C shall do for D. . . . In all the discussions attention is concentrated on A and B, the noble social reformers, and on D, the 'poor man.' I call C the Forgotten Man, because I have never seen that any notice was taken of him in any of the discussions."[27] "The State cannot get a cent for any man without taking it from some other man, and this latter must be a man who has produced and saved it. This latter is the Forgotten Man," he concluded.[28]

Rendered silent by the arrogant neglect of the state and progressive reformers, forced to fund the bad decisions of the derelict poor, and compelled by their society, like Isocrates had been in ancient Greece, to testify that being wealthy was somehow wicked, Sumner's forgotten man was the progenitor of Nixon's silent majority. This forgotten man was, like Nixon's, the victim of the tyranny of the minority—though in Sumner's case, this tyrannical minority wasn't antiwar activists or civil rights protestors, but progressive activists who were advocating for the good-for-nothing poor, a class of people who Sumner believed should be left alone to die in the gutters.

Sumner's *What Social Classes Owe Each Other* stoked the resentment of rich Americans who were forced by liberal reformers to pay for social "justice." Sumner thus modeled the move away from external enemyship to a domestic politics of resentment that Nixon and other conservatives would make in the 1960s. These politicians made this turn by explicitly rejecting another definition of the forgotten man circulating in American public discourse—that of Franklin Delano Roosevelt in his fireside chat of April 7, 1932.

For President Roosevelt, the forgotten man was Sumner's group "D," the poor men and women who needed money and work but could not get them. These Americans suffered, through no fault of their own, extreme and almost unthinkable privation during the Great Depression. Roosevelt framed his New Deal as a project of social reform that would help the majority of forgotten Americans to get back on their feet: "These unhappy times call for the building of plans that rest upon the forgotten, the unorganized but the indispensable units of economic power, for plans like those of 1917 that build from the bottom up and not from the top down, that put their faith once more in the forgotten man at the bottom of the economic pyramid."[29] While Sumner employed the rhetoric of the forgotten man to redefine social reform as theft, Roosevelt defined such reform as vital to the future of American democracy because, he argued repeatedly, if citizens' basic needs (the "four freedoms") were not satisfied, they could not develop into contributors to the common weal. Here we see battle lines being drawn. With this speech "the Democratic Party found its agenda for the next half-century."[30] It was against Roosevelt's ideals of social reform aimed at raising the forgotten man up (as practiced by President Johnson) that conservative politicians mobilized during the 1960s.

These politicians, including Nixon, defined the forgotten man—the silent majority—in Sumner's terms, not Roosevelt's, and they gained political power by directing the resentment of Americans against the New Deal that had originally been pitched as an initiative that could mitigate democratic resentment by opening up access to the American Dream to more citizens. Sumner positioned the majority of Americans as the victims of liberal reform efforts, and Nixon followed his lead. Moreover, putting the insights of his adviser Phillips into play about how to consolidate the emerging Republican majority, Nixon encouraged white, middle-class Americans to find moral validation in their status as victims of liberal social engineering that produced race riots in the cities and disobedient youth on the campuses. During his presidential campaign and then his presidency, Nixon encouraged white, middle-class Americans to indulge their inner Hazel Bryans. He courted this resentment with his talk of "law and order," which promised to punish those who upset the quiet norms of suburban life. This language of victimhood was familiar to most Americans: according to *Newsweek*, the term *silent majority* was "a prototypical expression of the middle-class majority."[31]

To harness and channel popular resentment, Nixon talked of the silent majority in his address of November 3, 1969.[32] This is, without question, one of the most astonishingly mendacious speeches ever given by a president in American history—one that purports to tell Americans "the truth" about the Vietnam War while narrating a highly dubious history of the conflict, explicitly lying about strategy, touting progress in "Vietnamization" that was shadowy, and promising a victory that we now know neither Nixon, nor his predecessor, Johnson, believed was possible.

Though it was not the only such issue, Nixon rightly recognized that the most explosive problem dividing Americans was the war in Vietnam. He described witnessing protests and receiving letters against the war, and recognized the vehemence of such expressions. Yet he refused to allow himself to be shaken by these voices:

> But as President of the United States, I would be untrue to my oath of office if I allowed the policy of this nation to be dictated by the minority who hold that point of view and who try to impose it on the nation by mounting demonstrations in the street. For almost 200 years, the policy of this nation has been made under our Constitution by those leaders in the Congress and the White House elected by all the people. If a vocal minority, however fervent its cause, prevails over reason and the will of the majority, this nation has no future as a free society.

One trouble with these words was that opinion polling suggested that a majority of Americans stood firmly against the war, and Nixon himself was elected by promising peace. That those desiring peace were a "minority" at this point was questionable. Equally problematic was how the president framed the antiwar minority. Nixon divided Americans into a "vocal minority" standing against "the great silent majority" of Americans. And what were the markers of this silent majority? They were silent; they trusted the president; they believed in his promise to end the war. The great silent majority were the victors of the recent election, and they were under assault from loud protestors. According to Nixon, there was a war at the heart of American culture being fought for the highest stakes: "Let us be united for peace. Let us also be united against defeat. Because let us understand—North Vietnam cannot defeat or humiliate the United States. Only Americans can do that." The real enemy was inside the polis; he was internal to the citizenry. This enemy was the protestors, those shabbily dressed young people who, by questioning the authority of the president, by aligning themselves with the Black Panthers and others who protested the racial biases of American politics, and by mucking up the silence of the united American majority, gave comfort to the enemy. These protestors represented the real danger of defeat and humiliation in the Vietnam War.

Nixon called on Americans to be united, but his rhetoric only superficially displayed the characteristics of enemyship and the markings of *e pluribus unum*. Nixon began his speech in the customary way, by speaking to "my fellow Americans" in their totality, but at the crucial climax of the speech, the president spoke not to all Americans but to "the great silent majority": "So tonight, to you, the great silent majority of my fellow Americans, I ask for your support." America was divided between war protestors who, he suggested, sought to bring defeat and humiliation on the nation, and the good people who silently trusted the president. This silent majority was, primarily, a victim of loud, obnoxious, and fundamentally undemocratic minorities—and while this majority was silent, it was nevertheless justified in its resentment toward its enemies.

In his rhetoric, Nixon redefined the resentment that the silent majority felt as the mark of its civic righteousness. The silent majority was, he suggested, morally superior precisely because it resented. This moral righteousness was particularly clear in the rhetoric of Nixon's vice president, Spiro Agnew, who modeled, with his spite and sarcasm, the emotions that Americans should feel for the "loud minority" and the liberal politicians who supported them, those "nattering nabobs of negativity" who were soft on crime, who hated the troops as much as they hated capitalism, the social reformers who locked themselves in their ivory towers and there lost touch with real America.

The Tyranny of the Minority

Resentment is often an ugly emotion that, once brought out into the open, can seem inappropriate to liberal democratic norms of political discussion and civic engagement. A politics of resentment is therefore always in danger of appearing illegitimate. Nixon's rhetoric during the presidential election of 1968—including, especially, his talk of "law and order"—and during his first year of governing in 1969, worked to harness the resentment many middle-class white Americans felt for African Americans and student protestors by making it more respectable and rearticulating it in the language of liberal democracy. Resentment for other races became resentment for lawbreakers, and racial battles became a war between majorities and minorities for political power. The key point here was that resentment lived under the surface of public discourse, shaping it from the inside, and pushing it toward ever more hateful expressions.

Nixon announced in campaign commercials and speeches that Americans were at war, and there were only two sides: the majority position, occupied by Republicans, and the minority position, occupied by Democrats. Nixon linked the majority/Republican position to the law, and the minority/Democratic position to social disorder—transforming his political adversaries into anti-democratic crusaders preying on the majority of Americans. There was no neutral space in this war. In turn, Nixon dismissed Americans' complaints about the war and racial discrimination as "minority" positions. This meant two things. First, he did not have to listen to his critics, because in democratic culture, the majority rules. Thus, when asked what he would be doing during the national demonstration and teach-in against the war organized by the Moratorium to End the War in Vietnam on October 15, 1969—an event that saw the participation of millions around the world—he said he would be watching football.[33]

A month later, on November 15, there was a second Moratorium march on Washington, D.C., which turned out to be the
largest (and mostly peaceful) antiwar demonstration in American
history. The events of that day proved dramatic: five hundred
thousand Americans gathered on the Mall, and Pete Seeger led a
quarter million voices through a rendition of John Lennon's new
song "Give Peace a Chance." That evening, forty thousand peaceful protestors solemnly marched, single-file, down Pennsylvania
Avenue, each person calling out the name of a dead soldier as they
reached the sidewalk in front of the White House. About such
protests, Nixon said, "Now, I understand that there has been and
continues to be opposition to the war in Vietnam on the campuses,
and also in the Nation. As far as this kind of activity is concerned,
we expect it. However, under no circumstances will I be affected
whatever by it."[34]

Second, the very existence of "minority" opinions, no matter if
they fell on deaf ears, proved the health of Nixon's vision of
"democracy"—even as the elimination of a neutral subject position from which to make educated decisions demonstrated its
sickness. In his "Great Silent Majority" address of November 3,
1969, in which he dampened the enthusiasm generated by the
Moratorium by forecasting a peace that was not coming, President
Nixon told a story about his recent trip to San Francisco, where he
was welcomed by demonstrators with signs saying "Lose in Vietnam, bring the boys home." "Well," the president said, "one of the
strengths of our free society is that any American has a right to
reach that conclusion and to advocate that point of view." However, he had no obligation to listen. "But as President of the United
States," he continued, "I would be untrue to my oath of office if I
allowed the policy of this nation to be dictated by the minority
who hold that point of view and who try to impose it on the nation
by mounting demonstrations in the street."[35] Here, Nixon justified
not just unresponsiveness but open disdain for minority voices by
arguing that protestors violated the democratic process of major-

ity rule. In contrast to this vocal minority, and in perhaps his most famous phrasing, Nixon positioned himself as the leader of "the great silent majority."

The contrast between silence and shouting was central to Nixon's politics of resentment, for the metaphor of "silence" allowed the president to position those Americans who refused to raise their voices, and who suffered in silence, as the victims of rhetorical violence. In his Inaugural Address of January 20, 1969, Nixon argued that what democracy needed most was for Americans to stop shouting at one another. He transformed the "majority" of Americans, those who voted for him, into the victims of a tyrannical minority—impolite, indecorous protestors who refused to lower their voices and who thus committed rhetorical violence against the silent majority. Shouting, here, was a metaphor for aggressiveness and irrationality that acted as proof that anti-Nixon forces were intent on anarchy, not democracy. Having studied the body politic, Nixon diagnosed what ailed it: Americans were suffering from "a fever of words," from "inflated rhetoric," from "angry rhetoric that fans discontents into hatreds." "We cannot learn from one another until we stop shouting at one another—until we speak quietly enough so that our words can be heard as well as our voices," he asserted.[36]

By talking in terms of silence and shouting, Nixon constituted his audience—the silent majority—as victims. He encouraged these victims to loathe their victimizers, the domestic enemies who were polluting the quiet of American public discourse. The problem with American society, the president proclaimed, was not war, racism, economic injustice, or other forms of objective violence. The problem was not technocratic elites who made decisions about war behind closed doors without consulting those most affected by the war or thinking of the public good. The problem was that minorities had disregarded the democratic process and had begun yelling at the (silent) majority, constituted in Nixon's rhetoric as victims needing him to voice their grievances and achieve redemption by punishing the victimizers. Good Americans were quiet—the ideal demos, in fact the only acceptable demos, was silent, passive, and acquiescent.

The rhetorical violence of (loud) minorities was a marker of democratic violence, for these minorities had broken the rules by refusing to defer to the majority's will. Americans had a duty to play by the rules of democracy. There was a time for debate, so long as the participants talked quietly and politely about important issues. Once the vote was complete, however, the minority had the duty to submit quietly to the majority's decision. With his talk of a great silent majority, Nixon argued that an all-too-vocal minority had declared war on democracy. Moreover, praising silence was a crucial act of depoliticization in Nixon's rhetoric, for by describing his constituents as silent, he discouraged their ability to speak out against his decisions. This was how he shifted agency away from an empowered demos and toward the president as "author" of national destiny.

While we usually think of persecuted minorities as harboring resentment for the majorities who have trampled on their rights, Nixon managed to capture, direct, and intensify civic resentment in the *majority.* He did this by deploying a metaphor—*the silent majority*—that reinscribed the resentment of white Americans in the language of liberal democracy. In the late 1960s, Nixon embraced, and then reversed, Alexis de Tocqueville's famous argument about the tyranny of the majority by drawing Americans' attention to *the tyranny of the minority.* This was the second master term of Nixon's politics of resentment, and it worked to codify the resentment of the silent majority in the vocabulary of liberal democracy—hence co-opting that vocabulary in the interests of stratification.

The idea that the majority should rule, even while it respects the rights of the minority, is central to the liberal democratic vocabulary. James Madison expressed concerns about tyrannizing majorities in his discussion of factions in *Federalist* No. 10. In this essay, he adopted Hobbes's argument that rich and poor were factions inappropriate to the liberal political state, and invented the poor-as-faction trope to condemn any politics interested in promoting the interests of the many. Tocqueville, too, foresaw the problems of majority government in the 1830s, for he realized that it is easy for majorities to persecute minorities—thus inspiring those minorities to take up arms in order to have their opinions heard.[37] This happened in the 1960s, as persecuted minorities demonstrated for social justice. Black protestors rioted to overturn a racist culture, and students mobilized to overturn the war machine. Nixon dismissed these complaints as "minority" positions, arguing that it was the right of the majority to rule over the minority, even to ignore its wishes. Yet Nixon cut off any arguments about the tyrannizing majority by making the majority silent—how can something silent be a tyrant?

With rhetorical dexterity, Nixon transformed the mass of Americans into a victim—not of war or an economic system but of an unruly minority that refused to abide by the rules of democracy, which supposedly included rational discourse and majority rule. These symmetrical ideas, of a tyrannizing minority and a victimized majority, might be Nixon's most lasting contributions to the rhetoric of the American presidency, for they are the master terms, and the philosophical foundation, of the politics of resentment as it continues to be practiced today.

Nixon talked about silence, but his actions ensured that there was plenty of shouting to keep the silent majority agitated. Rather than attempting to address the causes of resentment, Nixon stoked the resentment Americans felt for lawbreakers and criminals with carefully choreographed political performances of anarchy during his presidency. Riots and student protests were dominant topics in his presidential rhetoric, and rather than fix the problems causing the protests, Nixon prolonged them. Indeed, fearing that a "Halloween peace" negotiated by President Johnson in 1968 might derail his presidential campaign, we now know that Nixon actively worked to undermine peace negotiations so that the Vietnam War continued to be a campaign issue.[38] Once elected president, he continually and perpetually dissembled before Americans about his plans for ending the war, especially in the "Great Silent Majority" address.[39]

Americans were rightly resentful over the Vietnam War. Yet Nixon's genius was to redirect this resentment away from the war itself and toward war protestors. He did this by developing a rhetoric that has become a staple of American public address about war: he encouraged Americans to "support the troops."[40] This rhetorical trump card was a brilliant deflection strategy, for it stifled dissent by turning civic discussion away from the reasons why the Vietnam War was being fought and toward how best to support the troops already fighting the war. Nixon was one of the first presidents to practice a war rhetoric aimed not at achieving support for war, but instead at cultivating acquiescence to war, which he did by making critique tantamount to opposing the troops (which few citizens will do), thereby teaching citizens that opposing war is futile.[41]

To ensure that Americans remained resentful—not at him for prolonging the war, but instead at the protestors who committed rhetorical and democratic violence against the silent majority—he planted war protestors at his campaign events so that there would be images on the evening news of him confronting crazies.[42] "The President feels that we are doing too good a job keeping the demonstrators out of the halls," wrote aide Dwight Chapin in an internal memo from 1970. "The President's whole pitch is built around having a few demonstrators in the hall heckling him so that he can refer to them and their 'obscenities.' We have a new role now. Once the hall is three-quarters full, we can let in fifty to a hundred demonstrators . . . This should give the President the opportunity to strike out at them should he desire to do so."[43]

Nixon's goal was never to solve the structural problems that created resentment, but instead to continually stoke the anger of the silent majority toward "revolutionaries" who spit on democracy, thereby keeping Americans resentful and in need of his leadership. This model of presidential leadership led to predictably ugly outcomes. When we think of the 1960s today, we tend to think of antiwar violence—and while we should not absolve protestors like the Weathermen who moved beyond rhetoric toward violence and destroyed the Students for a Democratic Society with its days of rage, we must also remember that the pro-war side struck first and was persistently vicious toward student demonstrators.[44] This was the consequence of the politics of resentment.

During the 1968 campaign, Nixon suggested that he would support violence against ghetto rioters and student protestors like those at Columbia University, arguing that "our first commitment as a nation in this time of crisis and questioning must be a commitment to order."[45] When such violence occurred at Kent State University, he initially blamed the students, not the National Guardsmen—a judgment echoed by many in the silent majority. The official reaction to this tragedy was, in essence, "this should remind us all once again that when dissent turns to violence, it invites tragedy," though eventually Nixon softened his tone.[46] More emblematic of the consequences of a politics of resentment was the "Hard Hat Riot." On May 8, 1970, students gathered in downtown New York City to lament the Kent State shootings and express their discontent with the invasion of Cambodia; they were greeted by over two hundred flag-carrying, patriotic-slogan-chanting construction workers who beat them black-and-blue with their hard hats.

In this moment, the democratic potential of resentment was completely upended. On that fateful day in Manhattan, the Hard Hats reversed the politics of the few and the many, becoming the reactionary soldiers of elite resentment. They struck out, voicing their hatred through violence, but their actions did nothing to address the causes of their suffering in a world of arbitrary hierarchy that punished construction workers and other members of the working class. These workers destroyed property and hurt peaceful demonstrators—and the president smiled. Civic resentment is perfectly acceptable to governing elites so long as it is channeled at the wrong targets, so long as it weakens the citizenry rather than empowering it as a demos. Nixon cried, "Thank God for the hard hats!"[47] Nixon's words encouraged Americans to freely indulge their hatred for their fellow citizens, recast as victimizers. The logical outcome of the politics of resentment, with its violent language of the tyranny of the minority, is not justice but street fighting.

There were many reasons that Americans in the 1960s were suffering. Much of the resentment felt during this decade—toward the exclusivity of the American Dream and the collapse of its industrial frontier, toward the military–industrial complex, toward frustrated democratic ambitions (what I have called elsewhere "democratic alienation"), toward technocratic elites and their "democracy" of numbers, toward lying politicians, toward capitalism, toward broken promises of political agency and economic prosperity—was legitimate.[48] Americans during the late 1960s rightly feared that their economic prospects were slowing, and they felt resentment that the American Dream seemed to be off-limits to them in a way it was not to their parents.[49] Having to live under the shadow of the draft turned a generation of young people to rage. Some of the resentment felt during the 1960s was definitely problematic—this was the hatred of favored groups trying to secure their racial, social, and economic privileges against the promise of equality and democratic dignity for all. Some was certainly misguided and naïve. All of this resentment made Americans easy prey for political manipulation. Having lived for nearly two centuries under the regime of *e pluribus unum*, it seemed that American citizens had lost their ability to think in terms of the classical democratic conflict between rich and poor—to think, in short, as a demos. The result was a lot of noise.

Like most politicians in his day, and in ours, Nixon was uninterested in addressing the causes of civic resentment. He could have alleviated much of the resentment Americans felt by steering national policy away from war and toward promoting civil rights. Yet he did not halt the Vietnam War; in fact, he repeatedly intensified it. Moreover, he facilitated the rise of neoliberalism by dismantling many of the financial regulations put in place during the

1930s to manage the horrors of the market. Nixon shaped our contemporary world in a number of ways, including by opening up the financial frontier of the American Dream and by setting the United States on the path of deregulation—as though the invisible hand of the market was interested in giving, not taking.

The 1960s was a decade of resentment. Resentment spurred on civil rights protestors and antiwar demonstrators and countercultural warriors just as much as it inspired the animus of those middle-class citizens fearful of too much change and desirous of sustaining their privileged access to the American Dream (such as it was). What hindered the expression of the resentment of the 1960s in a unifying demos organized toward the production of its own political might was Nixon's deft retargeting and restructuring of the possibilities of resentment—away from demos-production and toward spurious, uneconomic divisions of race and morality. With his rhetoric of the silent majority, Nixon captured the resentment felt by middle-class Americans during the 1960s and channeled this resentment into politically expedient directions. His rhetoric, in short, deftly retargeted and restructured the political possibilities of civic resentment.

In the face of social fracture, Nixon did not revert to old metaphors of oneness or to the rhetoric of enemyship. Instead, he confronted the fracturing of the American people during the 1960s by embracing division. Nixon's divisive politics rearticulated the classical ideal of democracy as a battle between conflicting social groups. He did not do this to alleviate civic resentment by promoting social justice; instead, he sought to promote discord and thereby undermine the power of citizens. Nixon engaged in that ancient practice of *divide et impera*, dividing to conquer, but he did not encourage Americans to think of themselves in the ancient democratic terms of *duas civitates*. Nixon's presidency inverted Lincoln's "House Divided" speech; Nixon, too, observed that the American house was divided, but rather than fostering brotherly unity, he called on citizens throw up rhetorical walls between themselves and their enemies.

Nixon stands at the culmination of profound changes in American definitions and practices of democracy enacted during the 1960s. On the biggest stage and with the biggest bullhorn, he did what other conservative politicians had been doing in their states and districts: he redefined the conflict at the heart of democracy. It was no longer the rich versus the poor or the few versus the many. Nixon divided "the people" between the great silent majority and the tyrannizing minorities seeking to oppress it. In this world of legitimated political warfare, democracy became what it remains today—the arena for open battle between personal enemies who were, properly, to be hated.

Nixon's politics of resentment cemented a new metaphor for the American people, *e unibus duo*, and articulated a new vision of democratic politics in which a legitimate, but silent, majority went to war with its many enemies. This war was directed against racial minorities and war protestors, and thus it never touched the "structural evils" causing Americans to suffer.[50] Let me repeat: Nixon argued that war protestors, and not the war itself, was the problem. By leading the war against Americans interested in achieving social justice, he in the guise of a smooth-tongued if truth-challenged general, Nixon found political success. But much was lost in this fundamental rearticulation of democratic resentment away from the politics of the few and the many.

Dialogue Under Distress, Communication Failure, and Democratic Leadership

The 1960s thus came full circle. The decade began on a high note, as students discarded many of the more restrictive deliberative assumptions indicative of the 1950s. "The fifties," Robert Westbrook writes, "marked the consolidation of the triumph of realism in American democratic theory," and with it the victory of the democratic elitism championed by Walter Lippmann in *The Phan-*

tom Public and *Public Opinion* that restricted the participatory dimension of democracy by celebrating the rule of technocrats, scientists, and "experts."[51] The liberal consensus of the 1950s and early 1960s was premised on science and the rule of technocratic experts.[52] The students gathered at Port Huron, Michigan, in the summer of 1962 countered this vision of liberalism by drawing on the work of John Dewey and C. Wright Mills to envision a more "participatory democracy" and to celebrate dialogue, discussion, and local community organizing—values the Students for a Democratic Society put in practice with PREP (Peace Research and Education Project) and ERAP (Education Research and Action Project).[53] "In social change or interchange," the *Port Huron Statement* argued, "we find violence to be abhorrent because it requires generally the transformation of the target, be it a human being or a community of people, into a depersonalized object of hate."[54] In place of violence, the authors expressed their preference for "peaceful dissent" and the "open discussion of all issues."[55]

By the end of the decade, however, the emphasis on dialogue had been replaced with a call for violence. In their first communiqué, the Weathermen—who took over, and eventually dismantled, the SDS—derided peaceful protests, marches, and sit-ins as ineffective, and expressed their belief that "revolutionary violence is the only way."[56] When they gathered students together in Chicago to attack "pig Amerika" beginning on October 8, 1969, the Weathermen pronounced that the time for dialogue closed and urged protestors to "Bring the War Home." Bill Ayers explained in the September 12, 1969, issue of *New Left Notes*, "We're not just saying bring the troops home. . . . We're saying bring the war home. We're going to create class war in the streets and institutions of this city."

Vietnam provoked a crisis in the national imagination. The war shook many Americans' sense that their nation was an unqualified force for good in the world. The PTSD experienced by returning soldiers also challenged traditional notions of American masculinity. These legacies of Vietnam have been studied in great detail.[57] Yet the war had another legacy that has gone without the systematic study it deserves, for Vietnam also provoked a crisis in the democratic imagination. As dialogue broke down, and as hope for consensus and amicable disagreement evaporated, American society experienced a crisis of confidence. While many liberals worried that it might not be possible to create an American democracy, the 1960s made it seem to many conservatives that democracy was no longer a desirable social ideal at all.

The Trilateral Commission, a private, nonprofit organization founded by David Rockefeller in 1973, concluded in its 1975 report *The Crisis of Democracy*, authored by Michael Crozier, Samuel P. Huntington (he of "clash of civilizations" fame), and Jôji Watanuki, that the democracies in Western Europe, Japan, and the United States were indeed in crisis, rocked by a "democratic surge" of increased citizen participation and demands on government during the 1960s. The authors called for a moderation of democracy, which, they claimed, had run amok. Huntington countered the mantra that "the only cure for the evils of democracy is more democracy" by noting that "some of the problems of governance in the United States today stem from an excess of democracy—an 'excess of democracy'" similar to "the Jacksonian revolution which helped precipitate the Civil War"—notice, here, the denial of slavery as a cause of the Civil War, which instead is attributed to too much democracy. This text thus models the obfuscation of objective violence characteristic of conservative rhetoric during this period. To avoid another civil war in an increasingly polarized society, Huntington concluded that "a greater degree of moderation in democracy" was needed.[58] Not everyone agreed. Many scholars called for more, not less, democracy. But they, like Huntington, had to face the difficult question of how to control the violence of politics after the rise of the politics of resentment. For many, the answer to the problems of the sixties would be found in the study of communication.

"What we've got here is failure to communicate," observed Paul Newman's character in the 1967 film *Cool Hand Luke*. This statement encapsulates a mood and a moment, for the 1960s was a time of communication failure. The systematic distortion of communication and its ultimate failure was, in fact, central to America's crisis of confidence. One unintended but welcome consequence of the 1960s was that scholars came to understand, once and for all, that communication matters.[59]

The study of democratic deliberation as we know it today was born out of fear that politics could again go off the tracks, and out of frustration with those who abandoned deliberation as the engine for social change. In her 1969 monograph *On Violence* Hannah Arendt ripped students for their celebration of violence over speech.[60] Similarly, while Jürgen Habermas admitted sympathy for the radical, democratic aims of student protestors, he denounced their violent methods as "left fascism."[61] Arendt's later work on judgment and the *sensus communis*, and Habermas's on communicative reason, can both be seen as responses to the apparent legitimation crisis of democratic politics in the 1960s.

American pragmatism, too, was affected by the 1960s. Louis Menand has argued that the Civil War haunted the first generation of pragmatists, which included Oliver Wendell Holmes, William James, Charles S. Pierce, and John Dewey. These philosophers attempted to create a philosophy that could meliorate social conflict. The pragmatists did this, in part, by developing a philosophy of communication.[62] In the 1970s and 1980s, scholars including Richard Rorty and Cornel West rediscovered, and popularized, pragmatism as their model for democratic renewal. This new generation of pragmatists was also haunted, not by the Civil War of the 1860s but by the breakdown of populism into civic strife during the 1960s.

"The sixties constitute the watershed period in contemporary American intellectual life," West wrote in his sweeping history of pragmatism, *The American Evasion of Philosophy*, because this period produced the "disorienting intellectual polemics and inescapable ideological polarization that tend to reduce complex formulations and traduce genuine conversations" that were characteristic of contemporary political life. The disorientation of the sixties, he concluded, "was initiated by the worst of the New Left and has been perfected by the best of the New Right."[63]

Rorty agreed that the 1960s brought out the worst in the New Left. For him, pragmatism's job was to the fix the damage that students and protestors did to the prospects for democracy in the United States during that pivotal decade. Nearly thirty years after the fact, he was still fuming. In his 1998 book *Achieving Our Country*, Rorty attacked "the people—mostly students—who decided, around 1964, that it was no longer possible to work for social justice within the system."[64] For Rorty, the Left's task is to keep the conversation going, not to shut it down; thus, the critique of U.S. government and militarism by the Left in the 1960s was far too severe, for it undermined the very point of the Left by leading students beyond argument.[65] Taking the work of Arendt, Habermas, and the pragmatists as exemplars, we can begin to see how profoundly the study of democratic deliberation has been shaped by the failures of the 1960s.

The social activists of the 1960s defined democracy as the means by which U.S. citizens could mobilize to ensure equal access to the benefits of the American Dream for everyone. Consequently, they asserted that democracy does not rest on the four freedoms; democracy is the means by which citizens can organize to achieve these freedoms. They understood that the agent of democratic might is the demos. We must not forget this today. Yet to better our democracy, we need to be able to critique the forces of demos-formation, lest democratic resentment be turned to nefarious ends. Though democracy literally means rule by the people, in a republic like our own democracy is dependent on good leaders who seek to facilitate democratic outcomes. While scholars writing about democratic deliberation have been right to develop a robust critique of the Weathermen and the students who turned to violence, we must remember that the perversion of democratic leadership has been just as much a part of the legacy of the 1960s. Even as rhetorical scholars focus on the project of improving deliberation among citizens, I believe that rhetorical scholars should also exhibit a renewed focus on the characteristics of political leadership—both as it is and how we would like it to be.

The mark of the politics of resentment is to capture and direct civic resentment away from objective violence and the individuals who profit from such violence, and toward scapegoats. Nixon's leadership relished the look of spite on the faces of those gripped by resentment, because such people did not *act* so much as *react*. Once the democratic public has been turned against itself, it becomes relatively easy for leaders to control. All that needs to be done is to constantly activate the victimage ritual, transforming personal guilt into political resentment by branding certain people or groups as victimizers. Nixon's rhetoric encouraged Americans to view democracy as war by other means. His rhetoric promoted a weak form of citizenship and a strong form of leadership—and it aimed at keeping this balance by prolonging problems and provoking hate.

Nixon's rhetoric was brilliant because he subverted the democratic possibilities of resentment by redefining the conflict at the heart of democracy. Rather than promoting social justice for the many by taming the outsized power of the few, Nixon prolonged Americans' resentment by facilitating structural violence and naming false scapegoats. This was how he ensured that Americans continued to need him as their leader. The politics of resentment as practiced in the decades since the 1960s splits the people into two warring factions, painting one with the colors of the scapegoat, and turning the other into a reactive body that can be penned in with talk of moral outrage. Fractured into simple, simplistic, and all-too-easy binaries-one side silent, the other shouting; one side victims, the other victimizers; one side red states, the other blue states; one side real America, the other unpatriotic—Americans fighting the culture wars find it difficult to imagine ourselves as a demos acting collectively as a mighty agent of change and justice. So we remain silent—at least, that is, when we are not yelling and raising our fists at one another.

Essay III

The Rhetoric of Violence

In the days following the Tucson shooting, many Americans pondering the effects of violent rhetoric on our political culture began to point their fingers at one person in particular: Sarah Palin. The former Alaska governor and 2008 Republican vice presidential candidate is cited by many as a central figure in the deterioration of American public discourse. And there is little question that her rhetoric has drawn much of its symbolic efficacy from appeals to violence. Palin's persona has been tied from the beginning to the violent side of the American psyche, the side that goes rogue, the side that calls for a duel at high noon and justice with a shotgun, the side that says don't tread on me; liberty or death; take no prisoners; full speed ahead; let's roll; bring it on. Her rhetoric taps into a long American tradition of violent talk and metaphor, a tradition built on the centrality of violence to the American experience. She is the paramount representative of the contemporary politics of resentment as practiced by the contemporary social movement known as the Tea Party.

The 2008 presidential election, which introduced Palin to the national stage, was a passing of the torch as President George W. Bush and his team of master wordsmiths (led by Karl Rove) turned over their politics of resentment to a new band. Frequently invoking the horrible images of September 11 in his speeches, President Bush tickled Americans with the promise of national unity, touting an *e pluribus unum* born in the joyful embrace of an enemyship that would punish those who orchestrated the attacks.[1] Ultimately, however, his was a politics of resentment in the tradition of Nixon, and he and his administration practiced the types of victimage ritual characteristic of the culture wars—which align conservatives against their domestic enemies, "the liberals." Backed by a powerful conservative media establishment and the colorful propaganda of Fox News, President Bush found great success by carving Americans into warring camps of the red-state culture warriors and the blue-state liberals who stupidly, and arrogantly, opposed them. Stoking evangelical fury by preaching a clash between red states and blue states, real America and liberal America, President Bush's dominant rhetorical strategy, according to one journalist, was "latte libel," abusing liberals for being rich, snobbish, and dangerously out of touch with the demands of a moral, Christian life.[2]

I understand the culture wars of the 1980s and 1990s, in which conservative leaders gained national traction by politicizing issues such as abortion and gay marriage, to be a continuation and intensification of the 1960s politics of resentment into new areas of moral condemnation. In turn, I understand President Bush's politics to be an intensification of the culture wars—and therefore very much in the tradition of the 1960s politics of resentment. Only a few days after the attacks of September 11, 2001, the president said, "Either you are with us, or you are with the terrorists."[3] Far from being a means to *e pluribus unum*, the president's many similar statements divided Americans into the flag-waving majority and the unpatriotic, freedom-hating beatniks who refused to support the troops and do whatever it took to *git 'er done*.[4]

President Bush did not speak alone. He was simply the most prominent and influential spokesperson for national rhetorical trends. On June 15, 2006, a Republican representative from Georgia, Charlie Norwood, told his colleagues, "It is time to stand up

and vote. Is it Al Qaeda, or is it America?"⁵ Vice President Dick
Cheney claimed that the victory of an antiwar candidate in the
2006 Connecticut Democratic primary encouraged "Al Qaeda
types" to attack America.⁶ In late summer 2006 President Bush
and Secretary of Defense Donald Rumsfeld both invoked the
rhetoric of fascism to describe terrorists, and Rumsfeld implied
that war critics would have appeased rather than confronted
Hitler.⁷ The year 2007 began with the newly appointed Secretary
of Defense Robert Gates agreeing with hawkish Connecticut
Senator Joe Lieberman that congressional debate about President
Bush's 21,500-soldier increase in Iraq "emboldens the enemy and
our adversaries."⁸ Conservative public intellectual Dinesh D'Souza's
The Enemy at Home (2007) went so far as to argue that following
September 11, 2001, progressives, Democrats, and other "leftists"
had joined hands with terrorists in an effort to undermine American soldiers and destroy the United States.⁹ Such claims, which
move from labeling protests unpatriotic to charging critics with
complicity in genocide, were obviously false and increasingly
ridiculous; they were also rhetorically dangerous because they
openly discouraged political dissent by criminalizing it as tantamount to appeasing evil.

It was difficult in 2008 to pass the torch of a fire-and-brimstone
politics of resentment to John McCain, the war vet and (often,
though not always) moderate politician who seemed poorly
equipped to play the culture warrior—though he tried, to disastrous
effect. And thus, at the time she was chosen to be McCain's running mate in the presidential contest, Palin seemed a stroke of
genius, for she appeared to be someone who could rally President
Bush's lukewarm "base," the evangelical Right, to McCain's side. I
understand Palin's politics to be a continuation of the culture war
rhetorics of the Bush administration—and thus she also stands
squarely within the lineage of the politics of resentment as Nixon
and other conservative leaders practiced it during the 1960s. Given
Palin's position as the newest spokesperson for the politics of resentment, and given McCain's difficulty in capturing and channeling

civic resentment, it should be no surprise that, to an unprecedented degree, the McCain campaign's focus moved to its vice presidential candidate after Palin joined the ticket.

Though it might have been an honest mistake when Palin spoke of McCain as "my running mate" and when she talked about "a Palin and a McCain" administration, these slips were indicative of not just a big ego but also political strategy.[10] The 2008 presidential election quickly became Palin's campaign, for, as commentator William Kristol wrote, "Hockey Mom knows best."[11] The goal was to position Palin as a walking, talking synecdoche for "real America," and, through the principle of dialectical opposition, to make Barack Obama seem effete and un-American. When Obama stood next to an American flag, it would be perspective by incongruity.

Palin became the rhetorical lynchpin of the McCain campaign, which positioned her as an everyday American, "Mrs. Joe Six Pack"—and thus as a representative of "real America." Palin bumbled through the following controversial statement at a fund-raiser in Greensboro, North Carolina, on October 17: "We believe that the best of America is in these small towns that we get to visit, and in these wonderful little pockets of what I call the real America, being here with all of you hardworking, very patriotic, um, very, um, pro-America areas of this great nation. This is where we find the kindness and the goodness and the courage of everyday Americans."[12] Palin later apologized—sort of, and halfheartedly—on CNN for these comments, but the rhetoric continued and was even amplified by other Republicans.[13]

Asked about McCain's chances in Virginia, Palin spokeswoman Nancy Pfotenhauer suggested on October 18 that while Obama might do well in fast-growing Northern Virginia, that was not "real Virginia."[14] Minnesota representative Michele Bachmann questioned Senator Obama's patriotism, and she tried to invent a new Red Scare by calling for a congressional investigation into which members of Congress were "pro-America" or "anti-America."[15] North Carolina representative Robin Hayes took the cake when he told supporters, "Liberals hate real Americans that work and accomplish and achieve and believe in God."[16]

Having positioned Palin as Mrs. Joe Six Pack, the McCain campaign proceeded to attack Obama as strange, foreign, and dangerous (charges the "birthers" took to the extreme). After introducing herself to Americans and relating her biography, Palin spent the majority of her prime-time address at the Republican National Convention attacking Obama as a *mere* community organizer, painting him as a *mere* rhetorician, a charlatan interested more in advancing his career than in helping Americans.[17] She amplified her attacks on the campaign trail, telling crowds that Obama is "not one of us." In Colorado, she accused Obama of "palling around with terrorists." "This is not a man who sees America as you see it, and how I see America," she announced.[18] The response to such comments was predictably toxic. Followers held a sign (also a popular bumper sticker) that read "The only difference between Obama and Osama is a little bs." Crowds yelled, "Kill him," "Traitor," "Terrorist," "Treason," "Liar," and, "Off with his head."[19] The *New York Times* complained that the campaign's tone veered "into the dark territory of race-baiting and xenophobia."[20] The Secret Service was called in to investigate.

Coming from a faraway and exotic place that few Americans have visited, during the 2008 presidential election—and then during her 2010 reality show *Sarah Palin's Alaska* on TLC—Palin was packaged as a down-to-earth denizen of the last real American frontier, a place where violence is natural because existence is hard, where guns are everywhere, where everyone hunts, and where it is perfectly acceptable to snipe wolves from a plane. Palin has drawn great rhetorical strength from her deft use of symbolic violence. During the 2008 campaign, she framed herself as a "Mamma Grizzly" (she then ran into a real-life Mamma Grizzly on the premiere of her reality show). During the 2010 midterm elections her rhetoric continued call upon, and channel, the resentment of her supporters and direct it toward violent speech and deed. One of her slogans was "Don't Retreat, Reload"; another urged supporters to

"Take Up Arms," and she posted a now-infamous map on her PAC website that marked seventeen winnable congressional districts held by Democrats with gun sights—including Giffords's district in Arizona. The crosshairs map was pulled down from Palin's website after the Tucson shooting and is no longer available. Of course, the "targeting" metaphor is common to a postmodern politics whose discourse has been thoroughly militarized.[21] And it must be admitted that both political parties talk about "targeting" vulnerable incumbents. Nevertheless, Palin's visualization of the targeting metaphor was particularly striking given that one of the politicians metaphorically "targeted" was subsequently shot by real bullets.

In the days following the Tucson shooting, many commentators condemned Palin for her crosshairs map and, more generally, for her rhetorical bluster. While Palin initially responded with several brief and dismissive Facebook posts and Twitter messages, she offered a more substantive rejoinder to her critics on January 12, 2011, in the form of an eight-minute video released online (the transcript was posted on her Facebook page).[22] The timing of the speech's release suggests that it was intended to preempt President Obama's speech at the University of Arizona that evening concerning the tragedy. If her goal was to dominate the day's news cycle, she was successful.

While Sheriff Clarence Dupnik attempted to place the shooting in context, seeing it as a *manifestation* of our political discourse, Palin's argument is emphatic that there was no context for the tragedy. It was the act of a crazy man, plain and simple, and that was that. Furthermore, those who blamed political discourse, in particular, *her* political discourse, for the shooting were engaged in anti-Palin slander or what she called "blood libel." Though the phrase has been used for a variety of purposes, it is derived from a notorious biblical passage, Matthew 27:25, that, during the Middle Ages, justified Christian persecution of Jews by claiming that they engaged in murder, in particular of children, and used the blood in their rituals.[23]

What are we to make of Palin's post-Tucson address? Should we dismiss it out of hand, as many people did, or should we take it seriously? If nothing else, we should pay attention because of Palin's celebrity. In his recent book *The Death of the Liberal Class*, Chris Hedges points to why Palin is important. According to Hedges, for much of American history it was the job of the liberal class to stand between corporations and the American people, acting as a buffer that would protect democracy from the outsized influence of the moneyed classes. The liberal class represented the many poor Americans in their battle to ensure that the rich did not use their outsized means to oppress them. In the smoke-filled, back-room negotiations of national governance, liberals spoke for Franklin Delano Roosevelt's "forgotten man." Moreover, liberals gave Americans a nonviolent, deliberative language for expressing their grievances, and hope that they could be rectified from within the system. Liberalism tamed the might of the citizenry without rendering it impotent. Whatever one might think about the virtues and vices of such political liberalism, it seems that today the liberal class has been bought off by corporate power and compromised by centrism, triangulation, and arguments like "too big to fail." Hedges therefore argues that citizens must look elsewhere for vocabularies for the battle between the few and the many.[24] And that is where Palin comes in, for she is the representative of a political movement, the Tea Party, which has provided Americans with a popular vocabulary for expressing their many resentments. This vocabulary, the outlines of which should be familiar from Essay II, redirects the force of democratic resentment away from our current economic system and toward our fellow citizens.

Of course, it is not just conservatives who appeal to citizens' resentment. Occupy Wall Street is another contemporary social movement that draws much of its rhetorical power from channeling and focusing democratic resentment. Yet there are fundamental rhetorical differences. OWS is animated by classical ideals of democracy as it attempts to call forth a demos in opposition to the contemporary oligarchy. Moreover, OWS stages democratic resentment as an opportunity for a cultural conversation about the problems we face as a society by developing a rhetoric for discussing objective violence. By contrast, the Tea Party was born from Rick Santelli's explosive rant on the floor of the Chicago Mercantile Exchange in February 2009, and does not promote civic discussion about what ails society. It is a movement that cashes in on the resentment felt by citizens during the Great Recession by turning the citizenry against itself. Moreover, while OWS indicts contemporary capitalism, turning our collective civic attention *ad ratio* toward the evils of a social structure, the Tea Party's arguments are largely *ad hominem* against liberals, who are said to be personally culpable for Americans' suffering.

Like OWS, the Tea Party appeals to those Americans hurt hardest by the Great Recession—it seeks to capitalize on widespread feelings of powerlessness, frustration, and victimhood. Yet the Tea Party is devious in its methods and aims. As Isaac William Martin documents in his revealing book *Rich People's Movements*, while the Tea Party adopts populist rhetoric and claims to represent the voice of everyday people, it is nevertheless the brainchild of a few hyper-rich Americans who, in their quest to lower taxes and achieve greater corporate control over the public welfare, have enlisted the resentment of poor Americans hit hardest by the Great Recession as their primary weapon against the social safety net.[25] The Tea Party cashes in on Americans' rage against the consequences of neoliberalism in order to defend the neoliberal status quo. In our days of hate and rage, the Tea Party is the most vocal practitioner of the neoliberal politics of resentment, and Palin the most vocal representative of such victimage.

Consequently, it is a mistake to dismiss Palin's rhetoric as the bluster of a would-be demagogue or the fanfaronade of a spotlight-seeking celebrity. We should focus on her post-Tucson oration because in Palin's comments she espouses a vision of democratic citizenship and civic discourse that is perfectly suited to our neoliberal age of political resentment. One of the crucial developments in our era is that the politics of resentment has been enlisted in the service of neoliberal capitalism, which stresses privatization, deregulation, corporate rights, and personal (versus social or collective) responsibility. Neoliberalism undermines the common good while putting the wealthiest Americans in a privileged position to dictate public policy. The Tucson shooting occurred in a neoliberal context, with funding for mental health care in Arizona slashed and the gun market deregulated. The nature of the Tucson shooting thus made the subject of Palin's speech violence and rhetoric, in particular the relationship between violence and rhetoric in a democratic society. I focus on Palin's address because in her response to the shooting, and in her attempt to protect her image, she produces a model of neoliberal rhetorical theory vis-à-vis violence. I thus read her speech as operative theory. The Tucson shooting staged a declarative moment when neoliberal concepts of discourse were called into service to defend incendiary speech. In the end, this speech is a perfect crystalization of neoliberal rhetorical theory mobilized in the service of the politics of resentment.

Privatizing Violence: Neoliberalism's Rhetoric of Violence

> President Reagan said, "We must reject the idea that every time a law's broken, society is guilty rather than the lawbreaker. It is time to restore the American precept that each individual is accountable for his actions." Acts of monstrous criminality stand on their own. They begin and end with the criminals who commit them, not collectively with the citizens of the state, not with those who listen to talk radio, not with maps of swing districts used by both sides of the aisle, not with law-abiding citizens who respectfully exercise their First Amendment rights at campaign rallies, not with those who proudly voted in the last election.
>
> —Sarah Palin, "America's Enduring Strength" (address of January 12, 2011)

The post-shooting debate over violent rhetoric began with Sheriff Dupnik's comments. The January 9, 2011, editorial page of the *New York Times* affirmed Dupnik's insights, labeling political speech a central factor in the shooting. "Many on the right have exploited the arguments of division, reaping political power by demonizing immigrants, or welfare recipients, or bureaucrats. They seem to have persuaded many Americans that the government is not just misguided, but the enemy of the people," the paper noted. Having habituated Americans like the shooter, Jared Lee Loughner, to view the government as an enemy, the Right's political discourse created a symbolic world in which violence like the Tucson shooting was possible. "Now, having seen firsthand the horror of political violence, Arizona should lead the nation in quieting the voices of intolerance, demanding an end to the temptations of bloodshed, and imposing sensible controls on its instruments." Paul Krugman put it simply: the "toxic rhetoric" of the Right created a "climate of hate" that enabled violence.[26]

In her January 12 speech, Palin fires back at critics like Dupnik, Krugman, and the *New York Times* by privatizing the blame for the shooting, arguing that "acts of monstrous criminality stand on their own." Even more strongly, Palin claims that society is never guilty for violence—that there is never a social, political, or rhetorical context for violence. Palin thus follows William Graham Sumner's foundational sociological argument in *What Social Classes Owe Each Other* that society cannot be guilty for the actions of bad men. "'Society' is a fine word, and it saves us the trouble of thinking," Sumner wrote, condemning progressive social reformers who hoped to eradicate crime by changing society, not men.[27] Much as President Bush blamed torture at Guantanamo and other black sites on a "few rotten apples," deflecting attention away from the structural nature of these abuses, Palin argues that violence is not social or political but instead solely the product of deranged individuals. Palin models the neoliberal privatization of responsibility by denying that this particular act had any context outside of Loughner's evil mind.

American neoliberalism is premised on the fantasy of a pre-social individual who is fully formed before social interaction and who, consequently, is in complete control of his destiny.[28] It values an absolute laissez-faire world in which public goods are privatized, the economy is deregulated, the earth is a resource to be exploited, corporations are treated like people, and the public welfare (such as it is) is trusted to the invisible hand of the market. Neoliberalism represents the Protestant ethic run amok, for it announces that citizens are absolutely responsible for both their successes and their failures. According to the neoliberal logic, the Great Recession was solely the fault of the poor Americans who took out toxic loans, and not the system of subprime lending itself—that is, of course, unless you were a massive corporation or bank, and then your mistakes were redeemed by a government bailout (to the tune of more than $600 billion in the Troubled Asset Relief Program of 2008), because such entities, unlike individuals, were deemed "too big to fail."[29] Neoliberalism is fundamentally hostile to the New Deal and the social welfare state because it downplays the value of public support for the citizenry.

Neoliberalism's great faults include its fundamental misunderstanding of context and its troping of the world in terms of profit. This becomes a problem when everything is about profit. There are some public, democratic goods that are above profit, and these should be nonnegotiable in any society claiming to be democratic. Yet neoliberalism runs directly counter to the democratic emphases on equality and the common good; its proponents chafe at any definition of democracy as a force for empowering the many and protecting them from the outsized influence of the rich, corporate, would-be oligarchic elite. In the end, and for the majority of citizens, neoliberalism contradicts itself by undermining the possibility for its promised happy, hands-off life of individual fulfillment outside the eye of the state.

Our contemporary economy has been called the "great American bubble machine."[30] That machine is a creature of finance and debt, which first fuels and then implodes the institutions long thought central to maintaining the American Dream as equal access to prosperity—that is, housing, education, and health care. The popping of these bubbles, while decimating Main Street, results in tremendous profits for Wall Street. We have all lived through the great bubble machine, whose dynamics were on full display during the implosion of the housing market fueled by sub-prime lending during the late 2000s.[31] Moreover, we live in an age of "disaster capitalism" in which natural disasters, such as Hurricane Katrina or Superstorm Sandy, and also wars like those in Iraq and Afghanistan, become brilliant investment opportunities for those who lack consciences.[32] The popping of economic bubbles devalues public goods and infrastructure, which can then be opened up for private investment—this seems to be the new and frankly perverse era of neoliberal capitalism.

Today we see the evaporation of the middle class and the most severe stratification of society into rich and poor since the Gilded Age. Yet in our time of corporate governance, where it is no longer "one person, one vote," but "one dollar, one vote," the political power of the poor to effect change has been greatly eroded. And thus in the wake of the 2008 financial crisis and the Great Recession, up to and including the present day, numerous commentators and not a few citizens have toe-tagged the American Dream.[33] The American Dream has long defused the tension between rich and poor by promising the chance for prosperity to all. Framed correctly, the American Dream has disarmed social tensions and legitimated political, social, and especially economic hierarchies. Today, however, the American Dream has lost much of its believability, and its failure is an epochal development in the rhetorical history of the politics of resentment in the United States.

The Nobel Prize–winning economist Joseph E. Stiglitz argues that the American Dream has always been mythical, even if perhaps somewhat true to the average American experience. Since the financial crisis of 2008, however, social inequality has rendered the Dream obsolete: "America has always thought of itself as a land of *equal opportunity*. Horatio Alger stories, of individuals who made it from the bottom to the top, are part of American folklore. But … increasingly, the American dream that saw the country as a land of opportunity began to seem just that: a dream, a myth reinforced by anecdotes and stories, but not supported by the data."[34] Stiglitz supplies a preponderance of such data that prove the mythic nature of the American Dream. He points, in particular, to a Pew poll taken in 2011 on the state of the American Dream in the wake of the Great Recession.[35] The poll illustrates a number of interesting conclusions, two of which are worth mentioning here. First, the overwhelming majority polled *aren't even interested in social mobility*—long considered the bedrock of the American Dream. Instead, most prefer "financial stability"—that is, economic inertia—to "social mobility." As soon as Americans become more interested in protecting what they have than in collectively rallying for a better world, democracy has lost much of its dangerousness.

Second, in the absence of economic mobility, the American Dream has become a rhetoric of self-blaming (or, to use Kenneth Burke's term, "mortification") that depends largely on ignoring structural, systemic inequality. Indeed, Americans in the Pew poll judged "personal attributes" as "more powerful than outside circumstances in determining financial success," which means that politicians can attribute poverty to bad character. The American Dream thus becomes a form of "cruel optimism" that actually fuels, rather than ameliorates, civic resentment.[36] Stiglitz concludes, "We can judge our system by its results, and if we do so, we have to give it a failing grade: A little while ago those at the bottom and in the middle got a glimpse of the American dream, but today's reality is that for a large segment of the population that dream has now vanished."[37] Neoliberalism encourages citizens to blame themselves for a frustrating economy—hence setting Americans on the path of the victimage ritual, which, as I demonstrated in Essay II, promises, but does not deliver, catharsis through scapegoating.

From the 1980s forward, neoliberalism has slowly but steadily killed the fiction our culture knows as the American Dream. It did this first by attempting to "roll back" the power of the state and thereby allow markets to flourish unfettered. When this did not work as desired—when, in fact, the rolling back resulted in market crashes and failures that nurtured deep and profound resistance on the part of citizens to postmodern capitalism—proponents of neoliberalism turned to a "roll out" of social programs that furthered neoliberal aims (such as the "Third Way" of the Clinton and Blair era and the Washington Consensus as enacted at the World Bank).[38] The rolling out of neoliberalism has weakened and undermined the American Dream, and we must mark this failure as an instance of structural violence. We must recognize that the destruction of public resources, and the weakening of the dangerousness of democracy, are not unintended consequences, but actual goals of contemporary neoliberalism.

It is precisely where the American Dream becomes a nightmare that the politics of resentment begins. It is only natural in an age of resource scarcity—and the scarcity of hope—that those Americans who, in the past, had been blessed by the promise of the American Dream, look to protect their privilege from encroachments. The Great Recession has put Americans on guard, and crushing debt has turned up the affective pressure. In lean times, like the present, Americans are particularly susceptible to xenophobic appeals. And thus Tea Party politicians encourage citizens to protect the American Dream tooth and nail from encroachments by minorities also claiming access to its benefits— even as these same politicians gut the Dream by espousing neoliberal financial policies. Politicians call on white Americans to rage at immigrants, affirming their privileged access to the Dream, when in fact they should be raging at Wall Street and the governmental entities that uphold corporate rule, including the Chamber of Commerce, the Fed, and the Supreme Court. This is the deflection maneuver at the heart of the contemporary politics of resentment.

While its most obvious consequences are economic, in many important ways neoliberalism has also affected the lived reality of postmodern violence. Nation-state sovereignty, as originally conceived by the 1648 Treaty of Westphalia, was intended to function as a force of control over both religious violence and the reign of the market. Neoliberalism undoes this sovereignty by reimagining government as a corporation and encouraging the state to speak the language of the market. Wendy Brown observes that as the nation-state's sovereignty is compromised, the forces of economic disaster and religious violence reemerge in full force; and nation-states, which have seemingly lost the monopoly on legitimate violence, are increasingly helpless to do anything about it. This is the terrifying reality of a violence that never crescendos: much like the evils of Pandora's box, violence has been released from its fragile nation-state container, resulting in a great magnification of carnage outside state control.[39] This violence explodes from non-state actors, and though we typically think of such actors as doing damage in faraway places with IEDs and suicide vests, they are also working at home. Indeed, neoliberalism weakens the state's monopoly on violence by framing government in market terms; it also engenders populist violence outside the control of state and market, as raging and resentful citizens, wronged by the violence of the market and seemingly lacking the ability to appeal to classical democratic norms of redress (the common good, the few versus the many), rise up.

With regard to violence, then, neoliberal rhetoric is aimed toward achieving two specific goals. The first is to turn attention away from the massive forms of objective, structural violence neoliberalism perpetuates.[40] While neoliberalism values a demobilized citizen, one unintended consequence of neoliberalism is civic violence. The second goal is therefore to discipline the resentful potential of the citizenry—directing the types of "rage capital" produced by neoliberalism in ways that are beneficial, rather than detrimental, to the market.[41] When political commentators dismissed Palin's reaction to the Tucson shooting they missed something significant, for in this speech Palin provides a critical snapshot of neoliberal rhetorical praxis.

In her address, Palin models the contemporary politics of resentment by promoting a psychologism of violence. This view is doubly useful for politicians looking to uphold the neoliberal status quo that benefits them and their corporate patrons. In the first place, neoliberalism works best when violence is privatized, because if all violence is private—that is, authored by evil individuals—then critics lose the vocabulary for discussing structural violence. Palin's rhetoric thus helps to maintain the current neoliberal status quo. Second, by privatizing the violence of the Tucson shooting, and by denying that public discourse contributed to the violent context, Palin defends herself from charges that political rhetoric—hers in particular—can be guilty of inciting violent behavior. By denying the connection between violent political rhetoric and violent deeds, Palin is able to pave the way for her continued use of violent rhetoric, without which she could not run for president (though she did not run in 2012, she repeatedly teased that she might) or keep herself in the news.

Language matters. The classical philosophers of both the East and West affirmed this, and it is an insight that has reemerged in recent decades in post-structuralist thought. If we want to get our minds right, a good place to start is by getting our language right. Thinking at one higher level of abstraction, if we want to improve our society, we will have to change our language, our rhetoric, our ways of relating to ourselves and to our fellow citizens, through discourse. Dupnik, Krugman, and the *New York Times* open up a productive social conversation by focusing on the social and political consequences of discourse, yet they do not take their concerns about violent language toward what Walter Benjamin called the "critique of violence." The problem is deeper than violent rhetoric; the problem is how violent talk is built right into the political and rhetorical economy of neoliberalism itself.

In his pivotal essay "Critique of Violence," Benjamin argues that violence is a "manifestation."[42] For Benjamin, violence cannot be separated from sociality, governance, and law. Jacques Derrida points out that the title of Benjamin's essay in German is "Zur

Kritik der Gewalt," and while *Gewalt* is translated into English as *violence*, "it also signifies, for Germans, legitimate power, authority, public force."[43] Benjamin's starting point is the assumption that violence cannot be separated from legitimate power, despite what many philosophers and legal theorists claim. Violence is a force that animates all forms of sovereignty. Indeed, Benjamin articulates the antithetical position to Hannah Arendt, who argues in one of the classic theoretical treatises on the subject, *On Violence*, for the strictest distinction between violence and power. For Arendt, violence can never be the means to power, and power only manifests signs of violence when in a legitimation crisis.[44] Benjamin's philosophy challenges the very premises of Arendt's theory that violence is antithetical to law, consent, and democracy: which is perhaps why Arendt never discusses Benjamin's work in *On Violence* even though she engages the writings of many other theorists of violence, including Hegel, Marx, Sorel, Fanon, and Sartre.

For Benjamin, the critique of violence is not about drawing lines between speech and violence, as Arendt does, nor is it concerned with utilitarianism or deontology, with fitting the proper relationship between means and ends or ends and means. Instead, the critique of violence focuses on the violence inherent to social order. This critique fundamentally denies the conservative argument that man is an island and thus that bad people are simply rotten apples. I believe Benjamin's critique to be essential, or else the great catastrophes and wasting plagues wrought upon humanity by humanity will appear random and nonsensical. We must "mark" structural violence, Robert Hariman notes, in order "to create a warrant for action to stop that violence."[45] Legal systems frame violence as an aberration, and this makes it easier for states to justify violence as exceptional. The critique of violence refuses to mark violence as exceptional; it looks for the violence within law and inside order—for, as Michel de Certeau writes, *pace* Benjamin, "Every order, every legal status has an origin marked in blood—even if, once established, it seeks to have this origin forgotten."[46]

The Tucson shooting created a rhetorical situation in which the critique of violence would have been tremendously useful to our democracy. The violence exploded as if from nowhere, and it is in just such moments that citizens must work to understand violence as a manifestation. In the weeks following the tragedy, however, most fledgling attempts at a critique of violence quickly ran up against the roadblock of the dominant neoliberal discourse. Indeed, Palin makes the critique of violence politically untenable by suggesting that any attribution of guilt beyond individual evil is tantamount to blaming all citizens for violence. Here, her invocation of Reagan is especially interesting, for the quote functions as a perlocutionary act; it denies that there is a context for violent acts, and it is given by Palin without context.

While Palin attributes the quote to "President Reagan," the words were in fact spoken long before he was president, on July 31, 1968, at a symposium on crime and violence in the days before the 1968 Republican National Convention in Miami Beach, Florida.[47] The significance of Palin quoting Reagan from 1968 cannot be underestimated, for during the late 1960s, conservative politicians like Reagan and Nixon rose to power by modeling a divisive politics of resentment that broke the nation into two, into the silent majority and its liberal victimizers. While Nixon and his vice president made the most visible use of this rhetoric on a national scale, they learned many of their maneuvers from Reagan.

Reagan's rhetoric was premised on well-worn rhetorical norms, for, as Michel Foucault demonstrates in *Discipline and Punish*, the state has structured itself on a core binary since the eighteenth century: the law-abiding citizen versus the criminal. Though this binary is foundational to modern societies, it is elastic. One of the insights of twentieth-century sociology, and in particular social psychology following World War II, is that crime and violence are social behaviors, sometimes learned, sometimes the product of broken social structures. While this line of research does not rule out psychological causes for crime, it advances the critique of violence by explicating the environmental factors of which violence is a manifestation. Reagan's neoliberal rhetoric countered this wisdom through a radical, neoliberal binary that sharply distinguished social theories of violence from psychological theories like his own. He then demeaned social theories as being soft on crime. Reagan's neoliberal rhetoric produced a criminal without context, a criminal who was simply a bad person, a rotten apple.

Reagan's successful campaign for California governor in 1966 characterized civil disorder and rising crime rates in California as the products of moral depravity on the part of irresponsible individuals, suggesting that violence had nothing to do with war, poverty, or racism. Society was not sick, he announced to great applause; perverse individuals, and the liberals who defended them, were the sick ones. Reagan spoke to the many fed-up Californians who were outraged at rising crime rates, civil rights legislation, antiwar activism, loud music, shirtless chests, and bare feet. Out of riots and Molotov cocktails, giant Afros, and anarchic facial hair, Black Panthers and hippies and druggies and draft-dodgers, conservative politicians redefined the people that they would then govern: their constituency was the conservative, law-respecting silent majority of middle-class white Americans.

Reagan took up the mantle of the culture war during the 1970s and 1980s, especially with his inflammatory rhetoric about "welfare queens" and other poor black Americans who supposedly bilked the system, to the detriment of white, working-class Americans—Nixon's silent majority. As president, Reagan was particularly astute at making coded racial appeals to his supporters, working from a rhetorical script that had well served Wallace and Nixon before him.[48] Reagan's politics of resentment named scapegoats to distract Americans as he advanced an economic revolution privatizing public goods and dismantling the social safety net that devastated the middle class. Indeed, Reagan's role in advancing neoliberal financial policies as president is well established.[49] However, not as widely discussed is that his either–or, bifurcating rhetoric privatizing violence was just as integral to the rise of neoliberalism in the United States as tax cuts or financial deregulation.

In the 1980s, Reagan's rhetoric attempted to shut down the critique of violence by denying that violence could ever be a manifestation.[50] In 2011, Palin updates and innovates on Reagan's rhetoric by denying any relationship between violent language and subjective violence. Here, Palin refines Reagan's neoliberal rhetoric by equating the critique of violence with "blood libel."

Palin's denial that rhetoric contributed to the shooting—or that violent language could contribute to violence at all—is complex. On the one hand, she dismisses the power of rhetoric to influence conduct and provoke violence, yet on the other she defends her conduct by recounting how she cautioned supporters against violence. Consequently, it might seem that, upon analysis, her speech devolves into contradiction, or worse, hypocrisy. Still, there is a theory underlining the incoherence that must be explained if we are to understand Palin's response to the Tucson shooting and, more generally, the neoliberal politics of resentment. Palin articulates a theory about the violence of language that is premised on a stark distinction between the advocacy of violence and the use of violent metaphors, as though metaphors have no effect on conduct. Thus, on the one hand she can announce that she hates violence—so she wrote in an e-mail to Glenn Beck that he read aloud on his talk show on the morning of January 10, 2011—while on the other hand she can approvingly cite in her autobiography, *Going Rogue*, a book like David Horowitz's *The Art of Political War* that talks about words and ideas as weapons for political warfare between the Left and the Right.[51]

It seems that the only violent rhetoric for Palin is the physical threat, meaning that to be violent, rhetoric would have to cross the threshold that separates the word from the gun, coercive rhetoric from coercion. To be violent, rhetoric would have to stop being rhetoric and leave the symbolic realm altogether: it would have to become the bullet. Palin forwards an "emancipatory" vision of speech that makes a clear distinction between discourse and violence.[52] Unlike another proponent of an emancipatory theory of discourse, Jürgen Habermas, however, Palin does not try to use this distinction to produce less systematically distorted communication. Instead, she affirms the nonviolence of rhetoric to defend her violent rhetoric. The trouble is that her impossibly high standard of what would count as rhetorical violence makes it difficult to recognize the wide range of rhetorical violence as it is experienced in our politics.

In the aftermath of the shooting, many commentators rightly pointed out that American political discourse has always employed violent metaphors. Martin J. Medhurst noted in an interview with the *Columbia Journalism Review*, "Metaphorical violence permeates American political language and always has."[53] Moreover, the metaphors of war are built right into how we conceptualize and talk about argumentation itself.[54] This does not mean, however, that violent metaphors have remained consistent in form or force. The metaphorical violence of the contemporary Right is especially inflammatory for two reasons. First, cultural and moral issues increasingly divide Americans, meaning that we have lost sight of any sense of the common good that might bring us together for productive deliberation. The people have been broken into two; the motto of the politics of resentment is *e unibus duo*, not *e pluribus unum*. Yet the two out of one are not the few and the many, as they were in classical Greece. In this way, politicians practicing the politics of resentment have armed our democracy for battle while sapping the potential for a demos to form and make democracy dangerous. Second, our practices of democratic deliberation are weak, and Americans are not habituated to engaging one another as political friends but instead as hated enemies.[55]

In an April 2009 report, the Department of Homeland Security expressed concern about the rising tide of right-wing extremism in United States.[56] Without a doubt, Palin's rhetoric has participated in this culture of extremism. When she accuses Obama of "palling around with terrorists," labels his health care reform "downright evil," and claims that he is "hell-bent on weakening America," she suggests that her opponent is an enemy who has no right to participate in democratic conversations.[57] *If* Obama is equivalent to a terrorist (a belief that the *New Yorker* parodied with the now-infamous fist-bump cover of its July 21, 2008, issue) and his supporters are jihadists who would cheerfully kill babies and geriatrics, then violence can start to seem like a good idea—especially when the stakes are raised with talk comparing abortion to "murder" and health-care reform to "death panels." Habituated to talk about our opponents as hated enemies, violence becomes logical, even necessary.

Blood Libel and Imagined Insults: Neoliberalism's Violent Rhetoric

> Vigorous and spirited public debates during elections are among our most cherished traditions. And after the election, we shake hands and get back to work, and often both sides find common ground back in DC and elsewhere. If you don't like a person's vision for the country, you're free to debate that vision. If you don't like their ideas, you're free to propose better ideas. But, especially within hours of a tragedy unfolding, journalists and pundits should not manufacture a blood libel that serves only to incite the very hatred and violence they purport to condemn. That is reprehensible.
>
> —Sarah Palin, "America's Enduring Strength"
> (address of January 12, 2011)

David Harvey explains that during the 1970s, neoliberal theorists seeking to advance their financial goals "actively sought to capture the Republican Party as their own instrument."[58] According to his analysis, they succeeded. Since that moment, Harvey frets at how deeply the GOP has been controlled by corporate interests espousing neoliberal rationalities; he laments that moderate forces have been expunged from the party in the interest of an "unholy alliance between big business and conservative Christians backed by the neoconservatives."[59] By taking hold of the Republican Party, neoliberalism gained a platform of influence from which it completely remade the U.S. and world economy. But neoliberalism also gained access, via its political agents, to a panoply of potent rhetorics employed by the Republicans who waged the "culture wars" of the 1980s and who courted Christian voters with metaphorically violent jeremiads concerning wedge issues like abortion and gay marriage. Such violent rhetoric has become as much a part of neoliberalism in the United States as the rhetoric of efficiency, deregulation, and free trade. In Palin's speech on the Tucson shooting, we see how violent rhetoric—in particular, a rhetoric of hateful resentment—can be deployed in the interest of neoliberalism.

Palin's post-Tucson video is classic politics—when in a pinch, redirect blame and claim the status of victim. Thus, Palin claims to be the victim of "blood libel" manufactured by "journalists and pundits," that is, the liberal press. Many on the Left found Palin's strategy of framing herself as a victim of the tragedy objectionable; at least a few intellectuals on the Right found it bankrupt. In his review of Palin's speech, *Weekly Standard* columnist Matt Labash argued that "she's becoming Al Sharpton, Alaska edition" for her frequent appeals to victimhood.[60] Putting Labash's dig at Sharpton aside, his analysis has merit. In the tradition of Nixon and Reagan, Palin positions herself as a victim of the liberal media elite, and she claims to speak for millions of Americans who are likewise victims. Like Nixon and Reagan, she leads by giving voice to the many resentments Americans feel and by channeling these resentments into a potent political force. Thus, she speaks out against those who besmirch "the greatness of our country," who defile "our foundational freedoms," "who embrace evil and call it good," and who aim to curtail free speech and shut conservatives up. Notice, however, that while Palin strikes out at her enemies with slash-and-burn rhetoric, she does not promise justice or victory. The rhetoric associated with the politics of resentment never achieves catharsis because it ignores structural violence—it does not hasten justice; it perpetuates suffering. The politics of resentment amplifies, rather than alleviates, the feelings of injustice and loss that generate resentment.

Palin's rhetoric is resentful—her tone makes it clear that she is hurt by the unjust attacks of her opponents. This sense of hurt is productive, for Palin draws much of her emotional power from the expression of grievance. Her rhetoric is also a representation of the politics of resentment. Against the backdrop of economic devastation wrought by neoliberal financial policies, and the corresponding feelings of helplessness and frustration as common folks struggle and the rich get richer, Palin expresses a grievance—the claim that her rhetoric contributed to the Tucson shooting, which she interprets as a personal attack and more generally as an assault on "free speech." Here, we see an act of displacement as the cause of suffering is misattributed. Though Americans today are suffering in large measure because of economic injustice, Palin asserts that liberal policies aimed at curbing free speech are the cause of Americans' pain. The grievance is then metonymically linked to other charges in a chain of resentments—thus, Palin speaks of loss and how her opponents have demeaned the nation's exceptional status and divine founding. These grievances are bundled, giving birth to a rhetoric that is consumed with the enemy. Palin's rhetoric would not exist if not for the battle, if not to scold liberals. Finally, the nature of the enemy is revised to fit the schema. Note that Palin accuses her enemies not just of being bad people but of acting in bad faith—liberal grievances against her are described as "shrill cries of imagined insults." Thus, Palin transforms the enemy from a legitimate adversary into a liar and a cheat who calls evil "good."

I believe that in the decades since the 1960s, the resentment that many Americans have been taught to channel toward their neighbors and fellow citizens—first in the conservative rhetoric of the 1960s, including that of President Nixon, then in the rhetoric of the culture wars, and today in the rhetoric of the Tea Party—has been intensified into a pernicious orientation to the world. The politics of resentment has achieved, over the past several decades, something like the metaphysical state of being that Friedrich Nietzsche dubbed *ressentiment* in his epic *On the Genealogy of Morals*. Nietzsche's *ressentiment* is an orientation that builds on feelings of resentment but is not reducible to them. It is a rhetorical projection that refigures the social world, especially the relationship between self and other, citizen and citizen. *Ressentiment* is the discursive articulation of resentful affect. Therefore, *ressentiment* represents a way of being in the world—it is the human being settling into hatred. In a state of *ressentiment*, the cause of suffering becomes constitutive of self-identity and produces a new moral code that validates hatred of enemies who are labeled evil. Nietzsche's *ressentiment* represents the articulation of resentment into all-encompassing hatred that completely reshapes how citizens live their lives. *Ressentiment* reorients the human condition: People are no longer heroic actors but victims of the enemy's evil designs. They are now encouraged to hate their enemies, because this hatred is the mark of moral goodness.[61]

Humans are resilient creatures that can bear even the worst hardships so long as we know why we must bear them. Even Job had questions for God. To suffer needlessly is to matter not. Unfortunately, the types of objective violence that cause meaningless suffering—poverty, war, inequality, racism, sexism—are the cornerstones of modernity. There is a reason that revolutions come from the oppressed, and there is a reason why governing elites have always feared the revolutionary potential of democracy—because democracy can be a vehicle for turning meaningless suffering into meaningful political change by tapping the latent power of a unified demos.[62] *Ressentiment* works against change and for the status quo by making even the most unconscionable suffering meaningful for its own sake. This suffering goes on and on, meaningfully but usefully, empowering only those who use its rhetoric to stir up hatred. *We suffer because we are good. We fight because you are evil.* What can be more clear, more certain, more easy, more comforting than that?

Resentment is a volatile emotion that is prone to explode into violence, especially when rhetorically articulated as *ressentiment*.

Equally problematic, as Nietzsche suggested, *ressentiment* is an enervating emotion. If I am resentful and have learned to find happiness in that resentment because it is a mark of my own superiority, then I become dependent on a culture war for my political salvation. The post-1960s politics of resentment shifted the target of Americans' resentment, directing it away from oligarchy and toward various other social groups. Nixon governed by encouraging the silent majority to view its fellow citizens as enemies who were legitimately hated. In so doing, he made democracy less dangerous by ensuring that resentment would no longer be the affective glue of the many locked in battle for its rights against the few. In this regard, Palin's rhetoric follows very closely in his footsteps.

According to Nietzsche's philosophical anthropology, *ressentiment* begins with a perverse psychology that then produces enervating rhetoric. I think the opposite might also be true, that *ressentiment* begins with discourses that nurture a reactive psychology and then that psychology, in turn, reinforces the discourses—if so, then the theory of *ressentiment* can become more than a moral critique (as it was for Nietzsche); it can become a theory of democratic leadership. In fact, Nietzsche's *Genealogy* is less interesting to me as an account of the violence of Western morality or as a critique of Christianity than it is as a description of political leadership and rhetorical strategy. Ultimately, Nietzsche allows us to think of *ressentiment* as a rhetorical stance: as an attitude toward politics. The politics of resentment aims not just to channel and direct resentment but also to intensify resentment into a vicious hatred that targets political enemies and demands their extermination.

Ressentiment is the amplification, habituation, internalization, and normalization of the force of resentment into hatred. In his *Rhetoric*, Aristotle described hatred as the opposite of friendship—he defined friendship as a state of wishing good to another for their own sake, and thus hatred was a state of wishing harm upon another simply because of who they were. Hatred is social. One tends to hate the enemies of one's friends, and the enemies of

one's polis. Unlike anger, which is personal, hatred is less immediate and more general—hatred represents settled antagonism
toward a particular group of people, such as thieves or informers,
believed to be *kakon*, bad. Aristotle tied hatred (*to misein*) to
enmity (*ekhthra*)—someone in a state of hatred wishes harm upon
his enemy, and treats him as savagely inhuman. Hatred leads naturally to violence because hateful citizens desire not just a return to
the status quo before an insult, but the active production of a new
status quo, *ante bellum*, in which hated enemies are eliminated.
Building on Aristotle's *Rhetoric*, the Stoic philosopher Diogenes
Laertius wrote, "Hatred is a desire for something bad to happen to
another, progressively and continuously."[63]

When resentment is shaped by rhetoric into the hatred characteristic of *ressentiment*, the dangerousness of democracy is weakened, not strengthened. To say that I hate, *miseo*, is to transform
politics into war by other means, hence setting the stage for battle.
Hatred within the citizenry perverts the possibilities for a productive democratic politics by subjecting a demos to unpredictable
reversals and manipulations.

Intensified into an orientation of *ressentiment*, the politics of
resentment has brought about a change in the nature of political
enemies—they are no longer bad but evil.[64] What distinguishes
the morality Nietzsche lauds as "noble" and the morality of *ressentiment* he derides as "slave" are precisely such rhetorics naming
the enemy. The noble person is secure in his identity, which is not
dependent on the existence of his enemies. In contrast, the man of
ressentiment is dependent on his enemies for his identity. The
morality of *ressentiment* is a "slave" morality not because it comes
from slaves but instead because it is captured by a Manichean
social field. In the metaphysics of *ressentiment*, there is no "good"
without "evil"—there is, in short, no good qua good; there was
only good contra evil.[65] *Ressentiment* begins by affirming evil, and
then defines itself as the opposite of evil—as good. The politics of
resentment alters democracy by transforming politics into a battle
between good and evil. As it is routinized, becoming over time

civic habit, this politics cultivates an orientation of *ressentiment* that encourages citizens to live reactive rather than active lives. Put on edge, and profoundly sensitive to the bad actions and intentions of its evil enemies, citizens find it difficult to even imagine the transformative power of democratic fraternity.

In her Tucson speech and elsewhere, Palin models the defensive reactiveness, the tendency to see all speech acts as insults, characteristic of a state of *ressentiment*. She tells her supporters that they are the victims of the enemy's evil designs—her opponents "embrace evil and call it good." By focusing attention on the grievance and encouraging Americans to feel wounded by the words of their enemies, she negates the citizenry's potential to become a demos, cleaving the body politic in half and making it even more difficult to rally against the structural violence of neoliberalism—if it could be recognized—and for the common good. The politics of resentment produces precisely the type of subject neoliberalism desires: one that is forever reacting and never acting, a subject consumed by a violence that cannot be escaped because it has been psychologically internalized. Neoliberalism produces this damaged subject because the citizen of *ressentiment* is easily led—just direct their animus at a scapegoat and promise victory over evil. Through rhetorical leaders such as Palin, neoliberalism makes the resentment it engenders politically productive.

The Violence of Historical Fundamentalism

There are those who claim political rhetoric is to blame for the despicable act of this deranged, apparently apolitical criminal. And they claim political debate has somehow gotten more heated just recently. But when was it less heated? Back in those "calm days" when political figures literally settled their disputes with dueling pistols? In an ideal world all discourse would be civil and all disagreements cordial. But our Founding Fathers knew they weren't designing a system for perfect

men and women. If men and women were angels, there would
be no need for government. Our Founders' genius was to
design a system that helped settle the inevitable conflicts
caused by our imperfect passions in civil ways.

—Sarah Palin, "America's Enduring Strength"
(address of January 12, 2011)

Neoliberalism is invested in producing a "new art of government"
in which the job of government is no longer to limit or regulate the
functions of the economy; instead, government is modeled on the
market, "a state under the supervision of the market rather than a
market supervised by the state."[66] Neoliberalism is animated by an
effort to produce responsible subjects, independent entrepreneur-
ial agents who govern themselves in accordance with certain identifiable and predictable norms—it aims to cultivate the type of
citizen who is governable, who goes to work and files his or her
taxes, who has a retirement account and votes with his or her wal-
let, but who is otherwise politically acquiescent.[67] In creating the
responsible, apathetic citizen, neoliberalism inadvertently tends to
erode state sovereignty by placing the individual as *homo æconomicus* above, and against, the individual as *homo politicus* (Aristotle's *zōon politikōn*) and thus the state itself.[68]

Yet sovereign figures must still tap the latent energy of collec-
tives for support, especially during election season. Despite the
fact that Americans repeatedly affirm their concern for the economy, and though the "free market" has become a God term in
contemporary political discourse, the truth is that pie charts and
bar graphs do not make riveting political rhetoric. In the political
realm, neoliberalism therefore manages the *homo æconomicus* by
promoting a politics of "civic demobilization."[69] Its preferred rhetorical form for this task is epideictic, the rhetoric of praise and
blame, of show and declamation. Neoliberal epideictic oratory
cultivates an apolitical citizen–subject by praising the excellences
of private life and downplaying the wisdom of democratic action;
it also attempts, according to Bradford Vivian, "to nullify the pro-

found inequities evident in a multicultural polity by acclaiming the historical transcendence of the nation's freedoms over historical crises."[70] History, here, is a primary conduit of demobilization, for by praising the past, citizens are encouraged to ignore the present.

Perhaps it should be no surprise, then, that in the Tea Party, if you're going to run for president, you need the blessing of a founding father—maybe several, but certainly one, a patron saint to call your own. One of the things that unites the diverse Tea Party is a rhetorical hagiography that valorizes the founders as gods and worships the Constitution (at least the good parts) as a timeless document of political and moral wisdom. Jill Lepore calls this the Tea Party's "historical fundamentalism."[71] This rhetoric offers a new spin on an old rhetorical form: the American jeremiad.[72] The Tea Party's history is a melancholy tale of loss that calls on Americans to return to founding ideals. Rather than upbraiding followers for failing to live up to the covenant, however, this rhetoric makes it seem that the founders of the United States are alive and well and with us (as we are with them)—it is, in short, a time warp that skips over the messiness of the nineteenth and twentieth centuries and takes us back to a simpler, purer time when the world shook with the force of American ideals and looked upon the City on a Hill with envy and fear.

In place of nuanced, complex, thoroughly researched historical accounts of America's checkered past by professional historians, the Tea Party advances a history of great men and deeds whitewashed of slavery, racism, and class conflict. "There were very few black people in the Tea Party, but there were no black people at all in the Tea Party's eighteenth century," Lepore concludes, "nor, for that matter, were there any women, aside from Abigail Adams, and no slavery, poverty, ignorance, insanity, sickness, or misery. Nor was there any art, literature, sex, pleasure, or humor. There were only the Founding Fathers with their white wigs, wearing their three-cornered hats, in their Christian nation, revolting against taxes, and defending their right to bear arms."[73] To the extent that the study of history gives citizens with equipment for living, this history provides a dose of ease for complicated times: it makes life triumphant, patriotic, and celebratory. This history cultivates precisely the type of citizen that neoliberalism values, for by erasing structural violence from the past, the Tea Party's history does not provide citizens with the necessary training to see it in the present. And when scholars do point out the structural violence inherent to American history, describing, for instance, how slavery and racial violence have shaped our political landscape, historical fundamentalists can reject their scholarship as unpatriotic.

The Tea Party's historical fundamentalism denies structural violence, and therein lies much of its appeal. Deity worship is easy. Democracy is not. The Tea Party's history provides an ideal frame for living in neoliberal times. In that vein, Palin's Tucson speech deserves special attention. In fact, Palin's historical fundamentalism does more than just deny the structural violence in the past. Palin's history paves the way for structural violence in the present by creating an undemocratic mood that valorizes structural solutions to democratic problems and, in the process, profoundly weakens the meaning of an active, critical democratic citizenship. Interestingly, Palin here invokes James Madison's famous statement from *Federalist* No. 51, "If men were angels, no government would be necessary." By choosing Madison as her patron saint—the same Madison, mind you, who as I say in Essay I invented the poor-as-faction trope and who compared democracy to a disease of the body politic—Palin articulates a pessimistic vision of American history that supports a demobilized, hierarchal articulation of democratic politics in which neoliberalism can thrive.

In her Tucson speech, it makes sense that Palin did not choose for her founder someone like Tom Paine, with his radical democracy and atheism, or Thomas Jefferson, who upheld a wall of separation between church and state. After all, conservatives turned on Paine after he launched his rhetorical fusillades against organized religion in *The Age of Reason* (a book that almost got him executed) and after he attacked the American Cincinnatus as an illiterate, elitist hypocrite in *Letter to George Washington*. Similarly, conservative textbook writers in Texas have all but banned Jefferson from American history, replacing him with free enterprise theorists and St. Augustine. It is curious, though ultimately telling, that Palin chooses Madison.

Madison has been overlooked for much of American history, eclipsed by his more famous friend. Much shorter than Jefferson in height, his memory has proved short, too. This neglect is unfortunate, for historians agree that Madison was one of the most brilliant founders, an architectonic mind who authored the Virginia Plan and championed the Bill of Rights in the House of Representatives. Though historians agree on Madison's importance, they diverge wildly in their evaluations of his contribution to American politics. Madison was one of the more pessimistic founders. He was haunted by nightmares of civic decline, believing that the U.S. government, like all past governments, was subject to forces that ensured its eventual corruption and decay.[74] Madison lacked Jefferson's democratic faith—the belief in the innate dignity and moral capacity of all individuals that is a must for self-government.[75] Gripped by *misodemia*, the hatred of the citizenry's potential to become a demos, Madison equated democracy with anarchy and found individuals untrustworthy, especially when they formed groups or factions—because he believed that passion trumped reason in such situations, making it all the easier for demagogues to work their magic.

In the same essay where he told Americans that men were not angels, *Federalist* No. 51, Madison likened factionalism to "a state of nature," evoking Thomas Hobbes. Like Hobbes, Madison favored a structural solution to democratic disorder, though of course his solution was different. Instead of the Leviathan, Madison hoped to tame democracy with a system of representation that would place better, more rational individuals in charge of government. In Madison, Bryan Garsten finds a realistic answer to the problem of demagoguery that does not resort to Hobbes's solution of alienating civic judgment in a unified sovereign.[76] Yet for Richard

Matthews, almost everything that is wrong with American politics today can be traced back to Madison—in particular, to his hatred of democracy, to his belief that citizens were necessarily slaves to their passions, to his lack of faith in the individual capacity for self-government, and to his repeated assertions that the primary job of government is to protect individual property rights from rampaging democratic factions like the Shaysites in Massachusetts.[77]

Palin and the Tea Party do violence to history by transforming it into a sacred text; yet Palin's history also does violence to democracy through her reading of history. Here, Palin's choice of Madison as her patron saint has profound implications for her vision of democratic citizenship. Invoking Madison creates a pessimistic rhetorical mood—in the Madisonian tradition not only are the people imperfect, they are fundamentally flawed. Moreover, with his poor-as-faction trope, Madison undermined classical definitions of democracy as the conflict between the few and the many. He saw no value in the politics of the united poor. For him, citizens were driven by their "imperfect passions" into uncivil discussions. For Palin, then, it is fortunate that the providential founders had the genius, and the foresight, to devise a "system" that could "settle" disputes. The Madisonian message is clear: The people need to be managed, tamed, and restrained because reason is too feeble to control the passions. In the absence of such discipline, citizens must put their faith not in themselves but in a system designed to manage them.

Once the people have been deemed suspect, civic goals can be altered. Under neoliberalism, the goal is not to enrich democracy but instead to develop techniques for disciplining it. Here, the Madisonian political tradition provides neoliberal politicians with a useful rhetoric of governing. Madison's solution to the danger of democracy was two-pronged: empire and representation. Madison dreamed of propelling the young nation westward, expanding its demesne to such an extent that no faction could ever dream of gaining undue sway over government. Today, empire has become a frontier for investment, for neoliberalism monetizes everything, even war. For its part, representation tames democracy by potentially purifying it of the popular prejudices of the poor mobilized against the rich. While the founders admitted that all political power theoretically began with the people, they denied the wisdom of *vox populi vox Dei*. They rejected as too democratic state constitutions such as Pennsylvania's and instituted a bicameral legislature and a strong executive to curb the influence of common folks. The Constitution was designed to temper and control democratic movements for local control, paper money, and economic equality that raged in most of the states following the Revolutionary War. It did this, in large part, through a system of representation that minimized citizens' direct power over the levers of government. While representatives were bound to their constituents through elections, once the vote was complete representatives gained space to act autonomously. This was especially true in the Senate, with its six-year terms for representatives who were initially appointed by representatives of the people in the state legislatures rather than by the people themselves—and especially once the colonial practice of citizens giving instructions to their representatives was discontinued.

The founders of the United States, including Madison, prized deliberation as a means to making good decisions, but only among well-educated elites gathered in congressional bodies. They did not believe that citizens had the capacity for deliberation; enslaved by their passions, citizens were too easily led astray by smooth-talking demagogues.[78] Complaining that citizens were too impressionable, Madison summarized the antidemocratic bent of post-Revolution America in *Federalist* No. 58 with a historical allusion: "In the ancient republics, where the whole body of the people assembled in person, a single orator, or an artful statesmen, was generally seen to rule with as complete a sway, as if a scepter had been placed in his single hands."[79] Tyranny was the inevitable outcome of the mobilization of the many. The drafters of the Constitution believed, however, that when educated elites gathered in the name of citizens but also in their absence, sparks would fly upward. Deliberation was originally intended not to represent public opinion but to shape it, which explains Madison's claim in *Federalist* No. 10 about a republican system of representation: "Under such a regulation, it may well happen, that the public voice, pronounced by the representatives of the people, will be more consonant to the public good, than if pronounced by the people themselves."[80] As the founders of the United States understood it, deliberation prized "reason, order, information, commonality of interests, and farsightedness."[81] By creating small legislative bodies elected from large territories, and by lengthening the terms served in office in order to insulate the deliberative bodies from the ups and downs of popular sentiment, the founders created a system that fostered such deliberation.

Over the course of the nineteenth century, with the expansion of suffrage, the rise of democracy, and the emergence of the discursive formation of *demophilia* (the love of the demos), this hierarchal, restricted system of representation was under pressure to become more democratic.[82] Nevertheless, representation—which is characterized by the rhetorical maneuver of synecdoche, or substituting a part for whole—at once connects citizens to, and divorces them from, government.[83] Michael Hardt and Antonio Negri argue that "representation fills two contradictory purposes: it links the multitude to the government and at the same time separates it. Representation is a *disjunctive synthesis* in that it simultaneously connects and cuts, attaches and separates."[84] Representation is ambivalent, and it can shade toward disjuncture or synthesis, depending on a society's governing conventions and rhetorical prescriptions.

Pessimistic lessons drawn from history solidify the vital importance of representation as a political innovation for controlling democracy. Declarations of the imperfect nature of citizens shade representation toward disjuncture, because deeply flawed subjects cannot govern themselves and must be governed by people who are "better." Claims that citizens are unable to resolve their own disputes enforce representational disjuncture by privileging structure as the answer to democratic controversy. In this way, Palin's reading of history sets up a vital disjunctive synthesis for neoliberal politics. It is significant that Palin refers twice to the United States as a "republic," in contrast to President Obama, who that evening spoke lovingly of "our democracy." By affirming the nation's status as republic, not democracy, in this address Palin reinforces the disjuncture between citizens and the government—a division that conservatives in the tradition of Edmund Burke have long praised as essential to political stability. Neoliberalism thrives on the disjuncture inherent to representation, for once citizens are divorced from power by pessimistic rhetoric that dubs them unfit to govern, it becomes easier for the neoliberal system to run unchecked by democratic energies and hence to perpetuate both subjective and objective violence against citizens. Moreover, Palin's Madisonian history encourages a deeply undemocratic form of deliberation between elites who deliberate in the name of the people. This is a vision of deliberation in which citizens do not speak but are spoken for. A celebrity who repeatedly affirms that it is her job to speak for common folks, Palin symbolizes such deliberation as well as anyone.

Deliberate Caution: Shaking Hands or Hands Shaking?

> America must be stronger than the evil we saw displayed last week. We are better than the mindless finger-pointing we endured in the wake of the tragedy. We will come out of this stronger and more united in our desire to peacefully engage in the great debates of our time, to respectfully embrace our differences in a positive manner, and to unite in the knowledge that, though our ideas may be different, we must all strive for a better future for our country.
> —Sarah Palin, "America's Enduring Strength" (address of January 12, 2011)

I participated in many productive conversations after the Tucson shooting, but one in particular sticks out. After presenting an early version of my critique of Palin's address at "The Violence of Language," a symposium I organized at Penn State University in April 2011, a colleague offered a strident rebuttal of my talk that boiled down to the following objection: if someone else had given this speech, I would be singing its praises. After all, my colleague argued, Palin talks extensively about the importance of democratic deliberation, and she calls on citizens to shake hands and get down to business once they have had their say—and these are surely good things, no matter who says them. My colleague concluded that the problem is not Palin's Tucson speech but instead that her positive message of democratic deliberation contradicts her past rhetorical performances. The problem, in short, is that Palin is a hypocrite. To put it a little differently, he argued that in this speech Palin is involved in what Habermas would call a pragmatic contradiction, since her rhetoric violates the norms that sustain her own speech community, which is premised on invective and the politics of attack, not reasoned discourse. Palin's rhetoric is about making hands shake with rage, not about promoting the shaking of hands.

I disagree with this assessment. My problem with the speech is not with the speaker; it is with the words spoken, with the vision of citizenship and politics forwarded, and with how the relationship between violence and rhetoric in a democratic society is imagined. Though Palin appeals to what are, on the surface, liberal democratic values like deliberation and compromise, in the end her rhetoric contradicts these values—so yes, it is hypocritical— but the problems with her speech are far greater, for her rhetoric contributes to larger neoliberal discursive trends that are detrimental to citizens.

The problems with Palin's speech transcend Palin. Michel Foucault cautions critics against fetishizing "the author."[85] For Foucault, focusing on "the author" is a way of coping with the dangerousness of discourse: with the twin facts that authors are nodes through which discourse is articulated, meaning that discourse transcends the author (as Kenneth Burke taught, we never really control language); and that discourse represents infinite and multiple possibilities for interpretation and action. Demonizing an author for dangerous speech is a feeble attempt to contain that speech. Removing a speaker from conversation does not kill discourse—though it can intimidate speakers into silence, which is one of the ways that political regimes have ruled throughout history, hoping to avoid outward violence against citizens. I read Foucault's work as a challenge to focus on rhetoric as a technique of governance. Such techniques transcend individual speakers, though they are most easily seen in a speaker's words. Dismissing Palin is not enough; in fact, singling her out for derision can distract from larger rhetorical patterns. Palin's post-Tucson speech is representative of certain techniques of governance particularly suited to a neoliberal rhetorical culture that reconstructs democratic politics as a war between liberals and conservatives for the future of the republic.

Character—ethos—is integral to persuasion, and it is vital for rhetorical critics to evaluate specific rhetorical acts as part of a broader story or biography. Audiences clearly do. Charges of "hypocrisy" are essential to democracy, for they are one of the ways citizens regulate the rhetorical production of elite speakers while drawing attention to the often-unnoticed sacrifices of the common folks. Yet the trouble with a focus on ethos and biography is that it cultivates patterns of interpretation. The critic knows what she is going to find because she has studied the speaker and knows his or her soul. There is always a danger in rhetorical criticism of what social scientists call the *confirmatory bias*: favoring information that proves a thesis, or, seeing only what we want to see. This works both ways. Critics are primed to praise or blame speeches from figures they praise or blame—but critics are also ready to praise themes they value in speeches by figures they do not. Thus, my colleague argued that we should praise Palin for striking a democratic tone even as we denounce her as hypocritical. I think this misses the point.

Palin's speech should be evaluated on its own terms—not just for who it reveals the speaker to be (though this is important), and not just for how it fits into her entire biography (also important), but for the vision of democracy it discloses (which to me is most important). This must be one of our central goals in rhetorical criticism today: *we must describe the social vision implicit in instances of public address.*[86] Just because Palin talks about democracy does not mean that she advances a vision of democracy critics should endorse. The same goes for her talk of deliberation. In the end, Palin's address does not articulate a viable way forward because her talk of democracy weakens and demobilizes citizens while solidifying the neoliberal status quo.

None of this is to say that the speaker doesn't matter. Speakers matter because their words reveal worlds—or better, worldviews. A speaker's words manifest how he or she imagines the relationship between speaker and audience and whether or not the speaker has respect for his or her interlocutors. Moreover, a speaker's words reveal a vision of the democratic social world, of how the various figures relate in the public sphere on the playing field of politics and power. However, Palin's Tucson speech is problematic not just because Palin spoke it or because it is hypocritical, but because of what it reveals—this massively influential politician and celebrity, who holds a podium, wields a *skeptron*, and commands an audience few others can rival, propounds a frightening vision of democratic politics and citizenship. It would be a problematic speech no matter who spoke it, liberal or conservative, Democrat or Republican, Left or Right. However, given my genealogy, it should be clear why a conservative politician of the Right, who proudly and loudly positions herself in the tradition of the culture wars, was uniquely poised to give this speech.

Such praise of deliberation is undermined by Palin's politics of resentment, which frames conservative, middle-class Americans—real America—as the victims of liberal elites. Rather than promote honest self-reflection or a critique of violence that focuses on the relationship between economic policy and structural violence, she says, "You did it!" and encourages Americans to say the same. With a wink of her eye and a sarcastic turn of phrase, Palin then calls on Americans to hate their evil enemies. In fact, sarcasm and the sneer are central to the mocking ethos of Palin's rhetoric, which turns the liberal ironism of the Left back on itself by transforming irony into a weapon of political warfare. Despite her pleas for deliberation, Palin repeatedly encourages Americans to indulge in violent rhetoric, to rage at their enemies who are said to rule by deception. The deflection and reaction characteristic of *ressentiment* creates a flammable context for violent outbursts—not necessarily shootings but certainly screaming, as when Representative Wilson yelled, "You lie!" at President Obama or when Tea Partiers organized to shout at politicians during the summer of 2009 healthcare town hall meetings. These outbursts foster an undemocratic mood, for it makes it seem as though citizens are too volatile to govern themselves.

Much as the development of the politics of resentment in the late 1960s led scholars to study democratic deliberation, today scholars again affirm deliberation's importance as an antidote to violence. But we must be cautious. Palin, too, talks extensively about civic deliberation. With her kind and loving words about deliberation making America wonderful and exceptional, Palin demonstrates just how challenging it will be to rethink our rhetorical politics and transcend the violent rhetoric of neoliberalism. It is hard to see the violence inherent in what we take to be normal—including our use of language. It is even harder when politicians like Palin deliberately obscure objective violence. In the outlook of *ressentiment*, it becomes nearly impossible to see the neoliberal rhetoric of violence as it functions in our daily lives. We just speak it.

And speak it we have. In the months after the Tucson shooting, Giffords began her long recovery. She was released from the hospital on June 15, 2011. She made her first public appearance on August 1, 2011, turning up on the floor of the House of Representatives—to rousing bipartisan applause—to vote in favor of raising the debt floor ceiling. She announced on January 22, 2012, that she would be retiring from Congress to focus full-time on her recovery. It is doubtful that she will ever recover fully from the traumatic wounds to her brain. American politics recovered, if by that we mean it returned to the new normal of rhetorical violence. It seems appropriate that Giffords returned to vote on the debt ceiling, as debates over whether to raise the ceiling were a focal point of GOP resentment and an opportunity for Obama opponents to unleash almost unprecedented invective against him and the Democratic Party, invective we should note that was largely detached from fact. Leading into the 2012 presidential election, the GOP primaries were as violent and divisive as any campaign to date. Hearing Rick Santorum and Newt Gingrich speak, and Mitt Romney echo their speech in an attempt to appeal to fundamentalist voters, quickly confirms that we do in fact live in an age of *ressentiment*. Palin chimes in from time to time, underscoring the fact that the politics of resentment has become the new normal.

Turning our attention back to Tucson, Giffords's retirement created a vacancy in the House that was filled by a June 12, 2012, special election. The GOP candidate was pro-gun Tea Party favorite Jesse Kelly, the same man who, when running against Giffords in 2010, held an event where voters could shoot an M16 with him. The announcement read, "Get on Target for Victory in November—Help Remove Gabrielle Giffords from Office—Shoot a Fully Automatic M16 with Jesse Kelly."[87] While he did not hold such an event in 2012, the fact that he did not apologize for the first event in the wake of the Tucson shooting is a telling admission of how he, and many, see the relationship between physical and rhetorical violence—or better, the absence of such a relationship.[88] Without acknowledging that we speak the rhetoric of violence, the rhetoric of violence continues to speak us, goading us on toward unpredictable outcomes. And without acknowledging the power of rhetoric to cause violence, we cannot understand the politics of resentment—which is the rhetorical context for the plague of shootings that haunt American society today.

Conclusion
Resentment *Ad Hominem* and *Ad Ratio*: A Plea for Rhetorical Criticism

Historically, many of our culture's most productive discussions about the health of our politics have occurred in the aftermath of tragedy. Following the Tucson shooting, one such conversation centered on the relationship between violent language and violent deed, an ancient topic of concern dating back to the classical Greek commentators on rhetoric that has lost none of its importance today.[1] The shooting in Tucson encouraged Americans to zero in on the violence of contemporary political speech, opening an opportunity for us to think about the violence of rhetoric in a more nuanced, sophisticated manner—not as "mere" words, but instead as the context for politics and the backdrop for social action.

Rhetoric is a powerful tool of creation and destruction. Cicero repeatedly affirmed the head-snapping, spine-bending power of a well-turned phrase. For him, rhetoric had force (*vis*) and was akin to a weapon (*armum*). Eloquence was so powerful "that it can not only make him upright who is biased, or bias him who is steadfast, but can, like an able and resolute commander, lead even him captive who resists and opposes."[2] Because of its great potential to do good and ill, he cautioned that rhetoric "should be united with probity and eminent judgment; for if we bestow the faculty of eloquence upon persons destitute of these virtues, we shall not make them orators, but give arms to madmen [*sed furentibus quaedam arma dederimus*]."[3] It was advisable, for Cicero, that rhetoric be kept out of the hands of those who were raving mad and in violation of civilized decorum—for the Latin verb *furere* means not just behaving crazily but also furiously or wildly, that is, without self-control. In the right hands, rhetoric can build cities and cultivate harmony and establish laws and bring justice to the wicked. In the wrong hands, rhetoric can promote discord, violence, and civil war, destroying everything.

Violence is a multilayered, complex phenomenon that is difficult to conceptualize. Slajov Žižek argues that violence occurs on at least three levels that are difficult to see simultaneously: *subjective violence* "performed by a clearly identifiable agent"; *symbolic violence* as manifested in our language, such as the scapegoating associated with the victimage ritual; and *objective violence*, "the often catastrophic consequences of the smooth functioning of our economic and political systems."[4] A "citizen critic," to use my friend and colleague Rosa Eberly's helpful phrase, would be able to identify and discuss violence at all three levels as manifested in our democracy.[5] In particular, a citizen would be able to triangulate an instance of subjective violence with its linguistic and social context—to see it, in short, as a "manifestation" of forces of subjectification. For Žižek, the trouble is that the explosive, terrible lure and TV-readiness of subjective violence blinds us to deeper forms of objective violence in the daily functioning of everyday life, like poverty or racism, which are much harder to picture and even harder to fight. "The overpowering horror of violent acts and empathy with the victims," he writes, "inexorably function as a lure which prevents us from thinking."[6]

The natural human inclination to focus on individual acts of violence—a car crash, a bar fight, the death of Caylee Anthony, the brawl at a basketball game, a crazy man opening fire at a strip mall—is, for Žižek, necessarily a narrowing of focus, as it is difficult, if not impossible, to simultaneously ponder subjective violence and objective violence in their "symbolic" and "systemic" manifestations.[7] For Žižek, symbolic violence is the violence of language, and systemic violence involves the uneven distribution of power, rights, and wealth that result from a society's political and economic structure. Subjective violence, in contrast, is violence seen against the background of an everyday state of things that is decidedly nonviolent.

Subjective violence is most often described as random or exceptional (or even "divine"), because it is thought to explode from a nonviolent status quo, as if from nowhere. To think differently would be to implicate the violence of the system—precisely what Sarah Palin, by framing the shooting in Tucson as an isolated, individual, random event, discouraged Americans from doing. It is against the psychologism of violence, against the interpretation of violent speech as ineffectual and merely ornamental, and in service of a rhetorical way of looking at our contemporary practices of democracy, that I have written *The Politics of Resentment*. While it is natural to focus on subjective acts of violence like the tragic shooting of Congresswoman Giffords and others in Tucson, we must not lose sight of how deeply violence is embedded in our culture or of the forces that gave rise to the shooting of political "enemies," including hateful speech.

The trouble with our contemporary political discourse is not necessarily resentment. Instead, it is how this resentment is *cultivated* and is *addressed* that is the problem. Rhetoric engaging civic resentment can direct this emotion in many ways, two of which are most relevant to rhetorical critics: *ad ratio*, at a social system, or *ad hominem*, at a person. Much of the powerlessness, frustration, and victimhood that engenders resentment today is caused by objective violence, in particular the violence perpetuated by neoliberal capitalism. Unfortunately, we Americans have always had difficulty developing a sophisticated political vocabulary for talking about structural violence. All too often, then, resentment that should be directed *ad ratio* goes in search of an interpersonal cause, becoming resentment *ad hominem*. This is the essence of conspiratorial thinking, which posits an agent behind complex social events. It is also the heart and the soul of what Richard Hofstadter has called "the paranoid style" long associated with American conservatism.[8]

Resentment *ad hominem* can be very comforting. Friedrich Nietzsche argues, rightly in my view, that humans have a difficult time living without "metaphysical comfort," the feeling that our actions are right, and our suffering is meaningful, in a cosmic or karmic sense.[9] As we bounce to and fro, hither and thither, in this eternal recurrence, we desire the comfort of knowing that it is more than nothing—that it all has meaning—the joy of *amor fati*. John Dewey, too, believed that the universal human need for comfort made what he called the "quest for certainty" a driving force in human history.[10] Humans crave certainty and meaning. If all the world's a stage, we desperately desire to play parts that are rewarding (and rewarded) in the end. I am no two-bit hired hack, a mere player of the part; I am the lead; my name should be in lights above the marquee for my local universe. We must recognize as human nature this heady hankering. It is only natural for someone who suffers—or who finds their paths to fulfillment blocked—to survey the world for a scapegoat, to desperately and relentlessly seek out someone to blame, to name a devil who is said to cause the pain. This hankering, too, is human. Understanding this, politicians have learned to direct resentment *ad hominem*, blaming their opponents for popular suffering, when, in fact, resentment would be better directed *ad ratio*, at instances of objective violence.

Sacrifice, victimization, and oppression are daily realities in democratic life, where minorities are always in danger of having their rights trampled by the majority, as are the poor by the rich. As such, it is vital that democratic citizens be able to claim the status of victims. Yet with its massive forms of objective violence, modern society greatly multiplies the opportunities for victimization while dispersing responsibility across vast bureaucratic structures and minimizing the opportunities for citizens to rectify perceived wrongs.[11] This is our trouble.

This became increasingly apparent to democratic theorists as early as the 1920s and 1930s. During this period, progressive reformers in the United States—especially those working in the pragmatist tradition—articulated a robust definition of democracy. For them, democracy begins with the recognition that every life is significant. Democracy denies that some people are born better than others; it refutes the ancient oligarchic delusion that money proves wisdom or righteousness—these are proved only by deeds. The democratic dogma is that every citizen should be empowered to set his or her path and walk it, and that everyone deserves to feel at home in this world. Consequently, for Dewey democracy is a way for citizens to collectively exercise control over their environment so that everyone—and not just the rich—can flourish. Yet as he noted in *Individualism Old and New* (1930), "individuals are groping their way through situations which they do not direct and which do not give them direction. . . . Their conscious ideas and standards are inherited from an age that has passed away; their minds, as far as consciously entertained principles and methods of interpretation are concerned, are at odds with actual conditions. This profound split is the cause of distraction and bewilderment."[12] In the coming decades, C. Wright Mills brilliantly chronicled the amplification of these feelings of distraction and bewilderment in his works *White Collar* and *The Power Elite*. Increasingly bureaucratized and hierarchal, the citizens of modern democracies are outrun by massive technological changes that transcend the individual, and are gripped by economic forces that affect them and their families deeply but are beyond their control. The result is that American citizens are left feeling weakened and uncertain.

At least in this regard the Greeks had it right, for they understood that the masses are more likely to be the victims of the few, and the poor more likely to be the victims of the rich, than vice versa. The classical Greeks and Romans, as well as the Levellers of the English Civil War and many Americans who fought the British for independence in the 1770s, constructed a politics premised on rhetorical performances designed to keep balance. The need for balance was overturned during the founding period of the United States and reasserted during the Progressive era. It was upset during the 1960s. During this decade, as the industrial frontier of the American Dream continued to weaken, people came to feel increasingly alienated and upset. As Mills observed in *The Power Elite*:

> The powers of ordinary men are circumscribed by the everyday worlds in which they live, yet even in these rounds of job, family, and neighborhood they often seem driven by forces they can neither understand nor govern. "Great changes" are beyond their control, but affect their conduct and outlook none the less. The very framework of modern society confines them to projects not their own, but from every side, such changes now press upon the men and women of the mass society, who accordingly feel that they are without purpose in an epoch in which they are without power.[13]

William James once argued that the most intellectually and politically energetic periods of history are those in which people believe that they have the power to change the world. If he is right, then the mass society of the 1950s and early 1960s, structured along bureaucratic lines and ruled by elites governing in the realist traditions of Walter Lippmann, was a perfect incubator for feelings of democratic powerlessness. Some Americans, like those students who crafted the *Port Huron Statement* in 1962, confronted their alienation by reasserting the importance of democratic action and the common good. Yet these life-affirming attitudes were subverted and transformed by the politics of resentment, which provided false relief for the guilt and pain of democratic citizenship without addressing the underlying, structural causes of despair.

The politics of resentment takes advantage of the basic human need to matter—of the dread of suffering without meaning—by naming a scapegoat—by, in short, putting a name and a face on the victimizer who frustrates the human desire for self-development and spiritual fulfillment that is blocked by structural violence. The scapegoat redeems the all-too-human feelings of guilt and mortification we feel when we fail. Yet the politics of resentment is not curative. It perpetuates, not relieves, civic resentment. *This failure is its success.* The politics of resentment encourages those who are labeled victims to hate those who are said to cause their suffering, thereby elevating hatred to a moral virtue. During the late 1960s, and building on widespread trends in conservative leadership, President Richard M. Nixon practiced the politics of resentment to great effect.

Nixon promised Americans quiet and relief even as he perpetuated and intensified civic resentment by prolonging the war and ensuring that the exposed wounds of 1960s protest stayed open. Nixon legitimated civic resentment by reframing it in the language of liberal democracy, talking about silent majorities and tyrannizing minorities. His rhetoric was not curative. Pronouncing the master tropes of the politics of resentment, Nixon's rhetoric did not aim to cure the deep, structural causes of Americans' resentment, but instead channeled and focused that resentment on political adversaries and anyone else who was working to upend unjust and exclusive political hierarchies.

In so doing, Nixon put American democracy on war footing, mobilizing the "good" people of the silent majority against their enemies, the tyrannizing minority and its liberal political defenders who, the president said, spit on the troops and the honor of the nation, the libertines who longed to corrupt the traditional morality of the family and undermine the sanctity of the law. This silent majority was "good" because it resented these enemies and because it suffered silently. With his rhetorical innovations, President Nixon set Americans on the path to our resentful times. Many of our primary symbols of resentment today—red states versus blue states, the makers and the takers, the 47 percent—owe their existence to the rhetorical ingenuity of conservative leaders of the 1960s, including Nixon.

The politics of resentment defines political adversaries as "enemies," and politics as war by other means, to cultivate hatred in addition to fear—and herein lies its toxicity for democracy. The politics of resentment discredits the old motto *e pluribus unum*—

itself an invention, we should remember, designed to tame democracy—and instead redefines "the people" as divided against itself, *e unibus duo*. The politics of resentment divides the people into two, but it does not return to the metaphor of *duas civitates*. Instead, it cleaves the people into victims and victimizers. The goal of the politics of resentment is to keep citizens weak and in need of elite leadership by keeping them perpetually hostile toward their purported victimizers. As such, it makes it that much more difficult for citizens to come together into a demos expressing their justified resentment of the abuses of the rich and powerful.

I began writing this book in the aftermath of the January 8, 2011, shooting in Tucson, Arizona. In the months and years since, it seems, unfortunately, that tragic acts of violence have become a new normal in our culture. After yet another shooting spree, this time in Southern California, in May 2014 *The Onion*—with its characteristic bitter, acerbic wit—parodied our cultural paralysis with the following headline: "'No Way to Prevent This,' Says Only Nation Where This Regularly Happens." When it comes to deadly shootings, the majority of Americans seem either uninterested or unable to formulate solutions. This is the trouble with engaging violence solely in its subjective register. If, in fact, these are all random events in which bad people go bang-bang, then commentators like Palin are right and there is nothing that can be done. Yet when it happens over and over and over again, we should not be excused if we fail to notice patterns. If we genuinely want solutions—and this is, I grant, an open question for those wealthy profiteers whose bank accounts runneth over from weapons and the fear and resentment that make those weapons sell—then these solutions will have to be aimed at changing patterns. Some of the solutions clearly will be material—and here I'm not talking interventions that beg the question, like bulletproof backpacks for our kids or glocks for our teachers. Other solutions will be symbolic—they will target how we are taught to view ourselves as citizens and how we learn to engage with our fellows. They will target, in short, our rhetoric.

We live in violent and resentful times—and this is no coincidence. Resentment is a powerful emotion that can be used, rhetorically, to refigure the relationship between self and other, citizen and citizen, in such a way that violence is not just *logical*, not simply *justifiable*, but positively *righteous*. Following the shooting in Tucson, I was buoyed by the fact that many Americans turned their attention to our contemporary rhetorical culture after the tragedy, realizing, at least for a moment, that rhetoric is not "mere" decoration but in fact the scaffolding of our social world. I was chagrined when figures like Palin denied that violent rhetoric could have any practical, real-world consequences, in a speech in which she accused rhetorical critics of "blood libel" and claimed that her political opponents "embrace evil and call it good." These are strong words that transform her critics into vicious, tacky monsters. These words imagine politics as a war between "good" Americans and their "evil" enemies.

We must recognize that such words are not just business as usual or fun and games or "mere" anything. It matters how we address our friends and enemies; in fact, the health of our democracy depends on such public address. Violence is the product of a rhetorical culture that has embraced the politics of resentment. And to the extent that our political problems are in large part rhetorical, then a significant element of the solution, too, will be rhetorical; it will be, to use one of my favorite Latin expressions, *vi et lingua*—by the force of tongues.

I began to write this book because I fretted over the fact that in the aftermath of the Tucson shooting, Palin (and other neoliberal politicians of her ilk) employed the politics of resentment to turn attention away from structural violence—including the lack of mental health care, the deregulation of the gun market, and especially, violent political rhetoric that frames politics as "war" and talks about "targeting" rival politicians. Palin, in short, used rhetoric to negate the force of rhetoric. In Essay III, I focused on Palin's discourse precisely because she is an example of how the politics of resentment has been enlisted today in the service of neoliberal *ressentiment.* Though clothing herself as a populist, Palin models how the politics of resentment is used in the contemporary United States to uphold unjust hierarchies of rich and poor facilitated by neoliberal capitalism. Though it claims to be so, this is not a democratic politics. And here I think Nietzsche was wrong—*ressentiment* is not inherently democratic, as he argued, but can in fact be used against a dangerous democracy in which the many work collectively to ensure that they are not exploited by the few.

Before she was shot, Giffords emphasized in many public speeches the importance of toning town the violence in our public discourse, because she was afraid the violent rhetoric would lead to physical violence. To the extent that Giffords was correct—and I believe that she most certainly was—and a healthy culture of political discussion is vital to democratic life, the politics of resentment presents a grave challenge to the possibility for democracy in the United States. The problem is more than just violent metaphors, though these are problematic insofar as they provide a background for subjective violence. The problem is the way that neoliberal *ressentiment* has carved up the political map and altered our political language.

The contemporary politics of resentment portrays good, conservative, ideally passive, and acquiescent Americans as the victims of "Democrats," "liberals," "progressives," and "big government"—the words function interchangeably as devil terms. Notice one thing that is common to the key tropes of conservative discourse today: the claim to victimhood and the accusation that political opponents are victimizers. The takers tyrannize the makers, the blue states abuse the red states of real America with their liberal values and elite, out-of-touch media; the 47 percent of Americans who pay no taxes game the system (much like Reagan's "welfare queens" of the 1980s), making it hard for the makers to live the American Dream of unbridled, unrestrained wealth.

Having carved up the political playing field into warring parties, this rhetoric cultivates hostility toward the perceived cause of suffering. This rhetoric is not curative. The Ryan budgets of 2012 and 2013, which stressed the privatization of Medicare, tax cuts for the rich, and substantial cuts in public services for the poor, would have worsened inequality and hit the poorest Americans hardest.[14] The politics of resentment touts redemption and economic salvation, but is backed by policies that do not sincerely address the causes of popular rage. This rhetoric perpetuates powerlessness by directing blame *ad hominem* rather than *ad ratio*. In so doing, this rhetoric cultivates, perpetuates, and intensifies feelings of resentment to score political points and achieve electoral victories.

When studying the politics of resentment, it is vital to investigate the rhetoric of representative figures including Nixon and Palin—yet we cannot forget that such figures speak for us, and can only speak because of us. The president and the would-be president are, without question, significant figures in the politics of resentment. Yet we as rhetorical scholars are often so wrapped up in describing the whiplash power of propaganda that we forget to study our own role as citizens in the orchestration of political war. Rhetoric is never purely unilateral; it is always a collaboration between speaker and audience. A president's power as speaker is granted largely by Americans as audience because the president fulfills certain civic needs and desires.

Over the course of American history, the president and his office have come to be imbued with magical, superhuman powers—a process Dana Nelson calls "presidentialism."[15] Nelson illustrates three figurations of presidentialism—the president as "the wizard" behind the curtain of Oz; the president as monarch; and the president as national father—each equally "bad for democracy," for each lends the president undue power to orchestrate war at home and abroad. Presidentialism reveals a very different understanding of what Karlyn Kohrs Campbell and Kathleen Hall Jamieson call "investiture."[16] For them, investiture during wartime is the process by which the president manipulates events in order to become the commander in chief; for me, investiture is the study of the investments that citizens make in the president as wizard, monarch, and father that allows him to act as though he is our savior.

Shifting away from a top-down model of political rhetoric as the production of assent, and toward the study of investiture in presidentialism, opens up new avenues for the study of public address. Rather than ask how presidents convince citizens to support war at home and abroad, we might ask: How do presidents participate in the construction of a symbolic landscape in which citizens can accept that our culture is at war with itself? At the same time, what are our own investments as citizens in the politics of resentment? What needs and desires does this rhetoric fulfill for us? Why is it so comfortable to look at domestic politics as a battle between us and them, between makers and takers? What certainty—what metaphysical comfort—what apocryphal power—is won by such fantasies? Why do some of us feel so good when demonizing our opponents as evil? Ultimately, confronting the politics of resentment must occur at this personal level, through self-study. It is only by learning to care for ourselves as citizens that we can make our democracy dangerous.

This book is a contribution in the hope of creating a stronger and more robust democratic politics in the United States. Because the words *people* (*dēmos*) and *power* (*krātos*) are themselves open to such widely varying interpretations and obfuscations, *democracy* can be co-opted by just about anyone to do just about anything. As the word *democracy* is filled with political content and connected to particular political practices, we get a range of possible democracies. To name just a few, off the top of my head and as suggested by friends: oligarchic democracy, deliberative democracy, managed democracy, democratic centralism, federalist democracy, democratic socialism, radical democracy, local democracy, direct democracy, constitutional democratic monarchy, theocratic democracy, neoliberal democracy, corporate democracy, dollarocracy, sociocracy, inclusive democracy, authoritarian democracy, beautiful democracy, representative democracy, digital democracy, hipster democracy, Christian democracy, party-state democracy, democratic anarchism, democracy to come, and so forth.[17] This does not mean, however, that to study democracy rhetorically is to begin from an understanding that the word is basically empty. It is not; it has a dangerous heritage—and by studying its ancestry, as in Essay I, we get a better sense of democracy's possibilities and paradoxes.

Political thinkers have often tried to imagine ways that resentment might be eliminated from public discussion. The thinking goes something like this: if we don't talk about this, or if we just refrain from using this type of language, then democratic discussion can be civil, happy, and productive.[18] President Barack Obama's post-partisan rhetoric of hope (which itself clothes a neoliberal agenda in smiley-face slogans) is a contemporary attempt to shape the contours of public address so that resentment is left at the door. And we see how well that has worked. Fundamentalist politicians identifying with the Tea Party, who are on Capitol Hill because they are skilled at appealing to and directing their constituents' resentment at convenient scapegoats, have stymied President Obama's admittedly centrist, corporate-friendly, and generally neoliberal policies at every turn. These politicians represent citizens crushed by the economic collapse and fretting over the death of the American Dream, and yet they bloviate in defense of the very same neoliberal ideologies of privatization and deregulation that caused the financial collapse and killed the American Dream. They encourage Americans to rage at their partisan enemies. They govern with guilty rhetoric that encourages Americans to see the world in terms of *ressentiment*. In short, they practice the politics of resentment. It is unproductive—and literally for sixteen days in October 2013, nothing got done when the government shut down. Problems remain problems. Citizens remain resentful. And so it goes, on and on, *ad infinitum*, with ever-increasing speed and intensity, for politicians today have learned to play the game of "democracy" with great skill and unparalleled acumen. They understand that popular sovereignty constitutes the legitimacy and power of government, yet government, while needing to act in the name of "the people," need not act on citizens' behalf.

If we want to want to create the conditions for a healthy democracy in the United States, it is not possible to ban resentment from the public sphere. Instead, we must address it, understanding from whence it comes, how its force is harnessed by political elites, and how it might be voiced differently in the interest of a more equitable promise of the American Dream.

The classical theorists recognized that because emotions were in large measure cognitive, rhetoric could shape the nature of resentment by altering the beliefs associated with this emotion. Rhetoric can direct resentment by situating it within a narrative context. Resentment is a re-sentiment (which is perhaps clearer in the French *ressentir* than the English *resentment*), an emotion built on the replaying of an injury in memory or imagination. Resentment is an emotion particularly prone to narrative, and rhetorical narratives can keep an injury fresh in front of the mind's eye while framing that injury's meaning. In the proper rhetorical context, resentment can be intensified into a metaphysics or orientation—such as Nietzsche's *ressentiment*—that colors red a person's way of being in the world.

The dangerousness of democracy does not depend on eliminating resentment; this is the goal of the sage, not the citizen (and it is a worthy goal, but perhaps not for everyone). Democracy's dangerousness depends on managing resentment, ensuring that its manifestations facilitate social justice and the common good rather than damage dignity and human relationships. To put it simply, resentment must be steered away from hatred—which all too easily leads to dehumanization of political adversaries—and toward a more righteous resentment focused on righting objective violence: toward *phthonos*. The Greek word *phthonos* was generally associated with "upward" resentment of the masses toward the elite—a resentment that was triggered by elite hubris and arrogance that harmed the poor.[19] While keeping in mind that resentment *ad hominem* is often perfectly justified, a rhetoric of righteous indignation would focus attention *ad ratio*, marking objective violence so it can be challenged. Such a rhetoric would be fragile and forever in danger of corruption. Yet it is a possibility. Resentment represents the rhetorical problem of hateful citizens misdirecting their enmity against our own interests and the common good (this is resentment's "dark side"). Resentment also represents the rhetorical possibility of righteous indignation, and thus relearning to use democratic muscles that have grown stiff from desuetude (this is resentment's "light side").

Resentment is often ugly and unpredictable. When undisciplined, it can be truly frightening. And it is precisely when resentment manifests itself in its most vitriolic forms, in hatred and enmity—when resentment is intensified into *ressentiment*—that this emotion can be used against the interests of the many and for the interests of the few. But there is hope for civic reform. Perhaps if citizens can become properly attuned to the valences of this emotion, and temper it with spiritual discipline and practices of self-care, resentment can act as a force stimulating democratic mobilization for a more just and equal world. This is one of my tender-minded democratic hopes. For better or ill, resentment is a bedrock emotion of democratic culture, so we had better take the time to understand it and how it can be managed.

What will it take to ensure that the inevitable resentments of democratic life will be expressed as indignation rather than hatred? How can the force of civic resentment be directed toward, rather than against, democratic ends of collective self-flourishing and the common good? I can only point to potential solutions, as there are no easy answers to such protracted problems. Moreover, any real rhetorical change in our political discourse will have to be both personal and cultural in nature, backed by the creation of robust institutions dedicated to ensuring that the many are not trampled by the few and the powerful, and by an educational system invested in cultivating strong civic habits that prepare students for the burdens and blessings of citizenship, not just to take tests.

Yet I think one area of intervention is clear—American citizens must become better rhetorical critics capable of understanding two things: first, how subjective violence can be a manifestation of objective violence; and second, the nature of rhetorical violence, of how politicians and advertisers push our buttons, using rhetoric to encourage us to treat our fellow citizens as enemies. By practicing a rhetorical criticism that shines the spotlight on how we are made to react to the world—that, in short, illuminates the force of the politics of resentment and how it plays on our civic vulnerabilities and capacities and faiths—it is my hope that citizens will learn to act, not just react.

It bears repeating that if citizens are to unite to pursue the foundational democratic goal of protecting the dignity of the many from the predations of the few—a first step toward a dangerous democracy—we need to become better rhetorical critics, or else the demoi we form (or that are formed through us and with our bodies) will be stupid, ineffectual, and violent. It is only by first learning to care for ourselves in and through language that we can become the type of people who can make democracy real, not just a word.

For Aristotle, deliberation was one of the three genres of rhetoric—the study of rhetoric, in other words, encompasses and encapsulates democratic deliberation. Forgetting this history, many philosophers and political theorists claim that rhetoric and deliberation are distinct forms of civic practice—or that rhetoric is somehow contrary to deliberation, that rhetoric is a faux and dangerous non-art tantamount to lying. Too many scholars today see rhetoric as John Locke did. Looking down on those who taught people how to persuade, Locke besmirched orators as "perfect cheats." "It is evident how much men love to deceive and be deceived, since rhetoric, that powerful instrument of error and deceit, has its established professors, is publicly taught, and has always been had in great reputation," he commented.[20] Scholars writing about democratic deliberation today often misunderstand rhetoric along such Lockean lines. Yet without rhetoric there can be no movement. It is true that rhetoric can pick up the speed of social life, encouraging citizens to move on so fast that they lose track of what's happening. Rhetoric cultivates reactivity, which is precisely what the politics of resentment feeds on. At the same time, the study of rhetoric and the practice of rhetorical criticism can encourage citizens to slow down and broaden their vision. To see the world rhetorically is to learn how the social world moves, and how we can be at home in that world.

In the tradition of John Rawls, deliberation is generally defined as reason-giving discourse, while not all rhetoric assumes this deliberative form.[21] This does not mean, however, that rhetoric and deliberation are opposed or that rhetoric is merely a pre-deliberative mode of engagement, as some scholars claim. Instead, we can think of deliberation as constituting a specific type of rhetorical practice.[22] Rhetorical training is the foundation of civic engagement and democratic deliberation. Drawing on the insights of the rhetorical tradition, I believe that to understand democracy, in all its beauty and ugliness, we must study rhetoric, which is nothing less than the grammar of social life. Those who complain that there is "too much" rhetoric today, or those who relegate rhetoric to the status of "mere," forget this. If we are going to get our democracy right, we need to get our rhetoric right.

Rhetoric enables political action, for it is through rhetorical exchange and political discussion that we make decisions under conditions of contingency and fallibility. Rhetoric makes democracy possible. Yet at the same time rhetoric enables all manner of violence, coercion, and deception. According to David Zarefsky, there are "two faces" of democratic rhetoric—rhetoric aimed at helping communities come together to hash out solutions to shared problems, and rhetoric aimed at manufacturing consent through propaganda and the manipulation of emotion. These two faces—the "open hand" and the "closed fist"—are ever-present possibilities in democratic culture. He notes that "we cannot have one without the other. A commitment to political equality, majority rule, and minority rights requires collective decision making under uncertainty. But the space we open for deliberation about these decisions is also, necessarily, open for the manipulative engineering of consent. We cannot separate the two faces, but we must try for a healthy balance between them."[23] Rhetorical scholars have long been interested in enumerating the conditions for deliberation that leads to good collective decisions.[24] To promote good deliberation, however, it is first necessary to study the negative face of democratic rhetoric. That is precisely what I have done in *The Politics of Resentment*.

Too often resentment is met with resentment, as scholars scoff at the shouts and scowls typical of politics today. I have no desire to scoff. I understand resentment as deeply human. It is, more often than not, an emotional response to real injuries. Resentment might be ugly, but it is not necessarily the currency of fools and idiots and weaklings (as Nietzsche incorrectly claimed in his *Genealogy*). Smooth talkers and would-be demagogues can misdirect it. And we Americans have never developed a sufficient vocabulary for discussing objective violence—the structural violence built right into the daily functioning of our society, our economy, and our laws. Yet the fact remains: the pain is real, and resentment is often a completely appropriate response to injury and wrongdoing.

There is no need to beat ourselves up over the resentment we feel; rhetorical criticism should not lead us to willfully darken the sky above us. There are already plenty of clouds. Instead, we should learn how best to discipline, express, and channel our resentment so that it serves democratic ends—for all too often today resentment is stoked by the rich and powerful to serve their own interests, not the common good or the hopes and dreams of the many. It is both because politicians find it to be an expedient way to get votes, and because it fulfills some needs for us as citizens, that the politics of resentment is a prominent feature of our contemporary rhetorical landscape.

The politics of resentment is the rhetorical backdrop to our days of rage. Resentment is a central political force in contemporary democratic politics. It is the context of the recent plague of school shootings, of calls to assassinate the president, and, in the fall of 2013, the shutdown of the U.S. government. It is the background for the shooting in Tucson. It is one of the main reasons that citizens shout across partisan lines and treat one another with such disdain. The politics of resentment is the worst sort of schooling for politics. It cultivates a destructive attitude toward the world and toward other people. While it is difficult to say with certainty that these words caused that person to do this thing, the politics of resentment encourages citizens to treat democracy as war and their fellow Americans as enemies—and lest we forget, in wartime the targeting is real, as are the bullets.

NOTES

Introduction

1. Terkel, "Gabrielle Giffords."
2. Wallsten, "In the Wake of Tragedy."
3. Zengotita, "Numbing of the American Mind."
4. Aristotle, *On Rhetoric*, trans. Kennedy, 1387b (144).
5. Konstan, *Emotions of the Ancient Greeks*, 111–28.
6. Isocrates, *Antidosis*, section 115. Konstan translates φιλαπεχθήμονας as "fond of hatred," and suggests that it is a term Isocrates "associates with savage cruelty and misanthropy" (199). φιλαπεχθήμων is translated as "resentment" in Isocrates, *Antidosis*, trans. Mirhady and Too, 227. Liddell and Scott in *An Intermediate Greek–English Lexicon* define φιλαπεχθήμων as "fond of making enemies, quarrelsome." Elsewhere, Isocrates observes that his audience has heard certain things that are "true but φιλαπεχθήμονας," provoking negative reactions in an audience primed to feel hatefully toward his words about empire—*On the Peace*, 65. Thanks to Paul Harvey for his suggestions about how best to translate these Isocratean passages, and to Christopher Moore for the pleasure of sitting down to read Isocrates's Greek together.
7. Isocrates, *Antidosis*, sections 159–60.
8. Nietzsche, "On Truth and Lie," 46–47. Nietzsche posits truth as a rhetorical construction; on the importance of rhetoric for Nietzsche, see Blair, "Nietzsche's Lecture Notes."
9. This form of power often governs individuals through lifestyle norms—on norming as the intensification of biopolitical governance in our time of postmodern capitalism, see Nealon, *Foucault beyond Foucault*, 45–53.
10. It seems that what Michael Schudson calls the late twentieth-century civic ideal of the "monitorial citizen," who watches over, but does not intervene in, politics, has been superseded by what I have called elsewhere the *acquiescent citizen*. Schudson, *Good Citizen*, 310–11; on the production of apathetic, acquiescent citizens, see Engels and Saas, "On Acquiescence and Ends-Less War."
11. When the founders of the United States disparaged democracy as "mobocracy" and *anarchia*, they were participating in an ancient discourse that equated democracy with *ochlocracy*, mob rule. On "mobocracy," see Gilje, *Road to Mobocracy*. On ὀχλοκρατία (mob rule), see Polybius, *Histories*, 6.4.6–13; helpful on Polybius's theory of the cycle of constitutions is Von Fritz, *Theory of Mixed Constitutions*.

12. Following Ernesto Laclau and Chantal Mouffe in *Hegemony and Social-ist Strategy*, we might say that the democratic claim is itself a bid for hegemonic articulation, rather than an acknowledgment of a moral truth outside of and above human affairs. Of course, we must always remember to ask: which democracy is being claimed?

13. On the foundational hatred of democracy in the West, see Rancière, *Hatred of Democracy*.

14. For a description of the various modes of redistribution common to classical Athens, see Ober, *Mass and Elite*, 199–202. Ober concludes, "The rich were thus participants in a legal system and an ideological framework that gave the demos privileges in respect to the rich man's property. This system, in a sense, balanced the various privileges the rich man gained from the private possession of that same property" (243). For a very helpful and provocative Marxist analysis of Athenian democracy that focuses on class tensions as constitutive of social and political reality, see Ste. Croix, *Class Struggle in the Ancient Greek World*.

15. Dewey, "Creative Democracy."

16. Here, see the disciplinary histories in Gehrke, *Ethics and Politics of Speech*, and Medhurst, "History of Public Address." Contemporary departments of communication go by a number of names—"Communication Studies," "Speech Communication," "Communication," "Communication Arts."

17. Resentment is likely what Kenneth Burke calls a "universal experi-ence"—Burke, *Counter-Statement*, 149.

18. Booth, *Rhetoric of Rhetoric*, 107–47.

19. And thus rhetoric is a way of "doing, knowing, and being"—Benson, "Rhetoric as a Way of Being."

20. For social psychologists, the optimal word is "proprioception," which means knowing where one's body ends and others begin—see Gallagher, *How the Body Shapes the Mind*, 6–7.

21. The most detailed treatment of the rhetoric of identification is Burke, *Rhetoric of Motives*.

22. Booth, *Rhetoric of Rhetoric*, 171.

23. Burke, *Language as Symbolic Action*, 3.

24. Burke, *Permanence and Change*, 274–94. This essay, "On Human Behav-ior Considered 'Dramatistically,'" was added as an appendix to the second edition of *Permanence and Change*, published in 1954.

25. When speaking of the care of the self, I am drawing on Michel Foucault's important work in *Hermeneutics of the Subject*.

26. For helpful studies of the rhetoric of the culture wars, see Hunter, *Cul-ture Wars*; Frank, *What's the Matter with Kansas?* Lakoff, *Moral Politics*; Lakoff, *Whose Freedom?* and Rodgers, *Age of Fracture*.

27. Burke, *Attitudes toward History*, 41.

28. Rawls, *Theory of Justice*, 533–34—as opposed to the unjust, politically illegitimate emotion of "envy."

29. Žižek, *Violence*, 2; Hariman, "Speaking of Evil," 515.

30. I describe the "dilemmas of American nationalism" and the troubling legacy of revolution for American elites in my first book, Engels, *Enemyship*; for a helpful description of how civic traditions of revolution have been disciplined in the United States, see Bercovitch, *Rites of Assent*. In *On Revolution*, Hannah Arendt suggests that the American Revolution was resentful in the right measure, as opposed to the French Revolution, which was dominated by the wrong sort of resentment of the sansculottes.

31. Foucault, "Nietzsche, Genealogy, History"; for a very helpful reading of the utility of Foucault's work for rhetorical studies, see Phillips, "Spaces of Invention." Here, Foucault described his genealogical method in the positive terms of a "curative science" (90)—what Nietzsche in *On the Uses and Disadvantages of History for Life* called "history for the purpose of life," that is, history that enriches life rather than overburdening it with the debt of a past that can never be repaid, because this history is "in the service of the future and the present and not for the weakening of the present or for depriving a vigorous future of its roots" (66, 77).

Essay I

1. From the perspective of rhetorical scholars, invocations of the people are interesting because with their words politicians create a picture of the people that they will, in turn, act on. In this way, it can be said that politicians create the people, which "are not objectively real in the sense that they exist as a collective entity in nature; rather, they are a fiction dreamed by an advocate and infused with an artificial, rhetorical reality." McGee, "In Search of 'the People,'" 240.

2. An "attitude" being, in Burke's definition, "the point of mediation between the realms of nonsymbolic motion and symbolic action." *Attitudes toward History*, 394.

3. Ober, "Original Meaning of 'Democracy,'" 5. This point is explored in more detail in Ober, *Athenian Revolution*, 18–52, 107–39.

4. M. I. Finley observes that while there were a range of terms and euphemisms and puns in Greek and Latin for describing the people as divided into clashing classes, "the fact remains, however, that more often than not 'rich' and 'poor' render the sense better than a literal translation." *Politics in the Ancient World*, 2.

5. 4.2.37–39.

6. Demosthenes, *Against Timocrates*, trans. Murray, 24.171. One can also look to Pericles's funeral oration, in Thucydides, *History of the Peloponnesian War*, 144–51 (2.35–46).

7. Plato, *"Republic" of Plato*, 235 (557a).

8. Ibid., 557a.

9. Ober, *Mass and Elite*, 240.

10. Aristotle, *On Rhetoric*, 1390b–1391a. Aristotle listed *hubris* as one of the three causes of anger (*orgē*), the others being contempt and spite—1378b.

11. Ibid., Kennedy trans., 1378b, 1379b (117, 119).

12. Isocrates, *Antidosis*, section 131.

13. Ibid., trans. Mirhady and Too, section 138 (231).

14. Ibid., section 142 (232).

15. Ibid., sections 159–60.

16. Ibid., section 4.

17. Isocrates seems to capture this sense of *phthonos* in *Antidosis*, section 149, when speaking of his friends' advice to him: "Reasonable and sensible people might perhaps admire you for this, but others who are less talented and who generally are more upset at the honest success of others than at their own misfortune, can only be annoyed and resentful." *Antidosis*, trans. Mirhady and Too, 233. Liddell and Scott note that the adjective φθονερός, from the masculine noun φθόνος, means "envious, jealous, grudging." This is the sense of φθόνος in Matthew 27:18, ὅτι διὰ φθόνον παρέδωκαν αὐτόν, "that for envy they had delivered him."

18. Liddell and Scott define νέμεσις as "distribution of what is due; hence a righteous assignment of anger, wrath at anything unjust, just resentment." The goddess Νέμεσις was "the impersonation of divine wrath" and "the goddess of Retribution."

19. "It is true that, at least in democratic Athens, *phthonos* tended to be associated particularly with what we might call 'upward resentment,' that is, the anger of the lower classes towards the rich, whereas in Homer, *nemesis* seems more often to express 'downward resentment' on the part of superiors—whether gods or mortals—towards inferiors who overstep their station." Konstan, *Emotions of the Ancient Greeks*, 122, and for a more general discussion, see 111–28.

20. Ibid., 120.

21. Konstan writes, "The function of *phthonos* is to preserve the proper hierarchy in society. If a person attempts to exceed his station, he rightly incurs *phthonos*, as does an inferior who pretends to equality with his betters" (121).

22. On Aristotle's *Rhetoric*, see Gross and Walzer, *Rereading Aristotle's "Rhetoric,"* and Rorty, *Essays on Aristotle's "Rhetoric."*

23. Aristotle defined *phthonos* as "a certain kind of distress at apparent success on the part of one's peers in attaining the good things . . . not that a person may get anything for himself but because of those who have it." Aristotle, *On Rhetoric*, trans. Kennedy, 1387b (144); Aristotle distinguished *phthonos* from *to nemesan* in his *Rhetoric* at 1386b–1387a.

24. Aristotle, *On Rhetoric*, trans. Kennedy, 1387b (144).

25. Agamben, *State of Exception*, 74–75, 85–86.

26. The Romulus and Remus myth is explored as an expression of the social conflict between *plebs* and *patres* and the conflict of the orders in Wiseman, *Remus*. The emblem *SPQR*, much like our "USA," was emblazoned on the standard of the Roman legions and appeared on coins, on monuments, and at the end of official documents and pronouncements. Though a logo of unity, *Senatus* was

an office and *populus* was not. The opposition between ruler and ruled captured in *SPQR* is discussed in Boas, *Vox Populi*, 43–45.

27. Livy, *Ab Urbe Condita*, 2.44.9–10.

28. Sallust wrote histories of Catiline's conspiracy and the Jugurthine War; he also, like Thucydides, composed speeches for prominent historical figures in his *Histories*. Sallust, himself a tribune of the plebs in 52 BCE, protested the plebs' acquiescence to the rule of pompous, corrupt Roman aristocrats, and he took particular relish in writing screeds that affirmed the ultimate power of the people over the Roman aristocrats—see Sallust's *Oratio Macri* and also the speech of tribune Gaius Memmius to the people in Sallust's *Bellum Iugurthinum*. Sallust used the Greek distinction between mass and elite to rally the plebs against the Roman aristocrats—in Sallust's writings, "The opposition between the few and the many, the rich and the poor, is described as a struggle between those who desire liberty [*cura libertatis*] and those who lust or desire to dominate [*cura dominationis*]." Fontana, "Rhetoric and the Roots of Democratic Politics," 35.

29. Quintilian, *Institutio Oratoria*, 10.1.101–2.

30. "statui certaminis adversa pro libertate potiora esse forti viro quam omnio non certavisse," my translation.

31. On Cicero's view of violence in republican politics, see Lintott, *Violence*, 52–66; for a helpful discussion of homicide as a tool of political power in ancient Rome more generally, see Gaughan, *Murder Was Not a Crime*.

32. Cicero, *Speech on Behalf of Publius Sestius*, trans. Kaster, 32.

33. Cicero, *De Oratore*, 2.83.340.

34. Ibid., 2.82.337.

35. Ibid., 2.50.206.

36. Ibid., 2.52.209.

37. Cicero, *Letters to Atticus*, 5.19.3.

38. Cicero, *De Inventione*, trans. Hubell, 1.53.100 (151).

39. Cicero, *De Oratore*, 2.52.209. Here I am drawing on Sutton's translation in the Loeb Classical Library Edition, 351. Sutton translates *invidia* as "jealousy"; I translate it as "resentment."

40. Ibid., trans. Sutton, 2.52.209–210 (353).

41. Ibid., 2.52.210–211 (353).

42. Cicero, *Tusculanae Disputationes*, 3.34.82.

43. In *The Discourses on Livy*, a running commentary on key themes in Livy's *Ab Urbe Condita*, Machiavelli wrote, "Those who condemn the dissentions between the nobility and the people seem to me to be finding fault with what as a first cause kept Rome free, and to be considering the quarrels and the noise that resulted from the dissentions rather than the good effects they brought about; they are not considering that in every republic there are two opposed factions [*umori diversi*], that of the people and that of the rich, and that all the laws made in favour of liberty result from the discord." Machiavelli, *Discourses on Livy*, 1.4, quoted in Fontana, "Sallust and the Politics of Machiavelli," 89. Machiavelli reiterated these thoughts in *The Prince*, published just after his death in 1527. There, he noted that "in every city one finds these two opposed

classes [*umori diversi*], the populace and the elite," which "are at odds because the populace do not want to be ordered about or oppressed by the elite; and the elite want to order about and oppress the populace" (31).

44. The Levellers were concerned, primarily, with defending the rights of poor people against the wealthy. Enacting old democratic norms, Leveller emissaries attempted (in the words of one of their pamphlets) "to raise the servant against the master, the tenant against his landlord, the buyer against the seller, the borrower against the lender, the poor against the rich." Hill, *World Turned Upside Down*, 114, 121; on the Levellers and the democratic activism of the English Civil War more generally, see Linebaugh and Rediker, *Many-Headed Hydra*, 104–42, and Morgan, *Inventing the People*, 38–93. Machiavelli's ideas were clearly at play here, for classical ideals of democracy were transmitted to the Anglo-American world via Machiavelli and his followers in England, especially James Harrington of *Oceana* fame. On Machiavelli's influence on English political theory in the seventeenth and eighteenth centuries, see Pocock, *Machiavellian Moment*, 333–505, and Rahe, *Against Throne and Altar*.

45. Wood, *Creation of the American Republic*, 503.

46. On democracy as a central problem in post-Revolution America, see Wood, *Creation of the American Republic*, 471–518; Takaki, *Iron Cages*, 1–65; Linebaugh and Rediker, *Many-Headed Hydra*, 211–47; Nash, *Unknown American Revolution*, 366–422; Bouton, *Taming Democracy*; Holton, *Unruly Americans*; Fritz, *American Sovereigns*; and Engels, *Enemyship*.

47. Gerry quoted in Farrand, *Records*, 1:48.

48. James Madison, *Federalist* No. 10, in Hamilton, Madison, and Jay, *The Federalist*, 56.

49. Fisher Ames, speech at the Massachusetts Ratifying Convention, January 15, 1788, in Bailyn, *Debate on the Constitution*, 1:894.

50. "From the (New-York) Herald," *Catskill Packet and Western Mail*, May 23, 1795, 1.

51. Ali Kahn, "The Observer—No. III," *Boston Gazette*, March 24, 1803, 2.

52. John Adams to John Taylor, April 15, 1814, in Carey, *Political Writings*, 406.

53. I explore these charges against democracy in the context of Shays's Rebellion and the drafting of the Constitution in Engels, *Enemyship*, 67–111.

54. I offer a rhetorical theory of the state of exception in Engels, "Two Faces of Cincinnatus."

55. The "foot-stool" example is used by Spartanus, "The Interest of America, Letter III," *New-York Journal*, June 20, 1776, 1–2.

56. Minot, *History of the Insurrections*, 15.

57. Here, see James Madison's remarks at the Constitutional Convention on June 6, 1787, and June 26, 1787; and Alexander Hamilton's speech of June 17, 1787, in Farrand, *Records of the Federal Convention*, 1:135, 1:422, 1:299. See also Madison, *Federalist* No. 10, 53. Even Hamilton admitted, "If SHAYS had not been a *desperate debtor*, it is much to be doubted whether Massachusetts would have been plunged into a civil war." Hamilton, *Federalist* No. 6, 31. Both in Hamilton, Madison, and Jay, *The Federalist*.

58. Madison's remarks at the Constitutional Convention on June 6, 1787, in Farrand, *Records of the Federal Convention*, 1:135. Madison echoed these thoughts on June 26, noting that "in all civilized Countries the people fall into different classes havg. a real or supposed difference of interests. There will be creditors & debtors, farmers, merchts. & manufactures. There will be particularly the distinction of rich & poor." Farrand, *Records of the Federal Convention*, 1:422.

59. Hamilton's speech of June 18, 1787, in ibid., 1:299.

60. This discursive shift toward thinking of rich and poor as factions was already underway in the 1780s. See, for instance, Atticus, "For the Independent Chronicle, Letter II: From a Gentleman in the Country to His Friend in Town," *Independent Chronicle and Universal Advertiser* (Boston), October 18, 1787, 1. Note that contrary to the many frightened observers of Shays's Rebellion, Atticus found the conflict in Massachusetts and the broader United States between the "two factions" of the rich and the populace to be essential to national virtue.

61. Madison, *Federalist* No. 10, in Hamilton, Madison, and Jay, *The Federalist*, 52.

62. Rousseau, *Social Contract*, 49.

63. Rousseau, *Discourse on the Origin of Inequality*, 44. For a very helpful reading of Rousseau's *Discourse*, see Hartnett, "Prisons, Profit, Crime, and Social Control."

64. For Rousseau, "the more violent the passions are, the more necessary the laws are to contain them. But over and above the fact that the disorders and crimes these passions cause daily in our midst show quite well the insufficiency of the laws in this regard, it would still be good to examine whether these disorders did not come into being with the laws themselves." Rousseau, *Discourse on the Origin of Inequality*, 39.

65. Americans at the time were reading and grappling with Rousseau's ideas; see May, *Enlightenment in America*; Fliegelman, *Prodigals and Pilgrims*; and McFarland, *Romanticism and the Heritage of Rousseau*.

66. Madison, *Federalist* No. 10, in Hamilton, Madison, and Jay, *The Federalist*, 53.

67. Ibid., 54; Locke, *Second Treatise of Government*, ¶ 124, 350–51.

68. Madison, *Federalist* No. 10, in Hamilton, Madison, and Jay, *The Federalist*, 56.

69. Ibid.

70. Madison here spoke in line with a common belief shared by elites in post-Revolution America: that the United States could only compete with Europe if more money was centralized in the hands of wealthy investors—a belief that Terry Bouton calls "the gospel of moneyed men." Bouton, *Taming Democracy*, 70.

71. The Progressive historians of the early twentieth century, headlined by Charles Beard and his monumental *Economic Interpretation of the United States Constitution* (1913), claimed that that the founders, generally rich, elite, white men, were driven by their economic interests to write a Constitution that protected those interests at the expense of the economic well-being, and the political aspirations, of common men and women. This view of the founding period

came under attack in the 1950s, especially with Louis Hartz's *Liberal Tradition in America* (1955), which, troping John Locke as one of America's founding fathers, posited a liberal hegemony in which Americans from the founding period forward found stability and consensus in their shared commitment to negative liberty and private property. This liberal tradition downplayed the social conflict between rich and poor so central to Progressive historiography; Americans didn't need to fight because they were all liberals at heart. The Hartzian paradigm, such a natural expression of the post-Progressive liberalism of the 1950s, itself came under attack in the late 1960s and early 1970s with the rise of the republican paradigm. Gordon Wood, in his epic *Creation of the American Republic* (1969), argued that the republican injunction common to revolutionary-era America, that politics should be concerned with cultivating civic virtue, and promoting the public good, was overturned by the cold and calculating liberalism of the Constitution, which was concerned primarily with managing conflict and ensuring that the many did not rise up in revolution against the few. And thus Wood frames the Constitution as the culmination of a counter-revolution in the 1780s aimed at tempering the democratic impulses of revolution. Building on the work of the 1970s and 1980s, a number of historians in recent years have continued to excavate the antidemocratic foundations of the United States, articulating a neo-Progressive thesis focusing on social conflict. It is in this tradition—inspired by the work of Peter Linebaugh and Marcus Rediker, Terry Bouton, Christian Fritz, Woody Holton, Chris Castiglia, and Dana Nelson—that I position my work up to this point on eighteenth- and nineteenth-century U.S. politics. For a helpful discussion, and critique, of the Progressive historians, see Hofstadter, *Progressive Historians*; on the critique of Hartz's paradigm and the rise of the republican paradigm, see Rodgers, "Republicanism."

72. Sydney, *Discourses concerning Government*, 166. John Locke did not dictate the structure of an ideal constitution, but noted that from democracy, oligarchy, and monarchy "the Community may make compounded and mixed Forms of Government, as they think good." In *The Spirit of the Laws*, published in 1748, Montesquieu observed that there were three types of government—republican, monarchy, and despotism—and then further subdivided republics by arguing that they could take the forms of "democracy" or "aristocracy." Montesquieu advocated dividing political power according to its functions (executive, legislative, and judicial), but democracy was here in the background of his theory, framing discussions of political liberty and its corruption, and underpinning the republican aspect of the ideal mixed constitution. Locke, *Second Treatise of Government*, ¶ 132, 354; Montesquieu, *Spirit of the Laws*, 10–17, 154–66.

73. Madison, *Federalist* No. 10, in Hamilton, Madison, and Jay, *The Federalist*, 58.

74. Deutch, "E Pluribus Unum."

75. The official website for the Great Seal reports the same source: see http://www.state.gov/documents/organization/27807.pdf, page 6.

76. Deutch, "E Pluribus Unum."

It manus in gyrum; paullatim singula vires
Deperdunt proprias; color est E pluribus unus.

Spins round the stirring hand; lose by degrees
Their separate powers the parts, and comes at last
From many several colors one that rules.

77. John Adams wrote his wife with descriptions of each member's ideas—see John Adams to Abigail Adams, August 14, 1776, in *Familiar Letters*, 210–11.

78. Furthermore, there is a distinct possibility that the notion of strength in confederated unity was informed by the practices of the Iroquois nation. See Olson, *Benjamin Franklin's Vision*, 121–25.

79. Here, see Beard, *Economic Interpretation of the Constitution of the United States*. This move to deny inequality was also foundational to the first explicitly democratic rhetoric in the United States. See Engels, "Demophilia."

80. Jefferson, *Life and Writings*, 192.

81. I describe the development of enemyship as a technique for managing democracy in the United States in Engels, *Enemyship*.

82. Isocrates, *Panegyricus*, trans. Papillon, section 173 (69). This was a frequent argument in Isocrates's rhetoric: see also sections 15–17 and 187 of *Panegyricus*, and *To Philip*, section 9: "Going over these matters in my mind, I found that Athens would stay peaceful only if all the greatest cities would decide to put of hostilities among themselves and carry the war into Asia, and if they should plan to gain from the barbarians, the advantages that the barbarians now think they should get from the Greeks. This plan I advocated before in my discourse *Panegyricus*." Isocrates, *To Philip*, trans. Papillon, in *Isocrates II*, 77.

83. Isocrates, *Antidosis*, trans. Mirhady and Too, section 77 (220).

84. Livy, *Ab Urbe Condita*, 3.10.7–12, 3.16.1–6.

85. Ibid., 3.17.12.

86. Hobbes, *Leviathan*, 287.

87. Ibid., 368.

88. Ibid., 369.

89. Ibid.

90. Hovering over the countryside like a god, Hobbes's sovereign embodies the double-articulated provenance of medieval government, bringing together the *oikonomic*, taxonomic face of administration with the divine, acclamatory face of a semantically evacuated amen. These two faces of medieval government are explored in Agamben, *Kingdom and the Glory*.

91. Michel Foucault writes, "The justice of the king was shown to be an armed justice. The sword that punished the guilty was also the sword that destroyed enemies." *Discipline and Punish*, 50.

92. Foucault tracks the shift from sovereign violence to discipline and bio-politics in *Discipline and Punish*; for his description of sovereign violence as being too expensive to persist, see 80–89.

93. I describe Hobbes's gamble in Engels, *Enemyship*, 207–22. Hobbes concluded *Leviathan* with the following words: "And thus I have brought to an end my Discourse of Civill and Ecclesiasticall Government . . . without other designe, than to set before mens eyes the mutuall Relation between Protection and Obedience" (728). Carl Schmitt looked back on Hobbes as a political hero in his *Concept of the Political*: he lamented the decline of the "Leviathan image" in Western culture, and he claimed that Hobbes had grasped the "truth" of politics: "The *protego ergo obligo* is the *cogito ergo sum* of the state" (52).

94. Bailyn, *Ideological Origins*, 202–3, 205, 209, 216. Hobbes was, in fact, the theoretical enemy of American conceptions of divided sovereignty. Bailyn notes, "It was, nevertheless, in Hobbes who, in a series of writings in the mid-seventeenth century, first went beyond the immediate claims of monarchy to argue systematically that the only essential quality of sovereignty as such—whoever or whatever its possessor might be—was the capacity to compel obedience; and it was with his name, and with Filmer's, that the colonists came to associate the conception of the *Machtstaat* in its most blatant form" (199). Gordon Wood concludes similarly, "In the development of the idea of sovereignty its representational basis was always in danger of being forgotten and falling away, leaving the sovereign authority simply as the stark power to command—a frightening notion made famous by Hobbes in the seventeenth century and denounced but never really repudiated by almost all eighteenth-century thinkers." Wood, *Creation of the American Republic*, 348.

95. Alexander Hamilton, *Federalist* No. 8, in Hamilton, Madison, and Jay, *The Federalist*, 42.

96. Thomas Paine, *American Crisis* No. 1, in *Thomas Paine Reader*, 122.

97. This phrasing is from Paine, *Common Sense* (1776), in *Thomas Paine Reader*, 80.

98. Butler, *Fifteen Sermons*, 136–67; for a very helpful discussion of Butler's philosophy, see Griswold, *Forgiveness*, 19–47.

99. Smith, *Theory of Moral Sentiments*, 218.

100. Ibid., 86. For a later development of many of Smith's suggestions about resentment, see also Reid, *Essays on the Active Powers*, 172–73, 183, 319.

101. On the disciplining of resentment into its moral form, see Smith, *Theory of Moral Sentiments*, 160, 172.

102. Ibid., 69–70.

103. Ibid., 96.

104. Smith argued that society was a collection of "mirrors" in which citizens judged the merit of their own actions by observing how they were reflected in the eyes of others; Hume claimed, similarly, that "the minds of men are mirrors to one another," reflecting one another's emotions and passions. Smith, *Theory of Moral Sentiments*, 84–85; Hume, *Treatise of Human Nature*, 365.

105. Smith, *Theory of Moral Sentiments*, 70.

106. Ibid.

107. Ibid., 71.

108. Smith describes Hobbes's philosophy as "odious." Ibid., 318.

109. Hobbes, *Leviathan*, 262.

110. And, Hobbes insists, "feare and liberty are consistent." Ibid.

111. On the Scottish Enlightenment's influence on American conceptions of rhetoric, see Fliegelman, *Declaring Independence*, and Potkay, *Fate of Eloquence*.

112. Madison, *Federalist* No. 42, in Hamilton, Madison, and Jay, *The Federalist*, 236.

113. Ibid., 236.

114. Madison, *Federalist* No. 49, in ibid., 283, italics added.

115. Hamilton, *Federalist* No. 16, in ibid., 89.

116. I have written the first volume of this early history in Engels, *Enemyship*. Much work in extending this history through the nineteenth, twentieth, and twenty-first centuries still needs to be done.

117. Alperovitz, *Atomic Diplomacy*. In a review of the expanded 1985 edition published in the *New York Times*, Yale historian Gaddis Smith noted that the controversy over *Atomic Diplomacy* was largely the product of context, given that the United States began ground operations and widespread bombing in Vietnam in 1965, the year the book was originally published. About the expanded edition, he observed, "In 1985 'Atomic Diplomacy' seems less startling. The old flaws remain, but the preponderance of new evidence that has appeared since 1965 tends to sustain the original argument. It has been demonstrated that the decision to bomb Japan was centrally connected to Truman's confrontational approach to the Soviet Union." Smith, "Was Moscow Our Real Target?" For an expanded and further updated version of the argument of *Atomic Diplomacy*, see Alperovitz, *Decision to Use the Atomic Bomb*. Even more recently, on the sixtieth anniversary of the bombings, this perspective has been advanced by Peter Kuznick, director of the Nuclear Studies Institute at American University, and Mark Selden, historian at Cornell University—see Edwards, "Hiroshima Bomb." On the death tolls of the atomic bombs, see Committee for the Compilation, *Hiroshima and Nagasaki*, 113, 115, 367–69.

118. Gaddis, "Was Moscow Our Real Target?"

119. Alperovitz, *Atomic Diplomacy*.

120. Marcuse, *Essay on Liberation*, 74.

121. According to Hal Brands, "As a nation chiefly of immigrants, America has lacked many of the usual characteristics of nationhood, especially a shared ancestry, language, and cultural experience. For this reason, Americans' shared enemies have mattered the more." *Devil We Knew*, v.

122. NSA documents, declassified in December 2005, suggest that that there was no attack on August 4, 1964, and that in fact the charges were trumped up; see Shane, "Vietnam War Intelligence." NSA historians pushed to declassify these documents as early as 2002, but they remained secret as the intelligence justifying the Iraq War was called into question. See Shane, "Vietnam Study." In July 2010, the Senate Foreign Relations Committee released over one thousand

pages of documents showing that many senators at the time expressed deep doubts about the Tonkin event and other Vietnam intelligence. Bumiller, "Records Show Doubts."

123. Ivie, "Images of Savagery."

124. John Dewey recognized the need for certainty as a driving force in human behavior in *The Quest for Certainty*; on war as a force that provides certainty and shuts down critical inquiry, see Bernstein, *Abuse of Evil*.

125. The concept of "cultural fictions" is theorized in Hartnett, *Democratic Dissent*.

126. American Protestantism was tied to an acquisitive logic from the very beginning; see Bercovitch, *American Jeremiad*. On the Protestant ethic, see, for instance, Weber, *Protestant Ethic*, and "Protestant Sects."

127. For a helpful discussion of the rhetoric surrounding reconstruction, see Wilson, *Reconstruction Desegregation Debate*.

128. I theorize the "contract of blood" in Engels, *Enemyship*, 157–205.

Essay II

1. Allen, *Talking to Strangers*.
2. Burke, *Permanence and Change*, 284–85.
3. Burke, *Rhetoric of Religion*, 4–5.
4. Though he is more skeptical in his assessment of the curative function of Hitler's rhetoric in *The Philosophy of Literary Form*—putting "medicine" and "curative" in quotations and suggesting that Hitler's cure was really nothing more than "snakeoil"—he is less hesitant and more emphatic in works like *Permanence and Change*. Burke, *Philosophy of Literary Form*, 191, 202, 192.
5. Burke, *Permanence and Change*, 15, 16. Thus, in his 1963–64 essay "Definition of Man," in *Language as Symbolic Action*, a summary statement of his philosophy, Burke concludes that humans name the enemy in order to achieve "catharsis by scapegoat" (18).
6. Allen, *Talking to Strangers*, 29.
7. Ibid., 46–47.
8. Ibid., 20, 88.
9. Ibid., 5.
10. Ibid., 9.
11. Ibid., 19.
12. Perlstein, *Nixonland*, 5.
13. Ibid., 13.
14. On the American traditions of white privilege in the eighteenth and nineteenth centuries, see Takaki, *Iron Cages*; Saxton, *Rise and Fall of the White Republic*; Roediger, *Wages of Whiteness*; and Harris, "Whiteness as Property."
15. McGinnis, *Selling of the President*, 141.
16. Phillips, *Emerging Republican Majority*, 184.
17. Ibid., 195.

18. Hunter, *How to Defend Yourself*, 108.

19. DeGroot, *Sixties Unplugged*, 381–85.

20. Fulbright, "Great Society."

21. Ian Haney López describes Nixon's coded racial appeals in *Dog Whistle Politics*.

22. See Morris, "Pink Herring and the Fourth Persona."

23. "Troubled American," 29.

24. King and Anderson, "Nixon, Agnew, and the 'Silent Majority.'"

25. Windt, *Presidents and Protestors*, 118.

26. Lowndes, *From the New Deal*, 9.

27. Sumner, *What Social Classes Owe Each Other*, 21–22.

28. Ibid., 108.

29. Franklin Delano Roosevelt, "The 'Forgotten Man' Speech," April 7, 1932. Available at the American Presidency Project, http://www.presidency.ucsb.edu/ws/?pid=88408.

30. Egan, "When FDR Found 'The Forgotten Man.'"

31. "Troubled American," 29.

32. Richard Nixon, "The Great Silent Majority" address, November 3, 1969. Available at American Rhetoric, http://www.americanrhetoric.com/speeches/richardnixongreatsilentmajority.html.

33. Perlstein, *Nixonland*, 418–26.

34. Richard Nixon, "The President's News Conference," September 26, 1969. Available at the American Presidency Project, http://www.presidency.ucsb.edu/ws/?pid=2246.

35. Nixon, "Great Silent Majority."

36. Nixon, "Inaugural Address," January 20, 1969. Available at the American Presidency Project, http://www.presidency.ucsb.edu/ws/index.php?pid=1941.

37. Tocqueville, *Democracy in America*, 235–49.

38. See Hersh, *Price of Power*, 21–22; Clifford, *Counsel to the President*, 581–93; and Summers, *Arrogance of Power*, 297–308.

39. Karlyn Kohrs Campbell has used Nixon's rhetoric to make a crucial point about the practice of rhetorical criticism. Criticism is not an apolitical, amoral practice, as the neo-Aristotelians preached. On the contrary, criticism "plays a crucial role in the processes of testing, questioning, and analyzing by which discourses advocating truth and justice may, in fact, become more powerful than their opposites." It is the critic's duty to call Nixon out for lying and self-contradiction, and for dividing Americans, she argues, for "unless we become careful, discriminating critics, questioning and evaluating, we shall be constrained to make poor decisions and supporting policies destructive of ourselves, our society, and our world." Following Campbell's lead, I suggest we should be critical of Nixon's rhetoric because the politics of resentment uses the language of democracy to undermine a dangerous democracy. Campbell, "Conventional Wisdom," 144; Campbell, "Exercise in the Rhetoric," 125.

40. On the invention and rhetorical structure of "support the troops" appeals, see Stahl, "Why We Support the Troops."

41. On war rhetoric as aimed at acquiescence rather than support, see Engels and Saas, "On Acquiescence and Ends-Less War," 225–32.

42. Perlstein, *Nixonland*, 501–3.

43. Lichtman, *White Protestant Nation*, 289.

44. Perlstein, *Nixonland*, 81, 179, 339–40, 367.

45. *New York Times*, "Nixon Would Use Force in the Cities."

46. Perlstein, *Nixonland*, 497.

47. Cowie, "Nixon's Class Struggle," 265.

48. Engels, "Democratic Alienation."

49. "Troubled American."

50. Hariman, "Speaking of Evil," 515–16.

51. Westbrook, *John Dewey*, 543.

52. On the technocratic rhetoric of the early 1960s liberal consensus, see Murphy, "Language of the Liberal Consensus."

53. On PREP and ERAP, see Miller, *Democracy Is in the Streets*, 173–217.

54. Hayden, *Port Huron Statement*, 55.

55. Ibid., 137.

56. H. Jacobs, *Weatherman*, 509; on the Weathermen's turn to violence, see also R. Jacobs, *Way the Wind Blew*, 38–89.

57. On the legacy of Vietnam for the nation's sense of itself and its destiny, and on Vietnam's challenge to traditional notions of masculinity, see Capps, *Unfinished War*; Owen, "Memory, War, and American Identity"; Gibson, *Warrior Dreams*; Bates, *Wars We Took to Vietnam*; and Morris and Ehrenhaus, *Cultural Legacies of Vietnam*.

58. Crozier, Huntington, and Watanuki, *Crisis of Democracy*, 113.

59. For the history of rhetorical education during the twentieth century, see Gehrke, *Ethics and Politics of Speech*.

60. Arendt, *On Violence*, 13–19.

61. Tipton, *History of Modern Germany*, 592.

62. On the pragmatists' philosophy of communication, see Shepherd, "Pragmatism and Tragedy"; Keith, *Democracy as Discussion*; Crick, *Democracy and Rhetoric*; and Crick and Engels, "'Effort of Reason.'"

63. West, *American Evasion of Philosophy*, 238.

64. Rorty, *Achieving Our Country*, 43.

65. Ibid., 14. John Rawls represents a complimentary though distinct case. He was active in the antiwar movement at Harvard and Stanford, and did not denounce students in the harsh terms of Arendt, Habermas, and Rorty. His central work, *A Theory of Justice*, reevaluated the moral foundations of liberalism at a time when liberalism found itself in crisis. When he completed *A Theory of Justice* in 1969–70 it bore the stamp of the Vietnam War. This was especially true as Rawls attempted to theorize the "conflict of duties" inherent to the legitimacy of civil disobedience in a constitutional democracy. His conclusion that those engaged in civil disobedience must suffer their punishment would not have sat well with the Weathermen's decision to go into hiding to avoid punishment. Pogge, *John Rawls*, 19–22, 319.

Essay III

1. See Conley, "Joys of Victimage."
2. Frank, *What's the Matter with Kansas?* 16.
3. George W. Bush, "Address to Joint Session of Congress Following 9/11 Attacks," September 20, 2001. Available at American Rhetoric, http://www .americanrhetoric.com/speeches/gwbush911jointsessionspe ech.htm.
4. Ivie writes in *Democracy and America's War on Terror*, 127, "The president's profile of terrorism, it goes almost without saying, was the single most influential interpretation of the danger at hand. It was his role and the responsibility of his office to shape public opinion, to put events in perspective, and to set the nation on a sensible course of action."
5. Norwood quoted in Toner and Zernike, "Partisan Fight."
6. Cheney quoted in Nagourney, "Arrests Bolster."
7. For examples of this over-the-top rhetorical madness, which approaches the limits of enemyship and reveals the increasing rhetorical desperation of the war's proponents, see Cloud, "Rumsfeld Says," and Rich, "Donald Rumsfeld's Dance."
8. Secretary of Defense Robert M. Gates's January 26, 2007, press conference can be found on the Department of Defense website at the following link: http://www.defenselink.mil/Transcripts/Transcript.aspx?TranscriptID=3877.
9. D'Souza, *Enemy at Home.*
10. Gewargis, "A WHAT Administration?"
11. Kristol, "Wright Stuff."
12. Eilperin, "Palin's 'Pro-America Areas' Remark."
13. Layton, "Palin Apologizes."
14. Johnson, "McCain Aide Says."
15. Layton, "Palin Apologizes."
16. Ibid.
17. Sarah Palin, "Republican Vice Presidential Nomination Acceptance Speech," September 3, 2008. Available at American Rhetoric, http://www .americanrhetoric.com/speeches/convention2008/sarahpalin2008rnc.htm.
18. Palin quoted in Cooper, "Palin, on Offensive."
19. Sullivan, "Secret Service."
20. *New York Times*, "Politics of Attack."
21. On the militarization of postmodern political discourse, see Weber, *Targets of Opportunity*, and Agamben, *State of Exception*.
22. Palin, "America's Enduring Strength."
23. Bates, "Blood Libel."
24. Hedges, *Death of the Liberal Class*. Indeed, while my book focuses its critique on conservative rhetorics, a companion book critiquing liberal rhetorics would be equally valuable—only it seems to me that the trouble with the Left in the United States is not a politics of resentment but instead general passivity in the face of their corporate sponsors' demands.
25. Martin, *Rich People's Movements.*

26. Krugman, "Climate of Hate."

27. Sumner, *What Social Classes Owe Each Other*, 114.

28. Neoliberalism intensifies the problems with the liberal paradigm of "possessive individualism" described in Macpherson, *Political Theory of Possessive Individualism*; it represents a return to what John Dewey in *Liberalism and Social Action* called the "old" or "early" version of liberalism: "the underlying philosophy and psychology of earlier liberalism led to a conception of individuality as something ready-made, already possessed, and needing only the removal of certain legal restrictions to come into full play" (30). Of course, Dewey valorized a kind of positive liberty, arguing (in the tradition, he said, of Thomas Jefferson) that certain conditions must be in place for the growth of liberty. Dewey continues to be condemned on conservative message boards.

29. *Pro Publica*, "Bailout Tracker."

30. Taibbi, *Griftopia*.

31. On the implosion of the housing market, see *This American Life*, episode 355, "Giant Pool of Money," which originally aired on May 9, 2008, available online at http://www.thisamericanlife.org/radio-archives/episode/355/the-giant-pool-of-money.

32. Klein, *Shock Doctrine*. The "war on terror" is the neoliberal war par excellence—see Harvey, *New Imperialism*; Hartnett and Stengrim, *Globalization and Empire*; and Wolin, *Democracy Incorporated*.

33. See in particular Stiglitz, *Price of Inequality*.

34. Ibid., xv.

35. That research can be found here: http://www.pewstates.org/research/analysis/economic-mobility-and-the-american-dream-where-do-we-stand-in-the-wake-of-the-great-recession-85899378421.

36. The American Dream seems in many ways to be an example of what Lauren Berlant calls "cruel optimism." See Berlant, *Cruel Optimism*.

37. Stiglitz, *Price of Inequality*, 274.

38. These cycles of "roll out" and "roll back" neoliberalism are described Peck, *Constructions of Neoliberal Reason*.

39. Brown, *Walled States, Waning Sovereignty*.

40. Žižek, *Violence*, 1–2.

41. "Rage capital" is Žižek's phrase in "From Democracy to Divine Violence," 111.

42. Benjamin, "Critique of Violence," 294.

43. Derrida, "Force of Law," 6.

44. Arendt, *On Violence*, 51–54.

45. Hariman, "Speaking of Evil," 516.

46. de Certeau, *Culture in the Plural*, 35.

47. *New York Times*, "GOP Testimony on Violence."

48. For a helpful study of race-baiting rhetoric, see López, *Dog Whistle Politics*.

49. Davis, *Prisoners of the American Dream*, 181–255; Harvey, *Brief History of Neoliberalism*, 39–63.

50. Here, see especially Davis, *City of Quartz*.

51. Palin, *Going Rogue*, 363.

52. Dawes, *Language of War*, 21.

53. Meares, "Q&A."

54. Lakoff and Johnson, *Metaphors We Live By*, 62.

55. Allen, *Talking to Strangers*, 119–39.

56. Lovley, "Exclusive: FBI Details."

57. Dunn, "Sarah Palin's Obama Obsession," Wing, "Sarah Palin."

58. Harvey, *Brief History of Neoliberalism*, 48.

59. Ibid., 50.

60. Martin and Harris, "Palin 'Becoming Al Sharpton?'"

61. Nietzsche, *Genealogy of Morals*.

62. See Arendt, *On Revolution*.

63. Diogenes Laertius, *Lives of the Philosophers*, 7.113, quoted in Konstan, *Emotions of the Ancient Greeks*, 189.

64. Nietzsche, *Genealogy of Morals*, 39.

65. Gilles Deleuze writes, "We can guess what the creature of *ressentiment* wants: He wants others to be evil, he needs others to be evil in order to be able to consider himself good. You are evil, therefore I am good; this is the slave's fundamental formula.... This formula must be compared with that of the master: I am good, therefore you are evil." *Nietzsche and Philosophy*, 119.

66. Foucault, *Birth of Biopolitics*, 176, 116–17. Elsewhere Foucault explains that in neoliberalism, "the general form of the market becomes an instrument, a tool of discrimination in the debate with the administration. In other words, in classical liberalism the government was called upon to respect the form of the market and *laissez-faire*. Here, *laissez-faire* is turned into a do-not-*laissez-faire* government, in the name of a law of the market which will enable each of its activities to be measured and assessed. *Laissez-faire* is thus turned around, and the market is no longer a principle of government's self-limitation; it is a principle turned against it. It is a sort of permanent economic tribunal confronting government" (247).

67. "*Homo œconomicus* is someone who is eminently governable." Ibid., 270.

68. Here, see Foley, "From Infantile Citizens to Infantile Institutions."

69. Wolin, *Democracy Incorporated*, 239.

70. Vivian, "Neoliberal Epideictic," 4.

71. Lepore, *Whites of Their Eyes*, 16.

72. On the rhetoric of the jeremiad, see Bercovitch, *American Jeremiad*, and Murphy, "A Time of Shame and Sorrow."

73. Lepore, *Whites of Their Eyes*, 95.

74. "If the republican revolution had initially been defined as an escape from time, Madison had always acknowledged that, in the long run, such a revolution was doomed. Eventually the New World would come to resemble the Old." McCoy, *Elusive Republic*, 259.

75. On Jefferson's "democratic faith" as interpreted by John Dewey, see Engels, "Dewey on Jefferson."

76. Garsten, *Saving Persuasion*, 200–209.

77. Matthews, *If Men Were Angels*.

78. Ivie, *Democracy and America's War on Terror*, 19–20, 32, and Bessette, *Mild Voice of Reason*, 6–39.

79. Madison, *Federalist* No. 58, in Hamilton, Madison, and Jay, *The Federalist*, 326.

80. Madison, *Federalist* No. 10, in ibid., 56.

81. Bessette, *Mild Voice of Reason*, 21.

82. Engels, "Demophilia."

83. For two helpful discussions of the dynamics of representation, which is dependent on the rhetorical maneuver of synecdoche, see Burke, *Grammar of Motives*, 507–11, and Hartnett, *Democratic Dissent*, 132–72.

84. Hardt and Negri, *Multitude*, 241.

85. Foucault, "What Is an Author?"

86. As I see it, rhetoric is largely the spinning out of our foundational assumptions, propositions, and metaphysics (to use Burke's term, our "orientation"). Burke, *Permanence and Change*, 5–18.

87. Johnson, "Jesse Kelly."

88. Walsh, "Swearing Off."

Conclusion

1. See Foley, "*Peitho* and *Bia*."

2. Cicero, *De Oratore*, trans. Watson, 2.44.187 (134). The Watson translation does not provide the original Latin, which is essential for understanding Cicero's rhetoric; that can be found online or in the convenient Loeb editions of Cicero's works.

3. Ibid., 3.14.55–56 (207).

4. Žižek, *Violence*, 1–2.

5. Eberly, *Citizen Critics*.

6. Žižek, *Violence*, 4.

7. Ibid., 1–2.

8. Hofstadter, "Paranoid Style"; for a helpful clarification of his thesis, see Wood, "Conspiracy and the Paranoid Style"; for discussions of conspiracy theories in the formative rhetoric of the Revolutionary War at the beginning of our national consciousness, see Bailyn, *Ideological Origins*, 85–93, 95–102, 119–43, and Wood, *Creation of the American Republic*, 16, 22–23, 30–36, 40–43.

9. Nietzsche, *Birth of Tragedy*, 63.

10. Dewey, *Quest for Certainty*.

11. Žižek, *Violence*, 1–2; Hariman, "Speaking of Evil," 515.

12. Dewey, *Individualism Old and New*, 75.

13. Mills, *Power Elite*, 3.

14. See Krugman, "Ludicrous and Cruel," and "Ryan and Taxes."

15. Nelson, *Bad for Democracy*.

16. Campbell and Jamieson, *Presidents Creating the Presidency*, 234–42.

17. For a helpful discussion of many of the forms that democracy has taken historically, see Held, *Models of Democracy.*

18. To take just one classic example, the earliest writers in the United States to embrace democracy did so under very specific conditions—they encouraged Americans to participate in politics so long as they did not talk about slavery or class exploitation, which were of course the very forms of objective violence upon which wealthy white male democratic participation was premised in the early republic. By rendering certain appeals—claims about slavery, for instance—off-limits, these early Jeffersonians hoped to arrange the conversation in a way that democratic citizens from both North and South could meet on equal footing to confront shared problems. In short, they attempted to use their rational vision of democratic deliberation to discipline Americans to conform to an external ideal. And of course in the long run they failed. I explore the circumscribed conditions under which elite Americans embraced democracy in the early nineteenth century in Engels, "Demophilia."

19. Konstan, *Emotions of the Ancient Greeks*, 111–28.

20. Locke, *Essay Concerning Human Understanding*, 2:146–47.

21. Rawls, *Political Liberalism*, and "The Idea of Public Reason." For other works that stress the importance of reason-giving to deliberation, see also Gutmann and Thompson, *Democracy and Disagreement,* 52–127; Bohman, *Public Deliberation*, 23–70; and Cohen, "Deliberation and Democratic Legitimacy."

22. Here, see Hogan, "Rhetorical Pedagogy and Democratic Citizenship"; and Asen, "Discourse Theory of Citizenship."

23. Zarefsky, "Two Faces of Democratic Rhetoric," 127.

24. For one noteworthy example, see Farrell, *Norms of Rhetorical Culture.*

Adams, John, and Abigail Adams. *Familiar Letters of John Adams and His Wife Abigail Adams, during the Revolution*. New York: Hurd and Houghton, 1876.

Agamben, Giorgio. *The Kingdom and the Glory: For a Theological Genealogy of Economy and Government*. Translated by Lorenzo Chiesa. Stanford, CA: Stanford University Press, 2007/2011.

———. *State of Exception*. Translated by Kevin Attell. Chicago: University of Chicago Press, 2003/2005.

Allen, Danielle S. *Talking to Strangers: Anxieties of Citizenship since Brown v. Board of Education*. Chicago: University of Chicago Press, 2004.

Alperovitz, Gar. *Atomic Diplomacy: Hiroshima and Potsdam; The Use of the Atomic Bomb and the American Confrontation with Soviet Power*. Expanded and updated ed. New York: Elisabeth Sifton Books/Penguin, 1965/1985.

———. *The Decision to Use the Atomic Bomb*. New York: Vintage, 1995/1996.

Arendt, Hannah. *On Revolution*. New York: Viking, 1963.

———. *On Violence*. Orlando: Harcourt, 1969/1970.

Aristotle. *On Rhetoric: A Theory of Civic Discourse*. 2nd ed. Translated by George A. Kennedy. New York: Oxford University Press, 2007.

———. *Rhetoric*. Greek text edited by W. D. Ross. Perseus Digital Library. http://www.perseus.tufts.edu/hopper/text?doc=Perseus:text:1999.01.0059.

Asen, Robert. "A Discourse Theory of Citizenship." *Quarterly Journal of Speech* 90, no. 2 (2004): 189–211.

Bailyn, Bernard, ed. *The Debate on the Constitution: Federalist and Antifederalist Speeches, Articles, and Letters during the Struggle over Ratification*. 2 vols. Library of America. New York: Literary Classics of the U.S., 1993.

———. *The Ideological Origins of the American Revolution*. Cambridge, MA: Harvard University Press, 1967/1992.

Bates, Milton J. *The Wars We Took to Vietnam: Cultural Conflict and Storytelling*. Berkeley: University of California Press, 1996.

Bates, Stephen. "Blood Libel: What Does It Mean?" *Guardian*, January 12, 2011. http://www.guardian.co.uk/world/2011/jan/12/blood-libel-sarah-palin-arizona.

Beard, Charles A. *An Economic Interpretation of the Constitution of the United States*. New York: Free Press, 1913/1986.

Benjamin, Walter. "Critique of Violence." 1921. In *Reflections: Essays, Aphorisms, Autobiographical Writings*, edited by Peter Demetz. New York: Schocken, 2007.

Benson, Thomas W. "Rhetoric as a Way of Being." In *American Rhetoric: Context and Criticism*, edited by Thomas W. Benson, 293–322. Carbondale: Southern Illinois University Press, 1989.

Bercovitch, Sacvan. *The American Jeremiad*. Madison: University of Wisconsin Press, 1978.

———. *The Rites of Assent: Transformations in the Symbolic Construction of America*. New York: Routledge, 1993.

Berlant, Lauren. *Cruel Optimism*. Durham, NC: Duke University Press, 2011.

Bernstein, Richard J. *The Abuse of Evil: The Corruption of Politics and Religion since 9/11*. Cambridge, UK: Polity Press, 2005.

Bessette, Joseph M. *The Mild Voice of Reason: Deliberative Democracy and American National Government*. Chicago: University of Chicago Press, 1994.

Blair, Carole. "Nietzsche's Lecture Notes on Rhetoric: A Translation." *Philosophy and Rhetoric* 16, no. 2 (1983): 94–127.

Boas, George. *Vox Populi: Essays in the History of an Idea*. Baltimore: Johns Hopkins University Press, 1969.

Bohman, James. *Public Deliberation: Pluralism, Complexity, and Democracy*. Cambridge, MA: MIT Press, 2000.

Booth, Wayne C. *The Rhetoric of Rhetoric: The Quest for Effective Communication*. Malden, MA: Blackwell, 2004.

Bouton, Terry. *Taming Democracy: "The People," the Founders, and the Troubled Ending of the American Revolution*. New York: Oxford University Press, 2007.

Brands, H. W. *The Devil We Knew: Americans and the Cold War*. New York: Oxford University Press, 1993.

Brown, Wendy. *Walled States, Waning Sovereignty*. New York: Zone, 2010.

Bumiller, Elizabeth. "Records Show Doubts on '64 Vietnam Crisis." *New York Times*, July 14, 2010. http://www.nytimes.com/2010/07/15/world/asia/15vietnam.html.

Burke, Kenneth. *Attitudes toward History*. Berkeley: University of California Press, 1937/1984.

———. *Counter-Statement*. Berkeley: University of California Press, 1931/1968.

———. *A Grammar of Motives*. Berkeley: University of California Press, 1945/1962.

———. *Language as Symbolic Action: Essays on Life, Literature, and Method*. Berkeley: University of California Press, 1966.

———. *Permanence and Change: An Anatomy of Purpose*. Berkeley: University of California Press, 1935/1984.

———. *The Philosophy of Literary Form*. Baton Rouge: Louisiana State University Press, 1941.

———. *A Rhetoric of Motives*. Berkeley: University of California Press, 1950/1969.

———. *The Rhetoric of Religion: Studies in Logology*. Berkeley: University of California Press, 1961/1970.

Butler, Joseph. *Fifteen Sermons Preached at the Rolls Chapel*. 1726. In *The Works of Joseph Butler*, vol. 2, edited by W. E. Gladstone. London: Clarendon Press, 1896.

Campbell, Karlyn Kohrs. "'Conventional Wisdom–Traditional Form': A Rejoinder." In *The Practice of Rhetorical Criticism*, 2nd ed., edited by James R. Andrews, 144. New York: Longman, 1990.

———."An Exercise in the Rhetoric of Mythical America." In *The Practice of Rhetorical Criticism*, 2nd ed., edited by James R. Andrews, 121–27. New York: Longman, 1990.

Campbell, Karlyn Kohrs, and Kathleen Hall Jamieson. *Presidents Creating the Presidency: Deeds Done in Words*. Chicago: University of Chicago Press, 2008.

Capps, Walter H. *The Unfinished War: Vietnam and the American Conscience*. Boston: Beacon Press, 1982.

Carey, George W. *The Political Writings of John Adams*. Washington, DC: Regnery, 2000.

Cicero, Marcus Tullius. *Cicero on Oratory and Orators*. Translated and edited by J. S. Watson. Carbondale: Southern Illinois University Press, 1970.

———. *De Inventione*. Translated by H. M. Hubbell. Loeb Classical Library Edition. Cambridge, MA: Harvard University Press, 1949/2006.

———. *De Oratore*. Books I–II. Translated by E. W. Sutton. Loeb Classical Library Edition. Cambridge, MA: Harvard University Press, 1948.

———. *De Oratore*. Latin text edited by A. S. Wilkins. Perseus Digital Library. http://www.perseus.tufts.edu/hopper/text?doc=Perseus:text :1999.02.0120.

———. *Letters to Atticus*. Latin text edited by L. C. Purser. Perseus Digital Library. http://www.perseus.tufts.edu/hopper/text?doc=Perseus:text :1999.02.0008.

———. *Speech on Behalf of Publius Sestius*. Translated by Robert A. Kaster. Oxford: Clarendon Press, 2006.

———. *Tusculanae Disputationes*. Latin text edited by M. Pohlenz. Perseus Digital Library. http://www.perseus.tufts.edu/hopper/text?doc=Perseus :text:2007.01.0044.

Clifford, Clark, with Richard Holbrooke. *Counsel to the President: A Memoir*. New York: Random House, 1991.

Cloud, David S. "Rumsfeld Says War Critics Haven't Learned Lessons of History." *New York Times*, August 30, 2006, A4.

Cohen, Joshua. "Deliberation and Democratic Legitimacy." In *Deliberative Democracy: Essays on Reason and Politics*, edited by James Bohman and William Rehg, 67–91. Cambridge, MA: MIT Press, 1997.

Committee for the Compilation of Materials on Damage Caused by the Atomic Bombs in Hiroshima and Nagasaki. *Hiroshima and Nagasaki:*

The Physical, Medical, and Social Effects of the Atomic Bombings. New York: Basic, 1981.

Conley, Donovan S. "The Joys of Victimage in George W. Bush's War of Totality." *Cultural Studies <=> Critical Methodologies* 10, no. 4 (2010): 347–57.

Cooper, Michael. "Palin, on Offensive, Attacks Obama's Ties to '60s Radical." *New York Times*, October 4, 2008. http://www.nytimes.com/2008/10/05/us/politics/05palin.html.

Cowie, Jefferson. "Nixon's Class Struggle: Romancing the New Right Worker, 1969–1973." *Labor History* 43, no. 3 (2002): 257–83.

Crick, Nathan. *Democracy and Rhetoric: John Dewey on the Arts of Becoming*. Columbia: University of South Carolina Press, 2010.

Crick, Nathan, and Jeremy Engels. "'The Effort of Reason, and the Adventure of Beauty': The Aesthetic Rhetoric of Randolph Bourne." *Quarterly Journal of Speech* 98, no. 3 (2012): 272–96.

Crozier, Michael, Samuel P. Huntington, and Jôji Watanuki. *The Crisis of Democracy: Report on the Governability of Democracies to the Trilateral Commission*. New York: New York University Press, 1975.

Davis, Mike. *City of Quartz: Excavating the Future in Los Angeles*. New York: Vintage, 1992.

———. *Prisoners of the American Dream: Politics and Economy in the History of the U.S. Working Class*. London: Verso, 1986/1999.

Dawes, James. *The Language of War: Literature and Culture in the U.S. from the Civil War through World War II*. Cambridge, MA: Harvard University Press, 2002.

de Certeau, Michel. *Culture in the Plural*. Translated by Tom Conley. Minneapolis: University of Minnesota Press, 1974/1997.

DeGroot, Gerard J. *The Sixties Unplugged: A Kaleidoscopic History of a Disorderly Decade*. Cambridge, MA: Harvard University Press, 2008.

Deleuze, Gilles. *Nietzsche and Philosophy*. Translated by Hugh Tomlinson. New York: Columbia University Press, 1962/2006.

Demosthenes. *Against Timocrates*. Translated by A. T. Murray. Perseus Digital Library. http://www.perseus.tufts.edu/hopper/text?doc=Perseus%3Atext%3A1999.01.0074%3Aspeech%3D24%3Asection%3D171.

Derrida, Jacques. "Force of Law: The 'Mystical Foundation of Authority.'" In *Deconstruction and the Possibility of Justice*, edited by Drucilla Cornell, Michael Rosenfeld, and David Gray Carlson. New York: Routledge, 1992.

Deutch, Monroe E. "E Pluribus Unum." *Classical Journal* 18, no. 7 (1923): 387–407.

Dewey, John. "Creative Democracy: The Task before Us." 1939. In *John Dewey: The Later Works, 1925–1953*, vol. 14, edited by Jo Ann Boydston. Carbondale: Southern Illinois University Press, 1991.

———. *Individualism Old and New*. 1930. In *John Dewey: The Later Works, 1925–1953*, vol. 5, edited by Jo Ann Boydston. Carbondale: Southern Illinois University Press, 1988.

————. *Liberalism and Social Action*. 1935. In *John Dewey: The Later Works, 1925–1953*, vol. 11, edited by Jo Ann Boydston. Carbondale: Southern Illinois University Press, 1991.

————. *The Quest for Certainty*. 1929. In *John Dewey: The Later Works, 1925–1953*, vol. 4, edited by Jo Ann Boydston. Carbondale: Southern Illinois University Press, 1990.

D'Souza, Dinesh. *The Enemy at Home: The Cultural Left and Its Responsibility for 9/11*. New York: Doubleday, 2007.

Dunn, Geoffrey. "Sarah Palin's Obama Obsession." *Huffington Post*, August 29, 2009. http://www.huffingtonpost.com/geoffrey-dunn/sarah-palins-obama-obsess_b_271993.html.

Eberly, Rosa. *Citizen Critics: Literary Public Spheres*. Urbana: University of Illinois Press, 2000.

Edwards, Rob. "Hiroshima Bomb May Have Carried Hidden Agenda." *New Scientist*, July 21, 2005. http://www.newscientist.com/article/dn7706-hiroshima-bomb-may-have-carried-hidden-agenda.html.

Egan, Timothy. "When FDR Found 'The Forgotten Man.'" *New York Times*, August 28, 2008. http://www.nytimes.com/2008/08/28/opinion/28iht-edegan.1.15715387.html.

Eilperin, Juliet. "Palin's 'Pro-America Areas' Remark: Extended Version." *Washington Post*, October 17, 2008. http://voices.washingtonpost.com/the-trail/2008/10/17/palin_clarifies_her_pro-americ.html.

Engels, Jeremy. "Democratic Alienation." *Rhetoric and Public Affairs* 11, no. 3 (2008): 471–81.

————. "Demophilia: A Discursive Counter to Demophobia in the Early Republic." *Quarterly Journal of Speech* 97, no. 2 (2011): 131–54.

————. "Dewey on Jefferson: Reiterating Democratic Faith in Times of War." In *Trained Capacities: John Dewey, Rhetoric, and Democratic Culture*, edited by Gregory Clark and Brian Jackson, 87–105. Columbia: University of South Carolina Press, 2014.

————. *Enemyship: Democracy and Counter-Revolution in the Early Republic*. East Lansing: Michigan State University Press, 2010.

————. "The Two Faces of Cincinnatus: A Rhetorical Theory of the State of Exception." *Advances in the History of Rhetoric* 17, no. 1 (2014): 53–64.

Engels, Jeremy, and William Saas. "On Acquiescence and Ends-Less War: An Inquiry into the New War Rhetoric." *Quarterly Journal of Speech* 99, no. 2 (2013): 225–32.

Farrand, Max, ed. *The Records of the Federal Convention of 1787*. New Haven, CT: Yale University Press, 1911.

Farrell, Thomas. *Norms of Rhetorical Culture*. New Haven, CT: Yale University Press, 1993.

Finley, M. I. *Politics in the Ancient World*. Cambridge: Cambridge University Press, 1983.

Fliegelman, Jay. *Declaring Independence: Jefferson, Natural Language, and the Culture of Performance*. Stanford, CA: Stanford University Press, 1993.

————. *Prodigals and Pilgrims: The American Revolution against Patriarchal Authority, 1750–1800.* Cambridge: Cambridge University Press, 1982/1989.

Foley, Megan. "From Infantile Citizens to Infantile Institutions: The Metaphoric Transformation of Political Economy in the 2008 Housing Market Crisis." *Quarterly Journal of Speech* 98, no. 4 (2012): 386–410.

————. "*Peitho* and *Bia*: The Force of Language." *Symploke* 20, nos. 1–2 (2012): 173–81.

Fontana, Benedetto. "Rhetoric and the Roots of Democratic Politics." In *Talking Democracy: Historical Perspectives on Rhetoric and Democracy*, edited by Benedetto Fontana, Cary J. Nederman, and Gary Remer, 27–56. University Park: Pennsylvania State University Press, 2004.

————. "Sallust and the Politics of Machiavelli." *History of Political Thought* 24, no. 1 (2003): 86–108.

Foucault, Michel. *The Birth of Biopolitics: Lectures at the College de France, 1978–1979.* Edited by Michel Senellart. Translated by Graham Burchell. New York: Picador, 2004/2008.

————. *Discipline and Punish: The Birth of the Prison.* Translated by Alan Sheridan. New York: Vintage, 1975/1995.

————. *The Hermeneutics of the Subject: Lectures at the College de France, 1981–1982.* Edited by Frederic Gross. Translated by Graham Burchell. New York: Picador, 2005.

————. "Nietzsche, Genealogy, History." In *The Foucault Reader*, edited by Paul Rabinow, 76–100. New York: Pantheon, 1984.

————. "What Is an Author?" In *The Foucault Reader*, edited by Paul Rabinow, 101–20. New York: Pantheon, 1984.

Frank, Thomas. *What's the Matter with Kansas? How Conservatives Won the Heart of America.* New York: Henry Holt, 2004.

Fritz, Christian G. *American Sovereigns: The People and America's Constitutional Tradition before the Civil War.* New York: Cambridge University Press, 2008.

Fulbright, William J. "The Great Society Is a Sick Society." *New York Times Magazine*, August 20, 1967.

Gallagher, Shaun. *How the Body Shapes the Mind.* Oxford: Clarendon Press, 2005.

Garsten, Bryan. *Saving Persuasion: A Defense of Rhetoric and Judgment.* Cambridge, MA: Harvard University Press, 2006.

Gaughan, Judy E. *Murder Was Not a Crime: Homicide and Power in the Roman Republic.* Austin: University of Texas Press, 2010.

Gehrke, Pat. *The Ethics and Politics of Speech: Communication and Rhetoric in the Twentieth Century.* Carbondale: Southern Illinois University Press, 2010.

Gewargis, Natalie. "A WHAT Administration? A WHO Administration?" *Political Punch* (blog), ABC News, September 18, 2008. http://abcnews.go.com/blogs/politics/2008/09/a-what-administ/.

Gibson, James William. *Warrior Dreams: Violence and Manhood in Post-Vietnam America*. New York: Hill and Wang, 1994.

Gilje, Paul. *The Road to Mobocracy: Popular Disorder in New York City, 1763–1834*. Chapel Hill: University of North Carolina Press, 1987.

Griswold, Charles L. *Forgiveness: A Philosophical Exploration*. Cambridge: Cambridge University Press, 2007.

Gross, Alan G., and Arthur E. Walzer, eds. *Rereading Aristotle's "Rhetoric."* Carbondale: Southern Illinois University Press, 2000.

Gutmann, Amy, and Dennis Thompson. *Democracy and Disagreement*. Cambridge, MA: Harvard University Press, 1996.

Hamilton, Alexander, James Madison, and John Jay. *The Federalist*. Edited by Robert A. Ferguson. New York: Barnes & Noble Classics, 2006.

Hardt, Michael, and Antonio Negri. *Multitude: War and Democracy in the Age of Empire*. New York: Penguin, 2004.

Hariman, Robert. "Speaking of Evil." *Rhetoric and Public Affairs* 6, no. 3 (2003): 511–17.

Harris, Cheryl I. "Whiteness as Property." *Harvard Law Review* 106, no. 8 (1993): 1707–91.

Hartnett, Stephen John. *Democratic Dissent and the Cultural Fictions of Antebellum America*. Urbana: University of Illinois Press, 2002.

———. "Prisons, Profit, Crime, and Social Control: A Hermeneutic of the Production of Violence." In *Race, Class, and Community Identity*, edited by Andrew Light and Mechthild Nagel, 199–221. New York: Humanity Books, 2000.

Hartnett, Stephen John, and Laura Ann Stengrim. *Globalization and Empire: The U.S. Invasion of Iraq, Free Markets, and the Twilight of Democracy*. Tuscaloosa: University of Alabama Press, 2006.

Harvey, David. *A Brief History of Neoliberalism*. Oxford: Oxford University Press, 2005.

———. *The New Imperialism*. Oxford: Oxford University Press, 2003.

Hayden, Tom. *The Port Huron Statement: The Visionary Call of the 1960s Revolution*. New York: Avalon, 1962/2005.

Hedges, Chris. *Death of the Liberal Class*. New York: Nation Books, 2010.

Held, David. *Models of Democracy*. 3rd ed. Stanford, CA: Stanford University Press, 2006.

Hersh, Seymour M. *The Price of Power: Kissinger in the White House*. New York: Summit, 1983.

Hill, Christopher. *The World Turned Upside Down: Radical Ideas during the English Revolution*. New York: Penguin, 1972/1991.

Hobbes, Thomas. *Leviathan*. 1651. Edited by C. B. Macpherson. New York: Penguin, 1985.

Hofstadter, Richard. "The Paranoid Style in American Politics." In *The Paranoid Style in American Politics and Other Essays*, 3–40. London: Jonathan Cape, 1965.

———. *The Progressive Historians: Turner, Beard, Parrington*. New York: Alfred A. Knopf, 1969.

Hogan, J. Michael. "Rhetorical Pedagogy and Democratic Citizenship: Reviving the Traditions of Civic Engagement and Public Deliberation." In *Rhetoric and Democracy: Pedagogical and Political Practices*, edited by Todd F. McDorman and David M. Timmerman, 75–97. East Lansing: Michigan State University Press, 2008.

Holton, Woody. *Unruly Americans and the Origins of the Constitution*. New York: Hill and Wang, 2007.

Hume, David. *A Treatise of Human Nature*. 1739–40. Edited by L. A. Selby-Bigge. Oxford: Clarendon Press, 1888/1978.

Hunter, George. *How to Defend Yourself, Your Family, and Your Home*. New York: D. McKay, 1967.

Hunter, James Davison. *Culture Wars: The Struggle to Control the Family, Art, Education, Law, and Politics in America*. New York: Basic, 1991.

Isocrates. *Antidosis*. In *Isocrates I*, vol. 4 of *The Oratory of Classical Greece*. Translated by David C. Mirhady and Yun Lee Too. Austin: University of Texas Press, 2000.

———. *Antidosis*. Greek text edited by George Norlin. Perseus Digital Library. http://www.perseus.tufts.edu/hopper/text?doc=Perseus%3 Atext%3A1999.01.0143%3Aspeech%3D1.

———. *Panegyricus*. In *Isocrates II*, vol. 7 of *The Oratory of Classical Greece*. Translated by Terry L. Papillon. Austin: University of Texas Press, 2004.

———. *To Philip*. In *Isocrates II*, Volume 7 of *The Oratory of Classical Greece*. Translated by Terry L. Papillon. Austin: University of Texas Press, 2004.

Ivie, Robert L. *Democracy and America's War on Terror*. Tuscaloosa: University of Alabama Press, 2005.

———. "Images of Savagery in American Justifications for War." *Communication Monographs* 47, no. 4 (1980): 279–94.

Jacobs, Harold, ed. *Weatherman*. Berkeley, CA: Ramparts Press, 1970.

Jacobs, Ron. *The Way the Wind Blew: A History of the Weather Underground*. London: Verso, 1997.

Jefferson, Thomas. *The Life and Writings of Thomas Jefferson*. Indianapolis: Bowen-Merrill, 1900.

Johnson, Glen. "McCain Aide Says He's Strong in 'Real' Virginia." *Real Clear Politics*, October 18, 2008. http://www.realclearpolitics.com/news/ap/politics/2008/Oct/18/mccain_aide_says_he_s_strong_in__real__virginia.html.

Johnson, Luke. "Jesse Kelly, GOP Winner in Arizona Congressional Primary, Could Succeed Gabrielle Giffords." *Huffington Post*, April 19, 2012. http://www.huffingtonpost.com/2012/04/18/jesse-kelly-gabrielle-giffords-seat_n_1432603.html.

Keith, William M. *Democracy as Discussion: Civic Education and the American Forum Movement*. Lanham, MD: Lexington, 2007.

King, Andrew A., and Floyd Douglas Anderson. "Nixon, Agnew, and the 'Silent Majority': A Case Study in the Rhetoric of Polarization." *Western Speech* 35 (Fall 1971): 243–55.

Klein, Naomi. *The Shock Doctrine: The Rise of Disaster Capitalism*. New York: Metropolitan, 2007.

Konstan, David. *The Emotions of the Ancient Greeks: Studies in Aristotle and Classical Literature*. Toronto: University of Toronto Press, 2007.

Kristol, William. "The Wright Stuff." *New York Times*, October 5, 2008. http://www.nytimes.com/2008/10/06/opinion/06kristol.html.

Krugman, Paul. "Climate of Hate." *New York Times*, January 9, 2011. http://www.nytimes.com/2011/01/10/opinion/10krugman.html.

———. "Ludicrous and Cruel." *New York Times*, April 7, 2011. http://www.nytimes.com/2011/04/08/opinion/08krugman.html.

———. "Ryan and Taxes." *New York Times*, April 8, 2011. http://krugman.blogs.nytimes.com/2011/04/08/ryan-and-taxes/.

Laclau, Ernesto, and Chantal Mouffe. *Hegemony and Socialist Strategy: Towards a Radical Democratic Politics*. London: Verso, 1985/2001.

Lakoff, George. *Moral Politics: How Liberals and Conservatives Think*. Chicago: University of Chicago Press, 1996/2002.

———. *Whose Freedom? The Battle over America's Most Important Idea*. New York: Farrar, Straus and Giroux, 2006.

Lakoff, George, and Mark Johnson. *Metaphors We Live By*. Chicago: University of Chicago Press, 1980.

Layton, Lyndsey. "Palin Apologizes for 'Real America' Comments." *Washington Post*, October 22, 2008, A4.

Lepore, Jill. *The Whites of Their Eyes: The Tea Party's Revolution and the Battle over American History*. Princeton, NJ: Princeton University Press, 2010.

Lichtman, Allan J. *White Protestant Nation: The Rise of the American Conservative Movement*. New York: Atlantic Monthly Press, 2008.

Liddell, Henry George, and Robert Scott. *An Intermediate Greek–English Lexicon*. Oxford: Oxford University Press, 1889.

Linebaugh, Peter, and Marcus Rediker. *The Many-Headed Hydra: Sailors, Slaves, Commoners, and the Hidden History of the Revolutionary Atlantic*. Boston: Beacon Press, 2000.

Lintott, Andrew. *Violence in Republican Rome*. Oxford: Oxford University Press, 1999/2004.

Livy. *Ab Urbe Condita*. Latin text edited by Robert Seymour Conway and Charles Flamstead Walters. Perseus Digital Library. http://www.perseus.tufts.edu/hopper/text?doc=Perseus%3Atext%3A1999.02.0160%3Abook%3D2.

Locke, John. *An Essay Concerning Human Understanding*. 1690. Edited by Alexander Campbell Fraser. 2 vols. New York: Dover, 1959.

———. *Second Treatise of Government.* 1690. In *Two Treatises of Government,* edited by Peter Laslett. Cambridge: Cambridge University Press, 1960.

López, Ian Haney. *Dog Whistle Politics: How Coded Racial Appeals Have Reinvented Racism and Wrecked the Middle Class.* New York: Oxford University Press, 2014.

Lovley, Erika. "Exclusive: FBI Details Surge in Death Threats against Lawmakers." *Politico,* May 25, 2011. http://www.politico.com/news/stories/ 0510/37726.html.

Lowndes, Joseph E. *From the New Deal to the New Right: Race and the Origins of Modern Conservatism.* New Haven: Yale University Press, 2008.

Machiavelli, Niccolò. *The Prince.* 1521. Translated and edited by David Wootton. Indianapolis: Hackett, 1995.

Macpherson, C. B. *The Political Theory of Possessive Individualism: Hobbes to Locke.* New York: Oxford University Press, 1962/2011.

Marcuse, Herbert. *An Essay on Liberation.* Boston: Beacon Press, 1969/2000.

Martin, Isaac William. *Rich People's Movements: Grassroots Campaigns to Untax the One Percent.* Oxford: Oxford University Press, 2013.

Martin, Jonathan, and John F. Harris. "Palin 'Becoming Al Sharpton?'" *Politico,* March 14, 2011. http://www.politico.com/news/stories/0311/51218 .html.

Matthews, Richard. *If Men Were Angels: James Madison and the Heartless Empire of Reason.* Lawrence: University Press of Kansas, 1995.

May, Henry R. *The Enlightenment in America.* Oxford: Oxford University Press, 1976.

McCoy, Drew R. *The Elusive Republic: Political Economy in Jeffersonian America.* Chapel Hill: University of North Carolina Press, 1980.

McFarland, Thomas. *Romanticism and the Heritage of Rousseau.* Oxford: Clarendon Press, 1995.

McGee, Michael Calvin. "In Search of 'the People': A Rhetorical Alternative." *Quarterly Journal of Speech* 61, no. 3 (1975): 235–49.

McGinnis, Joe. *The Selling of the President.* New York: Penguin, 1969/1988.

Meares, Joel. "Q&A: Professor of Political Rhetoric Martin J. Medhurst." *Columbia Journalism Review,* January 10, 2011. http://www.cjr.org/ campaign_desk/qa_professor_of_political_rhet.php.

Medhurst, Martin J. "The History of Public Address as an Academic Study." In *The Handbook of Rhetoric and Public Address,* edited by Shawn J. Parry-Giles and J. Michael Hogan, 19–66. Malden, MA: Wiley-Blackwell, 2010.

Miller, James. *Democracy Is in the Streets: From Port Huron to the Siege of Chicago.* Cambridge, MA: Harvard University Press, 1987/2004.

Mills, C. Wright. *The Power Elite.* New York: Oxford University Press, 1956/2000.

Minot, George Richards. *The History of the Insurrections, in Massachusetts, in the Year MDCCLXXXVI, and the Rebellion Consequent Thereon.* Worcester, MA: Isaiah Thomas, 1788.

Montesquieu. *The Spirit of the Laws*. 1748. Edited by Anne M. Cohler, Basia C. Miller, and Harold S. Stone. Cambridge: Cambridge University Press, 1989.

Morgan, Edmund S. *Inventing the People: The Rise of Popular Sovereignty in England and America*. New York: W. W. Norton, 1988.

Morris, Charles E., III. "Pink Herring and the Fourth Persona: J. Edgar Hoover's Sex Crime Panic." *Quarterly Journal of Speech* 88, no. 2 (2002): 228–44.

Morris, Richard, and Peter Ehrenhaus, eds. *Cultural Legacies of Vietnam: Uses of the Past in the Present*. Norwood, NJ: Ablex, 1990.

Murphy, John M. "The Language of the Liberal Consensus: John F. Kennedy, Technical Reason, and the 'New Economics' at Yale University." *Quarterly Journal of Speech* 90, no. 2 (2004): 133–62.

———. "'A Time of Shame and Sorrow': Robert F. Kennedy and the American Jeremiad." *Quarterly Journal of Speech* 76, no. 4 (1990): 401–14.

Nagourney, Adam. "Arrests Bolster GOP Bid to Claim Security as Issue." *New York Times*, August 11, 2006, A8.

Nash, Gary. *The Unknown American Revolution: The Unruly Birth of Democracy and the Struggle to Create America*. New York: Viking, 2005.

Nealon, Jeffrey T. *Foucault beyond Foucault: Power and Its Intensifications since 1984*. Stanford, CA: Stanford University Press, 2008.

Nelson, Dana D. *Bad for Democracy: How the Presidency Undermines the Power of the People*. Minneapolis: University of Minnesota Press, 2008.

New York Times. "GOP Testimony on Violence." August 1, 1968, 20.

———. "Nixon Would Use Force in the Cities." March 8, 1968, 23.

———. "Politics of Attack." October 7, 2008. http://www.nytimes.com/2008/10/08/opinion/08wed1.html.

Nietzsche, Friedrich. *The Birth of Tragedy*. 1872. Translated by Clifton Fadiman. New York: Dover, 1995.

———. *On the Genealogy of Morals*. 1887. Translated by Walter Kauffman. New York: Vintage, 1967/1989.

———. *On the Uses and Disadvantages of History for Life*. 1874. In *Untimely Meditations*, edited by Daniel Breazeale. Cambridge: Cambridge University Press, 1997/2003.

———. "On Truth and Lie in an Extra-Moral Sense." In *The Portable Nietzsche*, edited and translated by Walter Kaufmann, 42–47. New York: Penguin, 1954/1976.

Ober, Josiah. *The Athenian Revolution: Essays on Ancient Greek Democracy and Political Theory*. Princeton, NJ: Princeton University Press, 1996.

———. *Mass and Elite in Democratic Athens: Rhetoric, Ideology, and the Power of the People*. Princeton, NJ: Princeton University Press, 1989.

———. "The Original Meaning of 'Democracy': Capacity to Do Things, Not Majority Rule." *Constellations* 15, no. 1 (2008): 3–9.

Olson, Lester C. *Benjamin Franklin's Vision of American Community: A Study in Rhetorical Iconology*. Columbia: University of South Carolina Press, 2004.

Owen, Susan A. "Memory, War, and American Identity: *Saving Private Ryan* as Cinematic Jeremiad." *Critical Studies in Media Communication* 19, no. 3 (2002): 249–82.

Paine, Thomas. *The Thomas Paine Reader.* Edited by Michael Foot and Isaac Kramnick. New York: Penguin, 1987.

Palin, Sarah. "America's Enduring Strength." Facebook, January 12, 2011. https://www.facebook.com/note.php?note_id=487510653434.

———. *Going Rogue: An American Life.* New York: Harper, 2009.

Peck, Jamie. *Constructions of Neoliberal Reason.* Oxford: Oxford University Press, 2010/2013.

Perlstein, Rick. *Nixonland: The Rise of a President and the Fracturing of America.* New York: Scribner, 2008.

Phillips, Kendall R. "Spaces of Invention: Dissension, Thought, and Freedom in Foucault." *Philosophy and Rhetoric* 35, no. 4 (2002): 328–44.

Phillips, Kevin P. *The Emerging Republican Majority.* New Rochelle, NY: Arlington House, 1969.

Plato. *The "Republic" of Plato.* Translated by Allan Bloom. New York: Basic, 1968/1991.

Pocock, J. G. A. *The Machiavellian Moment: Florentine Political Thought and the Atlantic Republican Tradition.* Princeton, NJ: Princeton University Press, 1975/2003.

Pogge, Thomas. *John Rawls: His Life and Theory of Justice.* Oxford: Oxford University Press, 1994/2007.

Potkay, Adam. *The Fate of Eloquence in the Age of Hume.* Ithaca, NY: Cornell University Press, 1994.

Pro Publica. "Bailout Tracker: Tracking Every Dollar and Every Recipient." May 29, 2014. http://projects.propublica.org/bailout/list.

Quintilian. *Institutio Oratoria*, Book 10. Latin text edited by Harold Edgeworth Butler. Perseus Digital Library. http://www.perseus.tufts.edu/hopper/text?doc=Perseus:text:2007.01.0068.

Rahe, Paul A. *Against Throne and Altar: Machiavelli and Political Theory Under the English Republic.* Cambridge: Cambridge University Press, 2008.

Rancière, Jacques. *Hatred of Democracy.* Translated by Steve Cocoran. London: Verso, 2005/2014.

Rawls, John. "The Idea of Public Reason." In *Deliberative Democracy: Essays on Reason and Politics*, edited by James Bohman and William Rehg, 93–141. Cambridge, MA: MIT Press, 1997.

———. *Political Liberalism.* New York: Columbia University Press, 1993/1996.

———. *A Theory of Justice.* Cambridge, MA: Harvard University Press, 1971.

Reid, Thomas. *Essays on the Active Powers of Man.* Edinburgh: John Bell, 1788.

Rich, Frank. "Donald Rumsfeld's Dance with the Nazis." *New York Times*, September 3, 2006. http://www.nytimes.com/2006/09/03/opinion/03rich.html?pagewanted=all&_r=0.

Rodgers, Daniel T. *Age of Fracture.* Cambridge, MA: Harvard University Press, 2011.

————. "Republicanism: The Career of a Concept." *Journal of American History* 79, no. 1 (1992): 11–38.

Roediger, David R. *The Wages of Whiteness: Race and the Making of the American Working Class*. New York: Verso, 1991.

Rorty, Amélie Oksenberg, ed. *Essays on Aristotle's "Rhetoric."* Berkeley: University of California Press, 1996.

Rorty, Richard. *Achieving Our Country: Leftist Thought in Twentieth-Century America*. Cambridge, MA: Harvard University Press, 1998.

Rousseau, Jean-Jacques. *Discourse on the Origin of Inequality*. Translated by Donald A. Cress. Indianapolis: Hackett, 1755/1992.

————. *The Social Contract*. 1762. Translated by Maurice Cranston. New York: Penguin, 1968.

Saxton, Alexander. *The Rise and Fall of the White Republic: Class Politics and Mass Culture in Nineteenth-Century America*. London: Verso, 1990/2003.

Schmitt, Carl. *The Concept of the Political*. Translated by George Schwab. Chicago: University of Chicago Press, 1932/1996.

Schudson, Michael. *The Good Citizen: A History of American Civic Life*. New York: Free Press, 1998.

Shane, Scott. "Vietnam Study, Casting Doubts, Remains Secret." *New York Times*, October 31, 2005. http://www.nytimes.com/2005/10/31/politics/31war.html.

————. "Vietnam War Intelligence 'Deliberately Skewed,' Secret Study Says." *New York Times*, December 2, 2005. http://www.nytimes.com/2005/12/02/politics/02tonkin.html.

Shepherd, Gregory J. "Pragmatism and Tragedy, Communication and Hope: A Summary Story." In *American Pragmatism and Communication Research*, edited by David K. Perry, 237–50. Mahwah, NJ: Lawrence Erlbaum Associates, 2001.

Smith, Adam *The Theory of Moral Sentiments*. 1759. Edited by D. D. Raphael and A. L. Macfie. Indianapolis: Liberty Fund, 1976.

Smith, Gaddis. "Was Moscow Our Real Target?" *New York Times*, August 18, 1985. http://www.nytimes.com/1985/08/18/books/was-moscow-our-real-target.html.

Stahl, Roger. "Why We Support the Troops: Rhetorical Evolutions." *Rhetoric and Public Affairs* 12, no. 4 (2009): 533–70.

Ste. Croix, G. E. M. de. *Class Struggle in the Ancient Greek World: From the Archaic Age to the Arab Conquests*. Ithaca, NY: Cornell University Press, 1981/1998.

Stiglitz, Joseph E. *The Price of Inequality: How Today's Divided Society Endangers Our Future*. New York: W. W. Norton, 2012.

Sullivan, Eileen. "Secret Service Looking into Obama Threat at Rally." *Fox News*, October 15, 2008. http://www.foxnews.com/printer_friendly_wires/2008Oct15/0,4675,ObamaSecret Service,00.html.

Summers, Anthony. *The Arrogance of Power: The Secret World of Richard Nixon*. New York: Viking, 2000.

Sumner, William Graham. *What Social Classes Owe Each Other.* 1883. Caldwell, ID: Caxton Printers, 1974.

Sydney, Algernon. *Discourses concerning Government.* 1698. Edited by Thomas G. West. Indianapolis: Liberty Fund, 1990.

Taibbi, Matt. *Griftopia: A Story of Bankers, Politicians, and the Most Audacious Power Grab in American History.* New York: Spiegel & Grau, 2010/2011.

Takaki, Ronald. *Iron Cages: Race and Culture in 19th-Century America.* Oxford: Oxford University Press, 1979/2000.

Terkel, Amanda. "Gabrielle Giffords Wrote Email Calling for 'Centrism and Moderation' on Eve of Shooting." *Huffington Post,* January 10, 2011. http://www.huffingtonpost.com/2011/01/10/gabrielle-giffords-email -centrism-mod eration_n_806791.html.

Thucydides. *History of the Peloponnesian War.* Translated by Rex Warner. New York: Penguin, 1954/1972.

Tipton, Frank B. *A History of Modern Germany since 1815.* Berkeley: University of California Press, 2003.

Tocqueville, Alexis de. *Democracy in America.* 1835. Translated by Harvey C. Mansfield and Delba Winthrop. Chicago: University of Chicago Press, 2000.

Toner, Robin, and Kate Zernike. "Partisan Fight over Iraq War Erupts on Hill." *New York Times,* June 16, 2006, A1.

"The Troubled American: A Special Report on the White Majority." *Newsweek,* October 6, 1969.

Vivian, Bradford. "Neoliberal Epideictic: Rhetorical Form and Commemorative Politics on September 11, 2002." *Quarterly Journal of Speech* 92, no. 1 (2006): 1–26.

Von Fritz, Kurt. *The Theory of Mixed Constitutions in Antiquity: A Critical Analysis of Polybius' Political Ideas.* New York: Columbia University Press, 1954.

Wallsten, Peter. "In the Wake of Tragedy, an Outspoken Sheriff Steps into the Spotlight." *Washington Post,* January 10, 2011. http://www.washington post.com/wp-dyn/content/article/2011/01/09/AR2011010904163.html.

Walsh, Joan. "Swearing Off the Rhetoric of Violence." *Salon,* January 8, 2011. http://www.salon.com/2011/01/09/stop_the_rhetoric_of_violence.

Weber, Max. *The Protestant Ethic and the Spirit of Capitalism.* 1904–5. Translated by Talcott Parsons. Los Angeles: Roxbury, 1998.

———. "The Protestant Sects and the Spirit of Capitalism." In *From Max Weber: Essays in Sociology,* edited and translated by H. H. Gerth and C. Wright Mills, 302–22. New York: Oxford University Press, 1958.

Weber, Samuel. *Targets of Opportunity: On the Militarization of Thinking.* New York: Fordham University Press, 2005.

West, Cornel. *The American Evasion of Philosophy: A Genealogy of Pragmatism.* Madison: University of Wisconsin Press, 1989.

Westbrook, Robert B. *John Dewey and American Democracy.* Ithaca, NY: Cornell University Press, 1991.

Wilson, Kirt H. *The Reconstruction Desegregation Debate: The Politics of Equality and the Rhetoric of Place, 1870–1875*. East Lansing: Michigan State University Press, 2002.

Windt, Theodore Otto, Jr. *Presidents and Protestors: Political Rhetoric in the 1960s*. Tuscaloosa: University of Alabama Press, 1990.

Wing, Nick. "Sarah Palin: Obama 'Hell-Bent on Weakening America.'" *Huffington Post*, January 7, 2011. http://www.huffingtonpost.com/2011/01/07/sarah-palin-obama-debt-ceiling_n_806014.html.

Wiseman, T. P. *Remus: A Roman Myth*. Cambridge: Cambridge University Press, 1995.

Wolin, Sheldon S. *Democracy Incorporated: Managed Democracy and the Specter of Inverted Totalitarianism*. Princeton, NJ: Princeton University Press, 2008.

Wood, Gordon S. "Conspiracy and the Paranoid Style: Causality and Deceit in the Eighteenth Century." *William and Mary Quarterly* 39, no. 3 (1982): 401–41.

———. *The Creation of the American Republic, 1776–1787*. Chapel Hill: University of North Carolina Press, 1969/1998.

Zarefsky, David. "Two Faces of Democratic Rhetoric." In *Rhetoric and Democracy: Pedagogical and Political Practices*, edited by Todd F. McDorman and David M. Timmerman, 115–37. East Lansing: Michigan State University Press, 2008.

Zengotita, Thomas de. "The Numbing of the American Mind: Culture as Anesthetic." *Harper's*, April 2002.

Žižek, Slajov. "From Democracy to Divine Violence." In *Democracy in What State?* edited by Giorgio Agamben et al., 100–120. New York: Columbia University Press, 2009/2011.

———. *Violence: Six Sideways Reflections*. New York: Picador, 2008.